I0005408

FORWARD/COMMENTARY

The National Institute of Standards and Technology (NIST) is a measurement standards laboratory, and a non-regulatory agency of the **United States Department of Commerce**. Its mission is to promote innovation and industrial competitiveness. Founded in 1901, as the National Bureau of Standards, NIST was formed with the mandate to provide standard weights and measures, and to serve as the national physical laboratory for the United States. With a world-class measurement and testing laboratory encompassing a wide range of areas of computer science, mathematics, statistics, and systems engineering, NIST's cybersecurity program supports its overall mission to promote U.S. innovation and industrial competitiveness by advancing measurement science, standards, and related technology through research and development in ways that enhance economic security and improve our quality of life.

The need for cybersecurity standards and best practices that address interoperability, usability and privacy has been shown to be critical for the nation. NIST's cybersecurity programs seek to enable greater development and application of practical, innovative security technologies and methodologies that enhance the country's ability to address current and future computer and information security challenges.

The cybersecurity publications produced by NIST cover a wide range of cybersecurity concepts that are carefully designed to work together to produce a holistic approach to cybersecurity primarily for government agencies and constitute the best practices used by industry. This holistic strategy to cybersecurity covers the gamut of security subjects from development of secure encryption standards for communication and storage of information while at rest to how best to recover from a cyber-attack.

Why buy a book you can download for free?   **We print this so you don't have to.**

Some are available only in electronic media. Some online docs are missing pages or barely legible.

We at 4th Watch Publishing are former government employees, so we know how government employees actually use the standards. When a new standard is released, an engineer prints it out, punches holes and puts it in a 3-ring binder. While this is not a big deal for a 5 or 10-page document, many NIST documents are over 100 pages and printing a large document is a time-consuming effort. So, an engineer that's paid $75 an hour is spending hours simply printing out the tools needed to do the job. That's time that could be better spent doing engineering. We publish these documents so engineers can focus on what they were hired to do – engineering. It's much more cost-effective to just order the latest version from Amazon.com

If there is a standard you would like published, let us know. Our web site is usgovpub.com

Many of our titles are available as eBooks for Kindle, iPad, Nook, remarkable, BOOX, and Sony eReaders. Buy the paperback from Amazon and get Kindle eBook FREE using MATCHBOOK. Go to https://usgovpub.com to learn more.

Why buy an eBook when you can access data on a website for free? HYPERLINKS

Yes, many books are available as a PDF, but not all PDFs are bookmarked? Do you really want to search a 6,500-page PDF document manually? Load our copy onto your Kindle, PC, iPad, Android Tablet, Nook, or iPhone (download the FREE kindle App from the APP Store) and you have an easily searchable copy. Most devices will allow you to easily navigate an ePub to any Chapter. Note that there is a distinction between a Table of Contents and "Page Navigation". Page Navigation refers to a different sort of Table of Contents. Not one appearing as a page in the book, but one that shows up on the device itself when the reader accesses the navigation feature. Readers can click on a navigation link to jump to a Chapter or Subchapter. Once there, most devices allow you to "pinch and zoom" in or out to easily read the text. (Unfortunately, downloading the free sample file at Amazon.com does not include this feature. You have to buy a copy to get that functionality, but as inexpensive as eBooks are, it's worth it.) Kindle allows you to do word search and Page Flip (temporary place holder takes you back when you want to go back and check something). Visit **USGOVPUB.COM** to learn more.

NIST SPECIAL PUBLICATION 1800-14

Protecting the Integrity of Internet Routing:

Border Gateway Protocol (BGP) Route Origin Validation

Includes Executive Summary (A); Approach, Architecture, and Security Characteristics (B); and How-To Guides (C)

William Haag
Doug Montgomery
William C. Barker
Allen Tan

Protecting the Integrity of Internet Routing: Border Gateway Protocol (BGP) Route Origin Validation

Includes Executive Summary (A); Approach, Architecture, and Security Characteristics (B); and How-To Guides (C)

William Haag
Applied Cybersecurity Division
Information Technology Laboratory

Doug Montgomery
Advanced Network Technologies Division
Information Technology Laboratory

Allen Tan
The MITRE Corporation
McLean, VA

William C. Barker
Dakota Consulting
Silver Spring, MD

June 2019

U.S. Department of Commerce
Wilbur Ross, Secretary

National Institute of Standards and Technology
Walter Copan, NIST Director and Undersecretary of Commerce for Standards and Technology

Protecting the Integrity of Internet Routing:
Border Gateway Protocol (BGP) Route Origin Validation

Volume A:
Executive Summary

William Haag
Applied Cybersecurity Division
Information Technology Laboratory

Doug Montgomery
Advanced Network Technologies Division
Information Technology Laboratory

Allen Tan
The MITRE Corporation
McLean, VA

William C. Barker
Dakota Consulting
Silver Spring, MD

June 2019

Executive Summary

- It is difficult to overstate the importance of the internet to modern business and to society in general. The internet is essential to the exchange of all manner of information, including transactional data, marketing and advertising information, remote access to services, entertainment, and much more.

- The internet is not a single network, but rather a complex grid of independent interconnected networks. The design of the internet is based on a trust relationship between these networks and relies on a protocol known as the Border Gateway Protocol (BGP) to route traffic among the various networks worldwide. BGP is the protocol that internet service providers (ISPs) and enterprises use to exchange route information between them.

- Unfortunately, BGP was not designed with security in mind. Traffic typically traverses multiple networks to get from its source to its destination. Networks implicitly trust the BGP information that they receive from each other, making BGP vulnerable to route hijacks.

- A route hijack attack can deny access to internet services, misdeliver traffic to malicious endpoints, and cause routing instability. A technique known as BGP route origin validation (ROV) is designed to protect against route hijacking.

- The National Cybersecurity Center of Excellence (NCCoE) at the National Institute of Standards and Technology (NIST) has developed proof-of-concept demonstrations of a BGP ROV implementation designed to improve the security of the internet's routing infrastructure.

- This NIST Cybersecurity Practice Guide demonstrates how networks can protect BGP routes from vulnerability to route hijacks by using available security protocols, products, and tools to perform BGP ROV to reduce route hijacking threats. The example implementation described in this guide aims to protect the integrity and improve the resiliency of internet traffic exchange by verifying the source of the route.

CHALLENGE

Most of the routing infrastructure underpinning the internet currently lacks basic security services. In most cases, internet traffic must transit multiple networks before reaching its destination. Each network implicitly trusts other networks to provide (via BGP) the accurate information necessary to correctly route traffic across the internet. When that information is inaccurate, traffic will take inefficient paths through the internet, arrive at malicious sites that masquerade as legitimate destinations, or never arrive at its intended destination. These impacts can be mitigated through a widespread adoption of BGP ROV.

To date, ISPs and enterprises have been slow to adopt BGP ROV for reasons that include an unavailability of detailed BGP ROV deployment, operation, and management guidelines, as well as lingering concerns and questions about functionality, performance, availability, scalability, and policy implications. These concerns need to be addressed so that potential users of BGP ROV can appreciate the feasibility of using BGP ROV and the increased security that it can provide.

SOLUTION

The NCCoE Secure Inter-Domain Routing (SIDR) Project is improving internet security by demonstrating how to use ROV to protect against route hijacks. The SIDR Project has produced a proof-of-concept example that demonstrates the use of BGP ROV in realistic deployment scenarios, has developed detailed deployment guidance, has addressed implementation and use issues, and has generated best practices and lessons learned. Project results are presented in this publicly available NIST Cybersecurity Practice Guide. This guide describes the following concepts:

- security objectives that are supported by implementing BGP ROV that uses Resource Public Key Infrastructure (RPKI) mechanisms

- an example solution of methods and tools that demonstrate and enable a practical implementation of BGP ROV

- how to protect your own internet addresses from route hijacking by registering them with trusted sources, thereby gaining assurance that traffic intended for your organization will not be hijacked when it is forwarded by entities that perform BGP ROV

- how to perform BGP ROV on received BGP route updates to validate, if possible, whether the entity that originated the route is in fact authorized to do so

- how to more precisely express your routing security requirements and/or service offerings

While the NCCoE used a suite of available products to address this challenge, this guide does not endorse these particular products, nor does it guarantee compliance with any regulatory initiatives. Your organization's information security experts should identify the products that will best integrate with your existing tools and information technology (IT) system infrastructure. Your organization can adopt this solution or one that adheres to these guidelines in whole, or you can use this guide as a starting point for tailoring and implementing parts of a solution.

BENEFITS

The NCCoE's practice guide is intended to improve the security and stability of the global internet by allowing networks to verify the validity of BGP routing information and strengthen the security and stability of traffic flowing across the global internet—benefitting all organizations and individuals that use and rely on it. This practice guide can help your organization:

- reduce the number of internet outages due to BGP route hijacks

- ensure that internet traffic reaches its destination

- make informed decisions regarding routes and what actions to take in cases when BGP ROV implementation has not been performed or has indicated that an advertised route is invalid.

SHARE YOUR FEEDBACK

You can view or download the guide at https://nccoe.nist.gov/projects/building-blocks/secure-inter-domain-routing. Help the NCCoE make this guide better by sharing your thoughts with us as you read the guide. If you adopt this solution for your own organization, please share your experience and advice with us. We recognize that technical solutions alone will not fully enable the benefits of our solution, so we encourage organizations to share lessons learned and best practices for transforming the processes associated with implementing this guide.

To provide comments or to learn more by arranging a demonstration of this example implementation, contact the NCCoE at sidr-nccoe@nist.gov.

TECHNOLOGY PARTNERS/COLLABORATORS

Organizations participating in this project submitted their capabilities in response to an open call in the Federal Register for all sources of relevant security capabilities from academia and industry (vendors and integrators). The following respondents with relevant capabilities or product components (identified as "Technology Partners/Collaborators" herein) signed a Cooperative Research and Development Agreement (CRADA) to collaborate with NIST in a consortium to build this example solution.

Certain commercial entities, equipment, products, or materials may be identified by name or company logo or other insignia in order to acknowledge their participation in this collaboration or to describe an experimental procedure or concept adequately. Such identification is not intended to imply special status or relationship with NIST or recommendation or endorsement by NIST or NCCoE; neither is it intended to imply that the entities, equipment, products, or materials are necessarily the best available for the purpose.

The National Cybersecurity Center of Excellence (NCCoE), a part of the National Institute of Standards and Technology (NIST), is a collaborative hub where industry organizations, government agencies, and academic institutions work together to address businesses' most pressing cybersecurity challenges. Through this collaboration, the NCCoE develops modular, easily adaptable example cybersecurity solutions demonstrating how to apply standards and best practices using commercially available technology.

LEARN MORE

Visit https://www.nccoe.nist.gov
nccoe@nist.gov
301-975-0200

NIST SPECIAL PUBLICATION 1800-14B

Protecting the Integrity of Internet Routing:
Border Gateway Protocol (BGP) Route Origin Validation

Volume B:
Approach, Architecture, and Security Characteristics

William Haag
Applied Cybersecurity Division
Information Technology Laboratory

Doug Montgomery
Advanced Network Technologies Division
Information Technology Laboratory

Allen Tan
The MITRE Corporation
McLean, VA

William C. Barker
Dakota Consulting
Silver Spring, MD

June 2019

DISCLAIMER

Certain commercial entities, equipment, products, or materials may be identified by name or company logo or other insignia in order to acknowledge their participation in this collaboration or to describe an experimental procedure or concept adequately. Such identification is not intended to imply special status or relationship with NIST or recommendation or endorsement by NIST or NCCoE; neither is it intended to imply that the entities, equipment, products, or materials are necessarily the best available for the purpose.

National Institute of Standards and Technology Special Publication 1800-14B, Natl. Inst. Stand. Technol. Spec. Publ. 1800-14B, 173 pages, (June 2019), CODEN: NSPUE2

FEEDBACK

As a private-public partnership, we are always seeking feedback on our Practice Guides. We are particularly interested in seeing how businesses apply NCCoE reference designs in the real world. If you have implemented the reference design, or have questions about applying it in your environment, please email us at sidr-nccoe@nist.gov.

All comments are subject to release under the Freedom of Information Act (FOIA).

National Cybersecurity Center of Excellence
National Institute of Standards and Technology
100 Bureau Drive
Mailstop 2002
Gaithersburg, MD 20899
Email: nccoe@nist.gov

NATIONAL CYBERSECURITY CENTER OF EXCELLENCE

The National Cybersecurity Center of Excellence (NCCoE), a part of the National Institute of Standards and Technology (NIST), is a collaborative hub where industry organizations, government agencies, and academic institutions work together to address businesses' most pressing cybersecurity issues. This public-private partnership enables the creation of practical cybersecurity solutions for specific industries, as well as for broad, cross-sector technology challenges. Through consortia under Cooperative Research and Development Agreements (CRADAs), including technology partners—from Fortune 50 market leaders to smaller companies specializing in IT security—the NCCoE applies standards and best practices to develop modular, easily adaptable example cybersecurity solutions using commercially available technology. The NCCoE documents these example solutions in the NIST Special Publication 1800 series, which maps capabilities to the NIST Cybersecurity Framework and details the steps needed for another entity to recreate the example solution. The NCCoE was established in 2012 by NIST in partnership with the State of Maryland and Montgomery County, Md.

To learn more about the NCCoE, visit https://www.nccoe.nist.gov/. To learn more about NIST, visit https://www.nist.gov.

NIST CYBERSECURITY PRACTICE GUIDES

NIST Cybersecurity Practice Guides (Special Publication Series 1800) target specific cybersecurity challenges in the public and private sectors. They are practical, user-friendly guides that facilitate the adoption of standards-based approaches to cybersecurity. They show members of the information security community how to implement example solutions that help them align more easily with relevant standards and best practices, and provide users with the materials lists, configuration files, and other information they need to implement a similar approach.

The documents in this series describe example implementations of cybersecurity practices that businesses and other organizations may voluntarily adopt. These documents do not describe regulations or mandatory practices, nor do they carry statutory authority.

ABSTRACT

The Border Gateway Protocol (BGP) is the default routing protocol to route traffic among internet domains. While BGP performs adequately in identifying viable paths that reflect local routing policies and preferences to destinations, the lack of built-in security allows the protocol to be exploited by route hijacking. Route hijacking occurs when an entity accidentally or maliciously alters an intended route. Such attacks can (1) deny access to internet services, (2) detour internet traffic to permit eavesdropping and to facilitate on-path attacks on endpoints (sites), (3) misdeliver internet network traffic to malicious endpoints, (4) undermine Internet Protocol (IP)-address-based reputation and filtering systems, and (5) cause routing instability in the internet. This document describes a security platform that demonstrates how to improve the security of inter-domain routing traffic exchange. The platform provides route origin validation (ROV) by using the Resource Public Key Infrastructure (RPKI) in a manner that mitigates some misconfigurations and malicious attacks associated with route hijacking. The example solutions and architectures presented here are based upon standards-based, open-source, and commercially available products.

KEYWORDS

AS, autonomous systems, BGP, Border Gateway Protocol, DDoS, denial-of-service (DoS) attacks, internet service provider, ISP, Regional Internet Registry, Resource Public Key Infrastructure, RIR, ROA, route hijack, route origin authorization, route origin validation, routing domain, ROV, RPKI

ACKNOWLEDGMENTS

We are grateful to the following individuals for their generous contributions of expertise and time.

Name	Organization
Tim Battles	AT&T
Jay Borkenhagen	AT&T
Chris Boyer	AT&T
Nimrod Levy	AT&T
Kathryn Condello	CenturyLink
Christopher Garner	CenturyLink
Peter Romness	Cisco Systems
Tony Tauber	Comcast
Jonathan Morgan	Juniper Networks
Carter Wyant	Juniper Networks
Oliver Borchert	NIST ITL Advanced Networks Technologies Division
Kotikalapudi Sriram	NIST ITL Advanced Networks Technologies Division
Sean Morgan	Palo Alto Networks
Tom Van Meter	Palo Alto Networks
Andrew Gallo	The George Washington University
Sophia Applebaum	The MITRE Corporation

Name	Organization
Yemi Fashina	The MITRE Corporation
Susan Prince	The MITRE Corporation
Susan Symington	The MITRE Corporation

The Technology Partners/Collaborators who participated in this build submitted their capabilities in response to a notice in the Federal Register. Respondents with relevant capabilities or product components were invited to sign a Cooperative Research and Development Agreement (CRADA) with NIST, allowing them to participate in a consortium to build this example solution. We worked with:

Technology Partner/Collaborator	Build Involvement
AT&T	Subject Matter Expertise
CenturyLink	1 gigabit per second (Gbps) Ethernet Link Subject Matter Expertise
Cisco	7206 VXR Router v15.2 ISR 4331 Router v16.3 2921 Router v15.2 IOS XRv 9000 Router v6.4.1 Subject Matter Expertise
Comcast	Subject Matter Expertise
Juniper Networks	MX80 3D Universal Edge Router v15.1R6.7 Subject Matter Expertise
Palo Alto Networks	Palo Alto Networks Next-Generation Firewall PA-5060 v7.1.10 Subject Matter Expertise
The George Washington University	Subject Matter Expertise

Contents

List of Figures

List of Tables

1   Summary

This National Institute of Standards and Technology (NIST) Cybersecurity Practice Guide addresses the challenge of using existing protocols to improve the security of inter-domain routing traffic exchange in a manner that mitigates accidental and malicious attacks associated with route hijacking.

A route prefix hijack occurs when an *autonomous system* (AS) accidentally or maliciously originates a Border Gateway Protocol (BGP) update for a route prefix that it is not authorized to originate. For example, a BGP update for Internet Protocol (IP) prefix 192.0.2.0/24 might legitimately be originated by one AS, but a different AS might fraudulently originate a BGP route update for that prefix. Many ASes for which the illegitimate AS is closer (i.e., in terms of a shorter routing path length) would trust the false update, and thus data traffic from them toward the said prefix would be misrouted to the illegitimate AS. The path to the prefix via the false origin AS will be shorter, on average, for about half of all ASes in the internet. So, nearly half of the internet ASes would install the false route in their Forwarding Information Base (FIB).

When an offending AS fraudulently announces a more specific prefix than the prefix announced legitimately by another AS, practically all of the internet ASes would install the false route in their FIB.

This Practice Guide implements and follows various Internet Engineering Task Force (IETF) Request for Comments (RFC) documents that define Resource Public Key Infrastructure (RPKI)-based BGP route origin validation (ROV), such as [RFC 6480], [RFC 6482], [RFC 6811], and [RFC 7115], as well as recommendations of [NIST SP 800-54], *Border Gateway Security*. To the extent practicable from a system composition point of view, the security platform design, build, and test processes have followed [NIST SP 800-160], *Systems Security Engineering: Considerations for a Multidisciplinary Approach in the Engineering of Trustworthy Secure Systems*.

The NIST Special Publication (SP) 1800-14 series of documents consists of the following volumes:

- Volume A: an executive-level summary describing the challenge that RPKI-based ROV is designed to address, the ROV solution, and its benefits

- Volume B: a rationale for, and descriptions of, RPKI-based internet routing platforms that perform BGP-based ROV

- Volume C: a series of How-To Guides, including instructions for the installation and configuration of the necessary services, that show system administrators and security engineers how to achieve similar outcomes

The solutions and architectures presented are built upon standards-based, commercially available, and open-source products. These solutions can be used by any organization providing or using internet routing services that is willing to perform the steps necessary to perform and/or benefit from RPKI-based ROV. Interoperable solutions are provided that are available from different types of sources (e.g., both commercial and open-source products).

This summary section (Section 1) describes the challenge addressed by Volume B (*Approach, Architecture, and Security Characteristics*), the solution demonstrated to address the challenge, and the benefits of the demonstrated solution. Section 2, How to Use This Guide, explains how each volume of this guide may be used by business decision makers, program managers, and information technology (IT) professionals, such as systems administrators. Section 3, Background, provides a high-level project overview. Section 4, Approach, provides a more detailed treatment of the project's intended audience, scope, assumptions, and the risks that informed it. Section 4 also describes the technologies and components that were provided by industry collaborators to enable platform development, and lists the *Cybersecurity Framework* Functions supported by each collaborator-contributed component. For each security characteristic supported, it lists not only the Cybersecurity Framework Categories and Subcategories, but also the *Security and Privacy Controls for Information Systems and Organizations* [NIST SP 800-53] controls and additional references, standards, and guidelines that apply to each security function being demonstrated. Section 5, Architecture, describes the RPKI-based ROV reference architecture and the usage scenarios that it supports, as well as the architecture of the laboratory-based solution that was implemented at the National Cybersecurity Center of Excellence (NCCoE). Section 6, Outcome, discusses lessons learned, best practices, and other items relevant to systems administrators' experiences with respect to integrating the new capabilities into their systems and in systems operations and maintenance. Section 7, Functional and Robustness Results, summarizes the tests that were performed to demonstrate security platform functionality and provides an overview of platform performance in the scenarios demonstrated. Section 8, Recommendations for Follow-on Activities, provides a brief description of future work that could be pursued to promote the adoption of Border Gateway Protocol Security (BGPsec) [RFC 8205] to provide protection for the path information in BGP updates. Appendices are provided for a description of the use of [NIST SP 800-160] in project design and development; recommended education and training requirements for internet service provider (ISP) operators and enterprises; further discussion of the mapping of the secure inter-domain routing (SIDR) security platform to the *Cybersecurity Framework Core*; informative security references cited in the Cybersecurity Framework Core; further discussion of assumptions; functional test requirements; results; acronyms; and references.

1.1 Challenge

Attacks against the internet routing functions are probably one of the greatest current threats to today's internet. Routing attacks can have regional, or even global, impact. There have been numerous incidents in recent years involving control plane anomalies, such as route hijacking, AS path modification attacks (e.g., an AS in the middle maliciously shortens a path to attract more traffic), route leaks, spoofing source addresses, etc., resulting in Denial-of-Service (DoS), unwanted data traffic detours, and performance degradation that is sufficiently severe to seriously disrupt the internet on a very large scale and for periods that can seriously harm organizations, the economy, and national security.

Protocols have been defined that are designed to provide protection against many of the routing attacks mentioned above. The technique that is the subject of this practice guide, RPKI-based ROV, enables operators to verify that the AS that has originated a BGP route advertisement is, in fact, authorized to do so. The use of RPKI-based ROV can provide protection against accidental, and some malicious, route hijacks. A second protocol, BGPsec, allows network operators to verify the validity of the entire routing path across the internet (referred to as path validation). The use of RPKI-based ROV in conjunction with BGPsec can provide protection against malicious route hijacks as well as other routing attacks. Unfortunately, the adoption of both ROV and BGPsec is still very limited. In the case of BGPsec, while the specification of the BGPsec-based path validation is complete [RFC 8205], [RFC 8207], [RFC 8208], [RFC 8210], and open-source implementations [NIST BGP-SRx] [Parsons BGPSec] are available, there is still a lack of commercial implementations available from router vendors.

BGPsec also has several other obstacles impeding its deployment, as compared with ROV, such as the fact that support for it will be resource-intensive because it increases the size and number of routing messages that are sent, and each message will require a cryptographic verification of at least one, and most likely multiple, digital signatures. Digital signature verification will be processing-intensive and may require hardware upgrades and/or software optimizations [NANOG69] [V_Sriram]. It also adds a level of complexity with respect to the acquisition and management of public keys for BGP routers, as well as the X.509 certificates used in sharing those keys.

Although the BGP path validation protections of BGPsec have not yet been incorporated into most vendor equipment, the state of implementation of BGP ROV, on the other hand, is more advanced. ROV capabilities have already been incorporated into the equipment of major vendors (e.g., they ship with Cisco, Juniper, and Alcatel/Lucent/Nokia routers). Further RPKI operations and repositories at all five Regional Internet Registries (RIRs) are in production. In some regions of the world, RIRs provide tools and support that facilitate an efficient implementation of RPKI-based ROV. However, commercial adoption to date has been slow, particularly in the North American region. This situation is beginning to change in other regions of the world. As of this writing, Europe, in particular, is approaching route origin authorization (ROA) coverage of approximately 43 percent of their announced Internet Protocol Version 4 (IPv4) address space, due, in part, to forward-looking adoption policies and favorable and flexible usage polices for RPKI services. North America trails Europe, Latin and South America, and Africa in its rate of adoption, with only approximately seven percent of its announced IPv4 address space covered by ROAs.

1.2 Solution

This Practice Guide (NIST SP 1800-14) describes how to use available security protocols, products, and tools to provide RPKI-based ROV in enterprises. This Practice Guide focuses on a proof-of-concept implementation of the IETF security protocols and the NIST implementation guidance needed to protect ISPs and ASes against the consequences of widespread and localized route hijacking attacks. Although it would have been preferable to protect against additional types of routing attacks by also focusing on the more comprehensive solution of BGP path validation in conjunction with ROV, the lack of commercial vendor implementation support for BGPsec makes providing a BGP path validation solution impractical at this time. Hence, this Practice Guide is focusing only on providing ROV.

The proof-of-concept implementation is used to demonstrate BGP ROV, using RPKI, to address and resolve route hijacking issues. The demonstration shows how, by using ROV, an AS can protect routes that it originates and flag and discard (or apply some other policy to, as desired) bogus routes that it receives that do not come from ASes that are authorized to originate the routes. The proof-of-concept implementation demonstrates RPKI-based ROV in realistic deployment scenarios. Also, some additional functionality, performance, robustness, and availability tests suggested by industry collaborators on the team were performed.

This Practice Guide offers detailed deployment guidance, identifies implementation and use issues, and generates best practices and lessons learned. Volume C of this Practice Guide serves as a detailed implementation guide to the practical steps required to implement a cybersecurity reference design that mitigates the inter-domain routing security challenge.

1.3 Benefits

The ROV capabilities demonstrated by the proof-of-concept implementation described in this Practice Guide improve inter-domain routing security by using standards-conformant security protocols to enable an entity that receives a BGP route update to validate whether the AS that has originated it is, in fact, authorized to do so. The capability demonstrated by the proof-of-concept can facilitate the adoption of ROV by ASes by making it easier for entities to use the RPKI to create and validate objects that explicitly and verifiably assert that an AS is authorized to originate routes to a given set of prefixes. The creation of ROAs can be accomplished independently by each address resource holder, and ROV can be deployed by each AS independently. Thus, there is clearly a benefit for early adopters, and deployment grows in a distributed manner. All organizations and individuals who are dependent on the internet stand to benefit greatly from the improvement to the security and stability of the global internet that can be achieved by providing a level of assurance that routing assertions come from the sources that are authorized to originate them. In particular, entities that issue ROA for the prefixes that they hold will benefit from the assurance that accidental hijackings and some malicious hijackings are prevented.

2 How to Use This Guide

This NIST Cybersecurity Practice Guide demonstrates a standards-based reference design and provides users with the information they need to replicate this approach to inter-domain routing security. This reference design is modular and can be deployed in whole or in part.

This guide contains three volumes:

- NIST SP 1800-14A: *Executive Summary*
- NIST SP 1800-14B: *Approach, Architecture, and Security Characteristics* — what we built and why **(you are here)**
- NIST SP 1800-14C: *How-To Guides* — instructions for building the example solution

Depending on your role in your organization, you might use this guide in different ways:

Business decision makers, including chief security and technology officers, will be interested in the *Executive Summary, NIST SP 1800-14A*, which describes the following topics:

- challenges that enterprises face in implementing and maintaining ROV
- an example solution built at the NCCoE
- the benefits of adopting the example solution.

Technology or security program managers who are concerned with how to identify, understand, assess, and mitigate risk will be interested in this part of the guide, *NIST SP 1800-14B*, which describes what we did and why. Section 4.4, Risk Assessment, will be of particular interest. This section provides a description of the risk analysis we performed and maps the security services provided by this example solution to NIST's *Framework for Improving Critical Infrastructure Cybersecurity* and to relevant security standards and guidelines.

You might share the *Executive Summary, NIST SP 1800-14A*, with your leadership team members to help them understand the importance of adopting standards-based ROV approaches to protect your organization's digital assets.

IT professionals who want to implement an approach like this will find the whole practice guide useful. You can use the How-To portion of the guide, *NIST SP 1800-14C*, to replicate all or parts of the build created in our lab. The How-To portion of the guide provides specific installation, configuration, and integration instructions for implementing the example solution. We do not recreate the product manufacturers' documentation, which is generally widely available. Rather, we show how we incorporated the products together in our environment to create an example solution.

This guide assumes that IT professionals have experience in implementing security products within the enterprise. While we have used a suite of commercially available and open-source software products to address this challenge, this guide does not endorse these particular products. Your organization can adopt this solution or one that adheres to these guidelines in whole, or you can use this guide as a starting point for tailoring and implementing parts of a solution that would support the deployment of an ROV-RPKI system and the corresponding business processes. Your organization's security experts should identify the products that will best integrate with your existing tools and IT system infrastructure. We hope that you will seek products that are congruent with applicable standards and best practices.

Section 4.5, Technologies, lists the products we used and maps them to the cybersecurity Functions called out in the Cybersecurity Framework.

2.1 Typographic Conventions

The following table presents typographic conventions used in this volume.

Typeface/Symbol	Meaning	Example
Italics	file names and path names; references to documents that are not hyperlinks; new terms; and placeholders	For detailed definitions of terms, see the *CSRC Glossary*.
Bold	names of menus, options, command buttons, and fields	Choose **File > Edit**.
`Monospace`	command-line input, on-screen computer output, sample code examples, and status codes	`Mkdir`
`Monospace Bold`	command-line user input contrasted with computer output	**`service sshd start`**
blue text	link to other parts of the document, a web URL, or an email address	All publications from NIST's NCCoE are available at https://www.nccoe.nist.gov.

3 Background

Most of the routing infrastructure underpinning the internet currently lacks basic security services. In most cases, internet traffic must transit multiple ISPs before reaching its destination. Each network operator implicitly trusts other ISPs to provide (via BGP) the accurate information necessary for network traffic to be routed correctly. When that information is inaccurate, traffic will take inefficient paths through the internet, arrive at malicious sites that masquerade as legitimate destinations, or never arrive at its intended destination. The consequences of these attacks can (1) deny access to internet services; (2) detour internet traffic to permit eavesdropping and to facilitate on-path attacks on endpoints (sites); (3) misdeliver internet network traffic to malicious endpoints, thereby providing the technical underpinning for other forms of cyber attack; (4) undermine IP-address-based reputation and filtering systems; and (5) cause routing instability in the internet. These impacts can be mitigated through the widespread adoption of current and emerging internet routing security protocols.

On April 8, 2010, nearly 15 percent of the world's internet traffic—including data from the United States (U.S.) Department of Defense and other U.S. government internet services—was redirected through computer networks in China [N Anderson]. Between February and May 2014, network traffic from 51 networks from 19 different ISPs was repeatedly hijacked in carefully crafted attacks aimed at stealing cryptocurrency [A Greenberg]. In June 2015, a third-party ISP in Asia asserted that it was the most efficient route to the entire internet, disrupting traffic worldwide and resulting in customers experiencing severe network problems [Saarinen]. In February 2008, YouTube became unreachable from most, if not all, of the internet. In an attempt to block access to a video that the Pakistani government considered blasphemous, Pakistan Telecom inadvertently redirected YouTube's traffic worldwide to an alternative site [Singel]. While, to date, the impacts of these events range from a loss of access to social media to potential issues of national and economic security, they share a root cause: the internet's routing infrastructure currently relies on protocols that lack basic security services.

This lack of security in the internet's routing infrastructure could be mitigated through the widespread adoption of current and emerging internet security protocols. The IETF, with significant contributions from the Department of Homeland Security and NIST, has developed standards and protocols to secure global internet routing. For example, the IETF has defined the RPKI, which is designed to secure the internet's routing infrastructure. The RPKI enables an enterprise to prove that it holds a range of internet addresses and to identify the ASes that the holder authorizes to originate routes to its addresses by using cryptographically verifiable ROAs. RPKI services are available today from the RIRs, which manage the allocation and registration of internet resources. Commercial routers are available today that are capable of using RPKI data to identify accidental errors in routing announcements by determining that the origin AS in the route contradicts an existing ROA in the RPKI.

ROV provides good protection against the accidental mis-origination of routes, but not necessarily against the intentional (e.g., malicious) mis-origination of routes. If an attacker adds the autonomous system number (ASN) (of the AS that is authorized to originate a route) to the beginning of the AS path in a bogus BGP route update in order to forge the origin AS in that update, then the bogus route update will pass ROV and will not be detected as bogus even though it is, because ROV assumes that the AS path is correct, rather than providing any sort of integrity checking on the AS path.

A separate protocol, BGPsec, augments RPKI-based ROV to detect these types of malicious route announcements by enabling network operators to verify the validity of the entire routing path across the internet (referred to as path validation), as opposed to just validating the authority of the originating AS. If widely implemented together, ROV and BGPsec would significantly improve the security and stability of global internet routing.

Unfortunately, the adoption of ROV and BGPsec security protocols has been slow due to impediments, such as usability, performance, and cost:

- Usability: Internet routing security mechanisms are implemented primarily by ISPs and ASes. As such, the usability impacts are felt mostly by systems administrators for those services. ISP and

AS administrators are faced with relatively few application choices, immature documentation, relatively immature products, and relatively complex installation and configuration processes. Furthermore, adding more data, data sources, and maintainers to the BGP decision and policy frameworks imparts several new failure modes. Thus, an already complex troubleshooting landscape can get significantly more complex.

- Performance: Some increase in processing latency may occur due to the processing associated with routing security protocols. With the use of RPKI to address ROV and the addition of an RPKI cache(s), new router operating systems (OSes) may have performance implications. A more significant performance issue is that longer paths to destinations are used due to fewer routing path choices from improper configuration. BGPsec path validation introduces a different set of performance issues. The reduction in available paths would be due to ISP/AS interdependencies that exacerbate the effects of connection refusals due to path validation failures in a path when an ISP/AS has not implemented the required integrity verification functionality. As in the case of Domain Name System Security, many of the connection refusals may be due to certificate management difficulties. The BPGsec protocol to be used for path validation is expected to be resource intensive. Each BGP update will have one or more digital signatures in it, thereby increasing the size of the message. Every one of the AS hops in the AS path will have an associated digital signature that must be verified. Also, each update will be able to carry only a single prefix, so updates will be more numerous.

- Cost: Much of the cost associated with the implementation of ROV using RPKI involves an integration of the few, and still relatively immature, products into existing systems that have an installed applications base, complete with restrictive support agreements. For example, some vendors prohibit the installation of software other than that distributed by themselves. Immature documentation and relatively complex installation and configuration processes add to this labor cost impact. Support contract impacts also represent a very significant cost-based impediment to ROV implementation at this time. If equipment needs to be upgraded, then its support contract may need to be updated or revised. The cost of implementing BGPsec in the future may be significantly larger than RPKI-based ROV. Because ISPs and ASes will need to support an additional type of certificate that binds their ASN to a public key, additional provisions for RPKI and router processing resources (upgraded hardware and router memory) will be needed to support path validation.

Other impediments to adoption include needed security features not being available from a vendor with which significant user sets have restrictive support contracts; incompatibility with potential users' installed bases; uncertainties associated with installation, integration, and activation processes; support concerns on the part of potential users who rely on software that is subject to frequent updates; resistance to making changes that might change the user experience (regardless of user-experience improvements that may accrue); and simply not being on the potential user's already-approved long-term system development, upgrade, and support plans (road maps).

The relative immaturity of available components and the lack of ubiquitous support for those components are also impediments to the implementation of route origin and path validation protocols.

Additional labor and support contract costs from equipment upgrades can result in competitive disadvantages. At least at first, mandating ROV can result in reduced routing path options (especially in the face of ISP/AS interdependencies), fewer partner relationship options, and fewer service delivery options.

Although the adoption of both ROV and BGPsec may have been hindered for the reasons mentioned above, the adoption and deployment of BGPsec is expected to be even slower relative to that of ROV. Commercial BGPsec implementations are not currently available. Also, the use of digital signatures in BGPsec adds a level of complexity with respect to the acquisition and management of router public keys, as well as the X.509 certificates used in sharing those keys. The relative scarcity of key management tools means that implementing organizations spend significant expert labor resources on complex cryptographic key-related acquisition, installation, configuration, and management.

ROV, on the other hand, has already been incorporated into the equipment of major vendors (i.e., it ships with Cisco, Juniper, and Alcatel/Lucent/Nokia routers), and all RIRs are in production mode with RPKI services. Furthermore, in some regions of the world, RIRs provide tools and support that facilitate the efficient implementation of these protocols. ROV adoption is sluggish in North America, where demand is insufficient to motivate the adoption of RPKI on a large scale. Customers do not demand ROV from their own network providers because the primary benefit would be to customers of other networks. Network providers are hesitant to invest in routing security because their customers do not demand it. Numerous governmental and industry road maps (e.g., Federal Communications Commission Communications Security, Reliability and Interoperability Council III Working Groups 4 and 6 reports) do call for the incremental deployment of new BGP security technologies. However, market pressure has been insufficient to overcome implementation constraints, and commercial adoption to date has been slow.

As previously mentioned, this situation is beginning to change in other regions of the world. Europe, in particular, is approaching an ROA coverage of approximately 43 percent of its announced IPv4 address space, due, in part, to forward-looking adoption policies and favorable and flexible usage polices for RPKI services. North America trails Europe, Latin and South America, and Africa in its rate of adoption, with only approximately seven percent of its announced IPv4 address space covered by ROA.

Given the lack of commercial vendor implementation support for BGPsec, other obstacles currently hindering its adoption, and the more favorable position of ROV with respect to being standardized and incorporated into vendor equipment, this effort is initially focusing only on BGP ROV.

The proof-of-concept implementation described in this Practice Guide demonstrates the use of available hardware and software to mitigate impediments to the adoption of ROV protocols. It takes advantage of available tools to facilitate implementation, operation, and maintenance; to improve the performance of administration functions; and to reduce the labor requirements that are major contributors to implementation costs. It is anticipated that a successful demonstration of currently available products and tools that mitigate the impediments preventing individual institutions from implementing ROV will foster the increased implementation of routing security protocols to the point that interoperability considerations will favor global implementation.

For hosted RPKI, an RIR provides the infrastructure to host the certificate authorities (CAs) and private keys used to sign the ROAs for address blocks registered in the RIR's region. An ROA authorizes one or more route prefixes to be originated from an AS and is signed with the private key associated with the prefix holder's digital end-entity (EE) certificate. The ROA also specifies a maximum prefix length (maxLength) [RFC 6482] so that an announcement of prefixes longer than the maxLength would be *invalid*. Address holders who are registered with the RIR and have received address allocations from it can access tools provided by the RIR to create and publish ROAs for those addresses. Those ROAs are stored in the RIR's RPKI repositories. Network operators around the world can retrieve the ROAs from the RIR RPKI repositories, validate their integrity and authenticity, and use the information in the ROAs to detect the validity of the origin AS in the received BGP updates. Depending on the ISP's or AS's policy, routes (i.e., updates) that fail ROV may be assigned a lower priority in the route selection or may be discarded. A failed ROV indicates that the ROV evaluation process determines the route to be *invalid*. For delegated RPKI, address holders (e.g., ISPs, large enterprises) operate a delegated RPKI CA and their own publication point to store associated certificates, keys, and ROAs. This implementation model allows an ISP or other entity to offer hosted or delegated RPKI resources to its customers. This project focused on both the hosted RPKI model and the delegated RPKI model.

4 Approach

4.1 Audience

This guide is intended for individuals responsible for implementing security solutions in organizations' IT support activities. The information provided in this Practice Guide permits the integration of ROV with minimum changes to the existing infrastructure and with minimum impact to service operations. The technical components will appeal to system administrators, IT managers, IT security managers, and others directly involved in the secure and safe operation of the business IT networks.

4.2 Scope

The scope of this project covers the roles of both address holders and network operators. Address holders are responsible for creating RPKI content, such as ROAs, that can be used to validate that specific ASes are authorized to originate routes to the addresses that they hold. Network operators are responsible for providing BGP-based routing services to clients and their peer networks in other ASes, and use the ROAs and other RPKI content to perform ROV. Note that the same entity may be both an address holder and a network operator.

For address holders, the scope of this project includes the demonstration of two implementation models of RPKI: hosted RPKI and delegated RPKI.

A determination of the vulnerability of the RPKI repository to intrusion and malicious alterations of data was outside the scope of the project. The project included partners and Community of Interest (COI) collaborators from various classes of enterprises, and service providers that contributed to the design and conduct of tests in these areas.

For network operators, the scope of the project focused on the deployment of, and scenarios for the use of, RPKI-ROA information in support of BGP ROV [RFC 6811]. The project tested the functionality of RPKI/ROV components and documented issues and best practices for the operation and use of RPKI validating caches (VCs) and ROV-capable BGP routers. It addressed issues about the robustness and responsiveness of these components, as well as routing policies that can be configured for them. The project included COI and National Cybersecurity Excellence Partnership (NCEP) partners to provide commercial off-the-shelf (COTS) and open-source products that implement the components necessary for BGP network operators to acquire, validate, and use RPKI information to implement BGP ROV. The project also included COI collaborators from various classes of network operators (e.g., enterprise, stub ISPs, regional networks, transit ISPs, internet exchange point operators) that contributed to the design and conduct of tests in realistic scenarios (e.g., BGP routing architectures, exterior border gateway protocol [eBGP] and interior border gateway protocol [iBGP], ISP architectures).

For each deployment scenario, RPKI-based ROV functionality was validated, including various scenarios for BGP ROV results (*valid*, *invalid*, and *not found* [RFC 6811]) and vendor implementation-specific options for RPKI-ROV-based filtering mechanisms. This project has resulted in this freely available NIST Cybersecurity Practice Guide describing steps to demonstrate, deploy, and manage RPKI-based ROV for both enterprises and network operators; identify implementation and interoperability issues; provide sample deployment architectures; and provide lessons learned from employing controls identified in [NIST SP 800-53].

The IETF has also developed a new protocol called BGPsec, which provides cryptographic protection for the entire AS path in a BGP update. This security extension to BGP would help prevent AS path modification attacks (e.g., maliciously shortening the AS path to redirect traffic). However, commercial router implementations of BGPsec are not currently available. Hence, this effort initially focuses on BGP ROV, and consideration of the BGPsec protocol is currently outside the scope of this project.

4.3 Assumptions

This project assumes that most potential adopters of the demonstrated build or any build components do not already have RPKI-based ROV tools or mechanisms in place, but that they do already have routing systems. This Practice Guide is intended to provide installation, configuration, and integration guidance, and assumes that an organization has the technical resources to implement all or parts of the build or has access to companies that can perform the implementation on its behalf. The guidance provided in this document may be used to provide a complete top-to-bottom solution or may be applied in a modular fashion to provide selected options based on need. It is intended that the benefits of adopting

RPKI-based ROV outweigh any additional performance, reliability, or security risks that may be introduced by instantiating the protocols.

RIRs play vital roles in RPKI, both in terms of assisting with the creation of RPKI content by address holders and in terms of making that content available to relying parties (RPs) via repositories that are hosted online. It is assumed that address holders understand the usage of RPKI resources. When using the hosted model, address holders must have agreements in place with an RIR or other hosting authority that enables the address holder to request that the host create, sign, and store ROAs for the address holders' addresses. When using the delegated model, the address holder must provide and manage its own RPKI infrastructure and CA to create, sign, store, and manage its own ROAs, rather than rely on a host to provide this infrastructure and services. For organizations that choose to use the delegated model and run their own CA, there is open-source software available to create the RPKI infrastructure and securely communicate with the RIR parent system. Network operators who provide BGP-based routing services are responsible for operating RPKI VCs and ROV-capable routers so that they can retrieve ROA information from RPKI repositories and can use it to perform ROV on BGP updates that they receive.

When a router applies ROV to a received BGP update, the router determines whether the update is *valid*, *invalid*, or *not found*. Based on this information, organizations can apply policies to the routes. *Valid* routes should typically be installed into the routing table, but what a router does with *invalid* and *not found* routes is the prerogative of the organization that operates the router, and will depend on local policy. Service provider policies may take into account whether there are requirements to forward routes to customers as well as local considerations. Enterprise policies will depend on enterprise-specific considerations. This project does not attempt to dictate the policies that any organization should implement. As a first step toward adoption, enterprises could simply perform ROV and mark all routes as *valid*, *invalid*, or *not found*. No further policy is needed beyond simply observing the number of routes that are *invalid* or *not found*.

4.4 Risk Assessment

While this guide does not present a full risk assessment as discussed in [NIST SP 800-30] or [NIST SP 800-37], it does describe the risks associated with unauthorized updates to routing information and identify some route hijacking risks that may be addressed in follow-on project activities.

NIST SP 800-30, *Guide for Conducting Risk Assessments*, states that risk is "a measure of the extent to which an entity is threatened by a potential circumstance or event, and typically a function of (i) the adverse impacts that would arise if the circumstance or event occurs and (ii) the likelihood of occurrence." The guide further defines risk assessment as "the process of identifying, estimating, and prioritizing risks to organizational operations (including mission, functions, image, and reputation), organizational assets, individuals, other organizations, and the Nation, resulting from the operation of an information system. Part of risk management incorporates threat and vulnerability analyses, and considers the mitigations provided by planned or in-place security controls."

The NCCoE recommends that any discussion of risk management, particularly at the enterprise level, begins with a comprehensive review of NIST SP 800-37, *Guide for Applying the Risk Management Framework to Federal Information Systems*—material that is available to the public. The Risk Management Framework (RMF) guidance, as a whole, proved to be invaluable in giving us a baseline to assess risks, from which we developed the project, the security characteristics of the build, and this guide.

4.4.1 Threats

The IETF's *Threat Model for BGP Path Security* [RFC 7132] points out that BGP routers themselves can inject bogus routing information either by masquerading as any other legitimate BGP router or by distributing unauthorized routing information as themselves. Historically, misconfigured and faulty routers have been responsible for widespread disruptions in the internet. As stated in [RFC 4593], legitimate BGP peers have the context and information to produce believable, yet bogus, routing information, and therefore have the opportunity to cause great damage. Cryptographic protections and operational protections cannot necessarily exclude the bogus information arising from a legitimate peer.

Threats to routing include deliberate exposure, sniffing, traffic analysis, spoofing, false route origination, interference, secure path downgrade, and overload. Of these, spoofing and false origination are most relevant to this project.

- Spoofing: occurs when an illegitimate device assumes the identity of a legitimate one. Spoofing, in and of itself, is often not the true attack. Spoofing is special, in that an attacker can use it as a means for launching other types of attacks. For example, if an attacker succeeds in spoofing the identity of a router, then the attacker can send out unrealistic routing information that might cause the disruption of network services. There are a few cases where spoofing can be an attack in and of itself. For example, messages from an attacker that spoof the identity of a legitimate router may cause a neighbor relationship to form and deny the formation of the relationship with the legitimate router. The primary consequence is that the authorized routers, which exchange routing messages with the spoofing router, do not realize that they are neighboring with a router that is faking another router's identity. Another consequence includes the spoofing router gaining access to the routing information.

- False route origination: occurs when an attacker sends false routing information. To falsify the routing information, an attacker has to be either the originator or a forwarder of the routing information. The attacker cannot be only a receiver. This project primarily addresses the falsification of route updates. Routers that legitimately forward routing protocol messages are expected to leave some fields unmodified and to modify other fields in certain circumscribed ways. The fields to be modified, the possible new contents of those fields, and their computation from the original fields—the fields that must remain unmodified, etc.—are all detailed in the protocol specification [RFC 4271]. These details may vary depending on the function of the router or its network environment. The primary threat here is misstatement, an action whereby the attacker modifies route attributes in an incorrect manner. In BGP, the attacker might delete some ASNs from the AS path. When forwarding routing information that should not be modified, an attacker can launch the following falsifications:

- Deletion – The attacker deletes *valid* data in the routing message.

- Insertion – The attacker inserts false information in the routing message.

- Substitution – The attacker replaces *valid* data in the routing message with false data.

The threat consequences of these falsifications by forwarders include the usurpation of some network resources and related routers, the deception of routers using false paths, and the disruption of the data planes of routers on the false paths. RPKI-based ROV provides protection against deletions, insertions, and substitutions that result in an AS that is not authorized to originate a BGP update being listed as the origin of that update. To protect against attacks on other parts of the AS path, however, BGPsec is needed.

A comprehensive treatment of threats to BGP path security (i.e., threats to other parts of the AS path, besides the origin) can be found in IETF [RFC 7132]. Of particular interest to this project are attacks on an RPKI CA (Section 4.5 of the RFC) because not only path security, but also BGP ROV, relies on the RPKI. Every entity to which Internet Number Resources (INRs) have been allocated/assigned is a CA in the RPKI. These resources include IPv4 or IPv6 address space and ASNs. ASNs are two-byte or four-byte numbers issued by a registry to identify an AS in BGP. Each CA is nominally responsible for managing the repository publication point for the set of signed products that it generates. An INR holder may choose to outsource the operation of the RPKI CA function and the associated publication point. In such cases, the organization operating on behalf of the INR holder becomes the CA, from an operational and security perspective. Note that attacks attributable to a CA may be the result of malice by the CA (i.e., the CA is the adversary) or may result from a compromise of the CA.

The RPKI, upon which BGP ROV and path security rely, has several residual vulnerabilities that are discussed in Sections 4.4 and 4.5 of [RFC 7132]. These vulnerabilities are of two principal forms:

- The RPKI repository system may be attacked in ways that make its contents unavailable, not current, or inconsistent. Such attacks assume that an adversary does not have access to the cryptographic keys needed to generate valid RPKI-signed products. The principal defense against most forms of such DoS attacks is the use of a VC by each RP. The VC ensures the availability of previously acquired RPKI data, in the event that a repository is inaccessible, or the repository contents are deleted (maliciously). Nonetheless, the use of a VC cannot ensure that every RP will always have access to up-to-date RPKI data. An RP, when it detects a problem with acquired repository data, has two options:

- The RP may choose to make use of its VC, employing configuration settings that tolerate expired or stale objects. (Such behavior is, nominally, always within the purview of an RP.) Using cached, expired, or stale data subjects the RP to attacks that take advantage of the RP's ignorance of changes to this data.

- The RP may choose to purge expired objects. Purging expired objects removes the security information associated with the real-world INRs to which the objects refer. This is equivalent to the affected INRs not having been afforded protection via the RPKI. Because the use of the RPKI is voluntary, there may always be a set of INRs that are not protected by these mechanisms. Thus, purging moves the affected INRs to the set of non-participating INR holders.

- Any CA in the RPKI may misbehave within the bounds of the INRs allocated to it (e.g., it may issue certificates with duplicate resource allocations or revoke certificates inappropriately). This vulnerability is intrinsic in any Public Key Infrastructure (PKI), but its impact is limited in the RPKI because of the use of the X.509 certificate extensions defined in [RFC 3779] to bind lists of prefixes or AS identifiers to the subject of a certificate. It is anticipated that RPs will deal with such misbehavior through administrative means once it is detected.

4.4.2 Vulnerabilities

Border Gateway Protocol 4 (BGP-4) was designed before the internet environment became perilous, and it was originally designed with little consideration for the protection of the information it carries. There were originally no mechanisms internal to BGP that protected against attacks that modified, deleted, forged, or replayed data, any of which has the potential to disrupt overall network routing behavior. (See IETF [RFC 4272] for a BGP security vulnerabilities analysis.) Except for RPKI-based ROV and mechanisms described in BGPsec [RFC 8205], BGP still does not include mechanisms that allow an AS to verify the legitimacy and authenticity of BGP route advertisements. BGP does, however, mandate support for mechanisms to secure peer-to-peer communication (i.e., the links that connect BGP routers).

The MITRE Corporation's Common Vulnerability and Exposures (CVE) lists more than 85,000 vulnerabilities that can affect the security of information carried over internet services. The full set of vulnerabilities includes elements beyond the scope of this project (e.g., Structured Query Language [SQL] servers, Domain Name System servers, firewalls, routers, other network components [https://cve.mitre.org]). The CVE includes specific vulnerabilities inherent in BGP protocols [RFC 4271]. As in the case of client systems vulnerabilities, NIST's National Vulnerability Database (https://nvd.nist.gov) is a frequently updated source of vulnerabilities that affect network servers.

4.4.3 Risk

There is a variety of risks resulting from the possibility that vulnerabilities to BGP routing may be exploited. Some examples include the unavailability of services on which revenue depends, legal liability, stimulation of regulatory initiatives, loss of productivity, and damage to organizational reputation. These breaches can be accidental, but they can also be intentional.

- With respect to both service availability and legal liability, failure to deliver services on which customers are dependent can result in multimillion-dollar torts or contract penalties.

- Harm to, or denial of access to, the critical infrastructure and its services have occurred and, if egregious or excessively frequent, may stimulate executive or legislative initiatives imposing security regulations on currently unregulated industries.

- The time and labor expended in recovering from routing-based attacks can result in the loss of operational and maintenance productivity.

- The loss of services on which customers depend can result in a loss of confidence in the reliability of the organization and can do long-term damage to the organization's reputation.

The use of the *Cybersecurity Framework Core* is recommended to reduce these risks. The Cybersecurity Framework Core, identified in NIST's *Framework for Improving Critical Infrastructure Cybersecurity*, is a set of cybersecurity activities, desired outcomes, and applicable references that are common across critical infrastructure sectors. The Core presents industry standards, guidelines, and practices in a manner that allows for the communication of cybersecurity activities and outcomes across the organization, from the executive level to the implementation/operations level. The Cybersecurity Framework Core consists of five concurrent and continuous *Functions*—Identify, Protect, Detect, Respond, and Recover. When considered together, these Functions provide a high-level, strategic view of the life cycle of an organization's management of cybersecurity risk.

4.4.4 Cybersecurity Framework Functions, Categories, and Subcategories Addressed by the SIDR Project

Implementation of the security platform described in this publication addresses aspects of the Protect (PR), Detect (DE), Respond (RS), and Identify (ID) functions of the *Cybersecurity Framework*, as shown in Table 4-1. For a more detailed discussion of how the various components of the SIDR reference architecture solution support specific subcategories of the Cybersecurity Framework, as well as a discussion of additional references, standards, and guidelines that informed the SIDR Project, refer to Appendix D.

Table 4-1 Security Control Mapping of Cybersecurity Framework Subcategories to Capabilities of the SIDR Reference Architecture Solution

Example Characteristic		Cybersecurity Standards and Best Practices			
Security Characteristics	Example Capability	Function	Category	Subcategory	Informative References
Integrity and Authenticity	Ensure that BGP routes are originated by authorized ASes	PROTECT (PR)	Data Security (PR.DS)	PR.DS-1, PR.DS2, PR.DS-6	[ISO/IEC 27001:2013] A.8.2.3, A.13.1.1, A.13.2.1, A.13.2.3, A.14.1.2, A.14.1.3 [NIST SP 800-53] Rev. 4 SC-8, SC-28
		DETECT (DE)	Security Continuous Monitoring (DE.CM)	DE.CM-4, DE.CM-7	[ISO/IEC 27001:2013] A.12.2.1 [NIST SP 800-53] Rev. 4 AU-12, CA-7, CM-3, CM-8, PE-3, PE-6, PE-20, SI-3, SI-4

Example Characteristic		Cybersecurity Standards and Best Practices			
Security Characteristics	Example Capability	Function	Category	Subcategory	Informative References
			Detection Processes (DE.DP)	DE.DP-3	[ISO/IEC 27001:2013] A.14.2.8 [NIST SP 800-53] Rev. 4 CA-2, CA-7, PE-3, PM-14, SI-3, SI-4
Anomalous Route Detection	Ensure the detection of unauthorized routes to block misrouting or to report the anomalous events	DETECT (DE)	Detection Processes (DE.DP)	DE.DP-4	[ISO/IEC 27001:2013] A.16.1.2 [NIST SP 800-53] Rev. 4 AU-6, CA-2, CA-7, RA-5, SI-4
System and Application Hardening	Adjust security controls on the server and/or software applications such that security is maximized ("hardened") while maintaining intended use	PROTECT (PR)	Information Protection Processes and Procedures (PR.IP)	PR.IP-1, PR.IP-2	[ISO/IEC 27001:2013] A.6.1.5, A.12.1.2, A.12.5.1, A.12.6.2, A.14.1.1, A.14.2.1, A.14.2.2, A.14.2.3, A.14.2.4, A.14.2.5 [NIST SP 800-53] Rev. 4 CM-2, CM-3, CM-4, CM-5, CM-6,

Example Characteristic		Cybersecurity Standards and Best Practices			
Security Characteristics	Example Capability	Function	Category	Subcategory	Informative References
					CM-7, CM-9, PL-8, SA-3, SA-4, SA-8, SA-10, SA-11, SA-12, SA-15, SA-17
Device Protection	Ensure the protection of devices, communications, and control networks	PROTECT (PR)	Access Control (PR.AC)	PR.AC-3, PR.AC-5	[ISO/IEC 27001:2013] A.6.2.2, A.13.1.1, A.13.1.3, A.13.2.1 [NIST SP 800-53] Rev. 4 AC-4, AC-17, AC-19, AC-20, SC-7
		PROTECT (PR)	Protective Technology (PR.PT)	PR.PT-4	[ISO/IEC 27001:2013] A.13.1.1, A.13.2.1 [NIST SP 800-53] Rev. 4 AC-4, AC-17, AC-18, CP-8, SC-7

Example Characteristic		Cybersecurity Standards and Best Practices			
Security Characteristics	Example Capability	Function	Category	Subcategory	Informative References
Incident Response	Ensure the integrity of network connections in the case of incidents that result in a compromise; the effects of the compromise can be limited by the exclusion of systems and devices that have not implemented the integrity mechanisms; when routes that originated from unauthorized ASes are received, these can be logged and reported	RESPOND (RS)	Communications (RS.CO)	RS.CO-2, RS.CO-3	[ISO/IEC 27001:2013] A.6.1.3, A.16.1.2, Clause 7.4, Clause 16.1.2 [NIST SP 800-53] Rev. 4 AU-6, CA-2, CA-7, CP-2, IR-4, IR-6, IR-8, PE-6, RA-5, SI-4
		RESPOND (RS)	Mitigation (RS.MI)	RS.MI-1	[ISO/IEC 27001:2013] A.16.1.5 [NIST SP 800-53] Rev. 4 IR-4

4.5 Technologies

Table 4-2 lists all of the technologies used in this project, and provides a mapping among the generic application term, the specific product used, and the security control(s) that the product provides.

Table 4-2 Products and Technologies

Component	Product	How Component Functions	Cybersecurity Framework Subcategories
ROV-enabled Router	Cisco 7206VXR Cisco 4331 Cisco 2921 Cisco IOS XRv 9000 Juniper MX80 3D Universal Edge	Receives BGP updates, evaluates routes, and installs routes according to policy. This protects network routing integrity and, by extension, data-in-transit and the communication network as a whole. The application of ROV monitors the network for routes that have been originated without authorization. *Invalid* and *not found* routes can be tagged and reported; the rejection of *invalid* routes may help contain or mitigate incidents.	ID.AM-3: Organizational communication and data flows are mapped. ID.AM-4: External information systems are catalogued. PR.AC-5: Network integrity is protected, incorporating network segregation where appropriate. PR.DS-2: Data-in-transit is protected. PR.DS-6: Integrity-checking mechanisms are used to verify software, firmware, and information integrity. PR.PT-4: Communications and control networks are protected. DE.CM-1: The network is monitored to detect potential cybersecurity events. DE.CM-6: External service provider activity is monitored to detect potential cybersecurity events. DE.CM-7: Monitoring for unauthorized personnel, connections, devices, and software is performed. RS.CO-2: Events are reported consistent with established criteria.

Component	Product	How Component Functions	Cybersecurity Framework Subcategories
			RS.MI-1: Incidents are contained. RS.MI-2: Incidents are mitigated.
RPKI CA	Dragon Research rpki.net RPKI toolkit	Functions as a CA that contains resource certificates attesting to holdings of IP address space and ASNs, and that can issue EE certificates and ROAs for addresses within this space.	PR.AC-1: Identities and credentials are managed for authorized devices and users.
RPKI Repository	Dragon Research rpki.net RPKI toolkit	Functions as a trusted repository of RPKI information that makes signed RPKI information, such as ROAs, available to RPs.	PR.AC-1: Identities and credentials are managed for authorized devices and users.
VCs	Réseaux IP Européens Network Coordination Centre (RIPE NCC) Validator	RP software; RPKI data from a trusted repository is downloaded to this component and validated; functions as a VC with which the ROV-enabled router interacts.	PR.AC-1: Identities and credentials are managed for authorized devices and users. PR.AC-3: Remote access is managed.
	Dragon Research rpki.net RPKI toolkit		
Circuit	CenturyLink 1 gigabit per second (Gbps) Ethernet link	Connectivity to the internet.	PR.AC-3: Remote access is managed.
Firewall	Palo Alto Networks Next-Generation Firewall PA-5060	Firewall protecting the lab network from the internet.	PR.AC-3: Remote access is managed.

4.5.1 ROV-Enabled Routers

The participating router vendors are Cisco and Juniper. These routers contain OSes that can perform ROV. The protocol used by these routers to communicate to the VCs is the RPKI-to-Router protocol [RFC 6810], [RFC 8210]. The routers connect to a 1 Gbps Ethernet link provided by CenturyLink. Route advertisements and updates are provided through this link. The routers connect to the virtual environments that represent their AS infrastructure through 1 Gbps Ethernet links.

4.5.1.1 Cisco Routers

Cisco routers used in the lab are Cisco 7206VXR routers. These "wide area network edge" routers have the following features: support for BGP ROV [RFC 6810], [RFC 6811]; Quality of Service; Multiprotocol Label Switching; and Voice over IP. They support various interfaces, such as Gigabit Ethernet (GbE) using copper or fiber, mixed-enabled T1/E1, and Packet over Synchronous Optical Network (SONET).

4.5.1.2 Juniper Routers

The Juniper routers used in this lab build are MX80 3D Universal Edge. These routers are described as best used for wide area network, Data Center Interconnect, branch aggregation, and campus applications. They have 10 GbE and modular interface capabilities for supporting a variety of interfaces, including [RFC 6810] and [RFC 6811].

4.5.2 RPKI CA

One of the components of the Dragon Research rpki.net RPKI toolkit is software that functions as a CA that enables resource certificates attesting to holdings of IP address space and ASNs, EE certificates, and ROAs to be created and signed. The Dragon Research rpki.net software is open-source and available via GitHub at https://github.com/dragonresearch/rpki.net.

Note: The above link provides the toolkit, which includes the RPKI CA, repository, and VC.

4.5.3 RPKI Repository

A second component of the Dragon Research rpki.net RPKI toolkit is software that functions as an RPKI repository that stores RPKI information and makes it available to RPs for use in ROV.

4.5.4 VCs

Two different open-source software products were used in the build to serve as VCs: the RIPE NCC Validator, which is recommended for use by the American Registry for Internet Numbers (ARIN), and a third component of the Dragon Research rpki.net RPKI toolkit, which ARIN also references.

4.5.5 Circuit

CenturyLink provided a 1 Gbps circuit that provided connectivity from our laboratory architecture to the internet, through which the RPKI repository system could be accessed, and a full BGP route table was provided.

4.5.6 Firewall

Palo Alto Networks provided a model PA-5060 firewall to protect the lab infrastructure from internet traffic. The firewall provides protection against known and unknown threats. In this deployment, only the ports and connections necessary for the build are configured. All other ports and connections are denied.

5 Architecture

5.1 Overall RPKI-Based ROV Reference Architecture

ROV depends on two separate, complementary functions being performed: ROA creation and ROV. To build a robust RPKI infrastructure to support ROV, all address holders (i.e., all entities that have been allocated IP address space) should ensure that ROAs for their addresses are created, signed, and stored in an RPKI repository system. The RPKI repository system will then make these ROAs and other RPKI information available for use by network operators to perform ROV on the BGP route updates that they receive. Hence, conceptually, there are two reference architectures necessary for supporting RPKI-based ROV: the ROV reference architecture, which is implemented by network operators and is used to perform ROV (Section 5.1.1, Figure 5-1), and the RPKI reference architecture, which is implemented by address holders and is used to create and store RPKI information (e.g., ROAs) (Section 5.1.2, Figure 5-2 and Figure 5-3).

Note that all network operators are also address holders, so network operators will typically implement both reference architectures. On the other hand, not all address holders are network operators, so some address holders (e.g., enterprises that rely on upstream ISPs to perform ROV on their behalf) may implement only the RPKI reference architecture; there is no reason for these address holders to implement the ROV reference architecture because they will not be performing ROV.

5.1.1 ROV Reference Architecture

Figure 5-1 depicts the reference architecture for ROV. As can be seen in Figure 5-1, only three components are needed to perform ROV: an ROV-capable router, a VC, and access to global RPKI repositories. Typically, but not necessarily, the trusted RPKI repositories will be repositories that are hosted by an RIR. This architecture is not intended to represent physical connectivity among the architecture components. Instead, it is meant to illustrate how they exchange information with each other.

Figure 5-1 The ROV Portion of the RPKI-Based ROV Reference Architecture

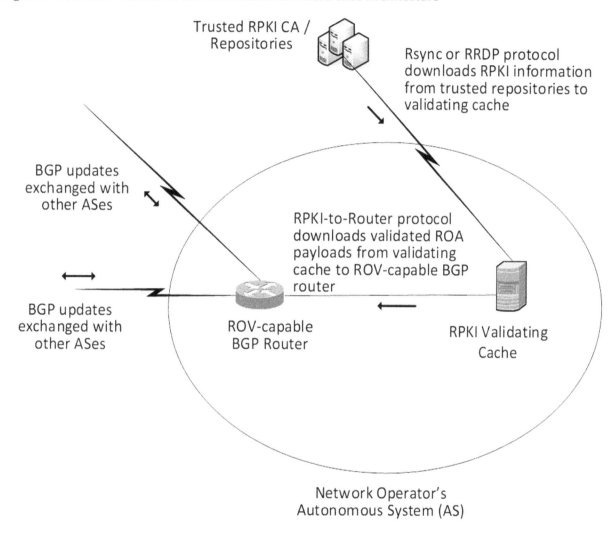

The network operator must deploy two components to perform ROV:

- RPKI VC

  - The Remote Synchronization (rsync) protocol is required to support interoperability between the RPKI VC and the trusted RPKI repositories. RPKI Repository Delta Protocol (RRDP) [RFC 8182] is also supported by some RIRs for this same purpose.

  - The RPKI-to-router protocol [RFC 6810] is required to support interoperability between the RPKI VC and the local ROV-enabled routers, route reflectors, and route servers.

- ROV-enabled BGP routers

  ROV policy options should be configured on these routers according to network operator policy and according to the network operator's status:

  - Stub AS (i.e., Enterprise) ROV policy configurations

  - Transit AS (i.e., ISP) ROV policy configurations

  - Intra-AS ROV policy configuration (iBGP ROV signaling [RFC 8097], monitoring, and management)

It is a matter of local policy regarding what action should be taken when an incoming BGP route update is determined to be *valid*, *invalid*, or *not found*. However, the particular actions that are configured to be performed will likely depend on the location of the BGP router that is validating the update (i.e., whether it is located within an ISP that the advertisement is transiting, whether it is located in a stub network, and whether it is an Internet Exchange Point router) as well as on the business model of the entity performing the ROV. More discussion of the considerations related to ROV policy are discussed in the Outcome section (Section 6).

5.1.2 RPKI Reference Architecture

The RPKI reference architecture is used by address holders to create, sign, manage, and store ROAs. ROA information is the foundation on which routers and networks perform ROV. However, not all address holders share a single, uniform perspective of the RPKI reference architecture. Address holders may create ROAs by using either the hosted model or the delegated model, and the structure of the RPKI reference architecture differs according to which of these models is being used. Figure 5-2 (Section 5.1.2.1) depicts the RPKI reference architecture as implemented by address holders using the hosted model, and Figure 5-3 (Section 5.1.2.2) depicts the RPKI reference architecture as implemented by address holders using the delegated model.

5.1.2.1 Hosted-Model RPKI Reference Architecture

Figure 5-2 The Hosted-Model RPKI Reference Architecture

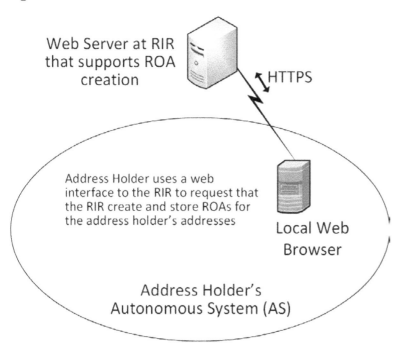

Figure 5-2 depicts the reference architecture for a hosted-model RPKI. As can be seen in the figure, an address holder wishing to use the hosted model of RPKI for ROA creation and storage needs to only have a web interface to the RIR or other authority from which it was allocated its addresses and other resources. As with Figure 5-1, this architecture is not intended to represent physical connectivity among the architecture components. Instead, it is meant to illustrate how they exchange information with each other.

In the hosted model, an RIR (or other authority) is responsible for operating an RPKI CA and repository. The RIR creates and signs ROAs for resources that are within the region that it oversees and that it has allocated. It also stores the ROAs in its repository. The address holder uses a tool (i.e., a web interface) to request that this RIR or other authority create, sign, manage, and store ROAs for its addresses on its behalf. In this model, the address holder does not have any responsibility to stand up or maintain a CA or repository or to directly create or maintain any of the RPKI information stored in it. All tools and applications for creating ROAs reside in the RIRs (or another organization that is hosting the RPKI service). RIRs provide the infrastructure and tools to create and store EE certificates, ROAs, and other RPKI information. Network operators are able to pull ROA information from the RIR (or other authority) repositories and use it to perform ROV.

Figure 5-3 The Delegated-Model RPKI Reference Architecture

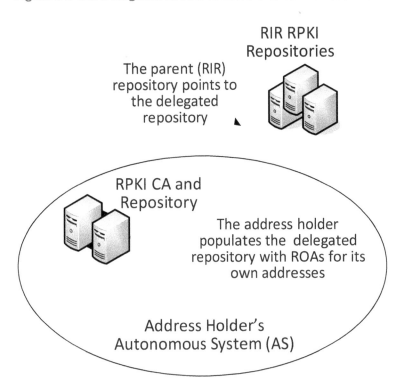

Figure 5-3 depicts the reference architecture for the delegated-model RPKI. As can be seen in the figure, the delegated model of RPKI for ROA creation and storage requires that two components be set up, operated, and maintained by the address holder: a CA and a repository. As with Figure 5-1 and Figure 5-2, this architecture is not intended to represent physical connectivity among the architecture components. Instead, it is meant to illustrate how they exchange information with each other.

In addition to setting up these components, the address holder must obtain an authorization to sub-allocate these resources from the RIR or other authority from which it received its address and other resource allocations as well as a CA certificate for these resources. The address holder must store the private key of its delegated RPKI key pair, exchange the public keys of the key pairs that it creates with its RIR, and store the resource certificates and ROAs in its repository. The CA certificate that the address holder receives from its RIR attests to the fact that the resources have been allocated. When it sub-allocates resources, the address holder may use its CA certificate to issue resource certificates that attest to these sub-allocations. If the address holder has customers to which it sub-allocates addresses, it can offer a hosted model of RPKI to its customers by creating and storing ROAs on behalf of those customers. Alternatively, if the resource holder has customers who want to set up their own delegated model of RPKI, it can authorize them to do so and can provide them with CA certificates attesting to their sub-allocations.

The address holder uses its CA certificate to generate EE certificates and thereby create and sign ROAs for addresses in its allocation, rather than rely on the RIR (or other authority) to do so. Once it creates and signs ROAs, it stores them in its repository and makes them available to VCs via the rsync or RRDP protocol. Network operators performing ROV are able to locate the delegated repository because the repository of the RIR (or other authority) that allocated the resources to the address holder will point to the delegated repository. Hence, although the parent repository is not actually part of the delegated RPKI reference model, the fact that it points to the delegated RPKI repository is crucial.

Because the applications and infrastructure for creating and storing ROAs reside in the address holder's network, the address holder itself, rather than an RIR or other outside entity, is responsible for the accessibility, robustness, and responsiveness of the delegated CA and repository. As the operator of the CA and repository, the address holder is also responsible for resource certification maintenance; ROA creation, maintenance, and revocation; as well as RPKI management, monitoring, and debugging, as needed. For many organizations, the responsibilities of running a delegated CA, such as the availability and complexity of setting up a CA in a secure fashion, the relative lack of availability of software products supporting the delegated model, developing a Certification Practice Statement, maintaining hardware security modules, and managing the delegated model repository, are found to be burdensome. In addition, there are many issues with running a CA in a delegated model [NIST SP 800-57 Part 2], [RFC 6484], [RFC 7382]. Available products for supporting the delegated model are limited and were not offered for this project. Consequently, the proof-of-concept demonstration focused mostly on the hosted model.

5.2 Combined ROV and RPKI Reference Architecture Example

Figure 5-4 depicts examples of all three reference architectures (ROV, hosted RPKI, and delegated RPKI) in one realistic network diagram. It shows three ASes (AS A, AS B, and AS C), each of which is capable of participating in RPKI-based ROV, both as a network operator and as an address holder. Figure 5-4 also includes icons representing RIR RPKI CAs and repositories.

Figure 5-4 Example ROV and RPKI Reference Architectures

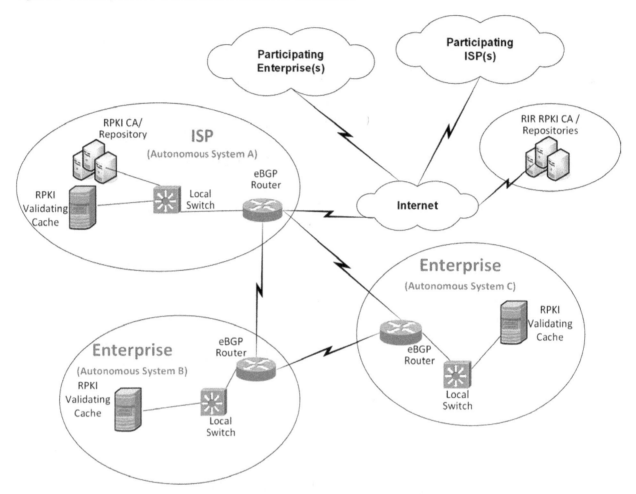

Viewing the architecture in Figure 5-4, in terms of its depiction of address holders, AS A represents an address holder that is implementing the delegated model of RPKI. This AS has set up its own CA and repository and is responsible for creating, signing, and storing ROAs for the addresses that it holds and for any addresses that it may sub-allocate to its customers. ROAs for all addresses that have been allocated to AS A must be downloaded from the repository that is associated with AS A. Assuming that AS A received its address allocation from an RIR, that RIR's repository will point to AS A's repository.

On the other hand, AS B and AS C represent address holders that are implementing the hosted model of RPKI. They have not set up their own CA or repositories. When they want to have ROAs created for the addresses that they hold, they must request that the entity that allocated the addresses to them creates, signs, and stores the ROAs on their behalf. AS B or AS C may have received its address allocation from its RIR, in which case it would use a tool (i.e., a web interface to an RIR tool) to request that the RIR creates, manages, and stores its ROAs. Alternatively, AS B or AS C may have received its address allocation from its ISP (i.e., from AS A). In this case, it would rely on AS A to create, manage, and store its ROAs.

Viewing the architecture in Figure 5-4, in terms of its depiction of network operators, all three ASes are network operators that are capable of performing ROV on all BGP updates that they receive. To perform ROV, a network operator must have an ROV-capable router, a VC (local or remote), and the ability for its VC to connect to its RPKI trust anchor (i.e., to the repository associated with AS A or to one of the RIR repositories).

Usage scenarios for ROV and for the RPKI hosted and delegated models are discussed in Section 5.3.

5.3 Usage Scenarios

5.3.1 ROV Usage Scenario

Figure 5-5 depicts the steps of an ROV usage scenario.

Figure 5-5 Route Origin Validation Usage Scenario

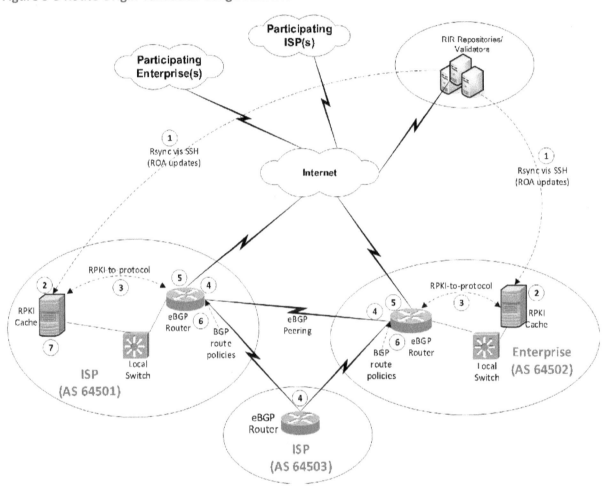

In this scenario, it is assumed that some address holders have created ROAs for the addresses that they hold. These ROAs are stored in the RPKI repository system, and network operators use these ROAs as the basis on which to perform the ROV. The steps of the ROV usage scenario, which are performed by AS 64501 and AS 64502 in their role as network operators, are as follows:

1. ROA information is pulled down to the RPKI VC (labelled "RPKI Cache") in AS 64501 and AS 64502 by using the remote file synchronization protocol rsync or RRDP between the RIR repositories and the VC.

2. The RPKI VC receives all ROAs and certificates from the RIR repositories and validates this information.

3. In AS 64501 and AS 64502, the RPKI VC communicates with the local eBGP router to send validated ROA payload (VRP) data to the router using the RPKI-to-Router protocol.

4. Each eBGP router receives BGP updates from its neighbors.

5. Each eBGP router checks the BGP updates against the VRP information received from the RPKI VC and uses this information to evaluate each update as *valid*, *invalid*, or *not found*.

6. Each eBGP router makes a routing decision, based on ROV policies, regarding what to do with the route. (Generally, if the route is found to be *valid*, then it will be accepted. How *invalid* or *not found* routes are acted upon depends on local policy.)

5.3.2 Hosted-Model Usage Scenario

To understand the hosted model of RPKI in the context of Figure 5-2, assume that both AS 64501 and AS 64502 (in their role as address holders) have received their IP address allocations from their RIRs. These ASes are responsible for ROA creation, maintenance, and revocation for the addresses that they hold. However, they do not have a locally deployed CA or repository. To create ROAs, these ASes would have to use the hosted model. They would register with their RIR and use its web interface to request that it create, sign, and store ROAs for the addresses that they were allocated by that RIR.

5.3.3 Delegated-Model Usage Scenario

In the context of Figure 5-6, the ISP in AS 64501 is hosting a delegated model of RPKI. It is authorized by the RIR from which it received its IP addresses to sub-allocate those addresses and issue CA certificates for those sub-allocations. It has set up its own CA to create and sign ROAs for these addresses, as well as a repository to store these ROAs and other RPKI data and make them available to network operators that want to perform ROV. It has also ensured that its parent RIR repository points to the repository that is associated with its own AS.

Figure 5-6 Delegated-Model RPKI Usage Scenario

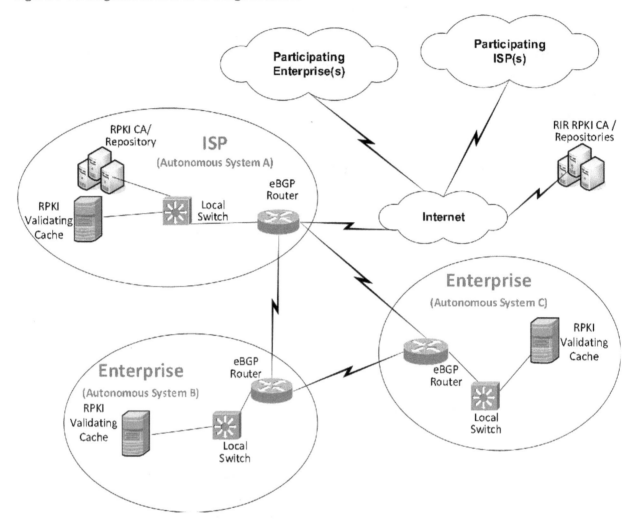

5.4 SIDR Laboratory Architecture

The SIDR laboratory's physical architecture is depicted in <u>Figure 5-7</u>. It consists of virtual and physical hardware and a physical circuit to CenturyLink, which provides connectivity to the internet where the RIRs reside. The architecture is organized into eight separate networks, each of which is designed to represent a different AS. For example, the network labelled 10.10.0.0/16 represents a transit ISP with AS 65501, the network labelled 10.50.0.0/16 represents a stub enterprise network of an organization with AS 65505, etc. The physical hardware mainly consists of the routers performing ROV and the firewalls that protect the lab infrastructure. The virtual environment hosts the various software components needed to implement the ROV and RPKI reference architectures: a local RPKI repository in AS 65501 that is needed to implement the delegated model of RPKI and various VCs in several ASes that are needed to perform ROV. Four network operators are capable of performing ROV, each of which is depicted as having a local VC: AS 65501, AS 65504, AS 65505, and AS 65507. AS 65500, AS 65502, AS 65503, and AS 65508 do not have VCs and therefore lack the necessary infrastructure to perform ROV. In Figure 5-7, AS 65508 is colored red to represent a malicious attacker that may originate unauthorized BGP updates in an attempt to hijack routes.

Figure 5-7 SIDR Lab Physical Architecture

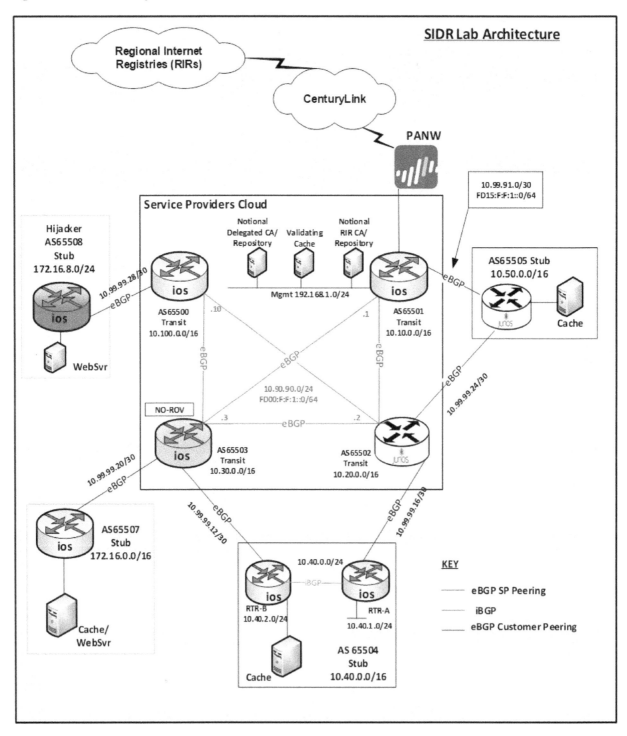

The architecture is designed to support a demonstration of both the hosted model and the delegated model.

Unfortunately, for the hosted model, we did not have address allocations from RIRs, or agreements in place with RIRs, that would give us access to the RIR to create and store ROAs at their repositories. To demonstrate the hosted model without access to RIR ROA creation tools, we set up a root CA and repository in AS 65501 (denoted by the *Notional RIR CA/Repository* icon in Figure 5-7) and used it to represent a notional RIR. ROAs for AS 65504 and AS 65507 could be stored in the Notional RIR repository just as they would typically be stored in an RIR repository if they had received their address allocations directly from an RIR rather than from our notional RIR.

In Figure 5-7, the delegated model is represented by the icon labelled *Delegated CA and Repository* that is located within AS 65501 in the Service Providers Cloud. This delegated CA is set up as a child of the *notional RIR* CA, which, for purposes of simplifying the design, resides on the same subnet. The delegated CA represents a delegated model of RPKI infrastructure that AS 65501 has set up in its own AS to host its own repository and to create and store certificates and ROAs for the addresses that have been allocated to it by the notional RIR. It can store ROAs not only for AS 65501 in this repository, but also for AS 65501's customer, AS 65505, to whom AS 65501 is assumed to have sub-allocated addresses. Hence, while the delegated CA and repository in AS 65501 represent a delegated RPKI model from the perspective of AS 65501, this model also offers a hosted RPKI service to AS 65505, which does not operate its own repository. As a customer of AS 65501, AS 65505 relies on AS 65501, rather than on the notional RIR, to create, sign, store, and maintain its ROAs.

For purposes of ROV, network operators in all ROV-capable ASes were able to pull down ROAs and other RPKI information not only from the real RIRs, but also from the notional RIR repository and the delegated repository in AS 65501.

6 Outcome

This section discusses ROV-related issues, lessons learned, and best practices.

6.1 ROV Policy Configuration Options

The action to be taken when an incoming BGP route advertisement is determined to be *valid*, *invalid*, or *not found* is determined by local policy. Ultimately, when RPKI adoption has attained a high level of maturity, it is expected that the recommendation will be to drop *invalid* routes. Until then, *invalid* routes can be observed and noted, or perhaps assigned lower local preference (LP) values to de-preference them by using policies.

Both Cisco and Juniper provided example policies for organizations to consider deploying with their ROV-capable routers. One candidate policy is to not drop *invalid* BGP updates. Another candidate policy is to associate varying LP values with routes, depending on how the update that advertised the route is evaluated. For example, routes received in *valid* updates may be given an LP value higher than the default, routes received in *not found* updates may be given the default LP value, and routes received in *invalid* updates may be given an LP value lower than the default.

In addition, researchers affiliated with NIST and the IETF SIDR Working Group are working to investigate and develop how the ROV-capable routers should best use the ROV state in route selection policy.

6.2 Implementation Status of RPKI Components

6.2.1 RPKI VC Component

The deployment or use of a VC (local or remote) is required for the support of ROV. As of this writing, we are aware of three open-source implementations of VCs that are available. The demonstration build used two of these VCs.

The third open-source VC implementation is also available from Raytheon BBN Technologies. Organizations wishing to adopt ROV may wish to investigate the use of this tool, which is called Rpstir. Its software can be found at https://github.com/bgpsecurity/rpstir.

Organizations that deploy open-source VC software should be aware of the possibility that they may eventually be required to assume some responsibility for keeping the software updated and maintained.

6.2.2 RPKI CA and Repository Components

Address holders willing to use the hosted model for ROA creation and storage can depend on their RIR to provide these services for them. Organizations wishing to deploy their own delegated model for ROA creation, maintenance, and storage will need CA and repository software. As of this writing, we are aware of one open-source implementation of CA and RPKI repository software that is available. We were able to use this software successfully to set up a delegated model CA and repository. However, it is not a turnkey product. Rather, its implementation requires a considerable staff investment. Organizations wishing to use the delegated model for RPKI to host their own CA and repository should be aware that, to do so, they will have to either develop their own software or take responsibility for maintaining and supporting the open-source implementation. We did not subject this demonstration implementation to stress, robustness, availability, or other testing that would typically be required before an organization would want to place it into operational use.

6.2.3 ROV-Capable Routers

The commercial implementations of ROV-capable routers that we demonstrated are well-documented and well-supported and can be used easily out of the box. See Section 7, Functional and Robustness Results, for details regarding their functionality.

6.2.4 Lessons Learned

- One of the most important lessons learned from the implementation and testing of the RPKI technologies is to ensure that software properly implements RPKI-based ROV based on the [RFC 6811] and [RFC 8210] specifications. Some versions of an OS may not have the capabilities specified in the RFCs.

- It is important to note that the default configuration for some routers is to exclude *invalid* prefixes from the routing table, whereas, for other routers, specific policy has to be defined to establish dispositions for *valid*, *invalid*, and *not found* prefixes. Some routers presume that all local routes, including iBGP learned routes, default to *valid*, especially when community strings are not sent [RFC 8097]. An additional lesson learned worth mentioning is that some routers may be configured for one additional state of "unverified" via a policy statement to indicate the case in which a router did not perform ROV on the particular route. Note: As of September 2018, [RFC 8481] states that all routes should be evaluated and have their state set. After the validation process is complete, the operator can apply any policy based on the evaluation state.

- With the use of RPKI, BGP ROV results in BGP routes that are evaluated as either *valid*, *invalid*, or *not found*. While accepting the *valid* routes for usage is the default recommendation and is non-controversial, organizations should use their local route selection policies for routes that are *invalid* or *not found*. Initially, organizations can simply log the fact that routes have been evaluated as *invalid* or *not found*, without changing the routes' behavior at all. This would be a risk-free method of initiating the adoption of RPKI ROV by monitoring how ROV would affect the routing if policies would be applied to the validation result. However, no increased level of route origin assurance would result from this level of adoption either. Such an initial adoption period—during which all routes are evaluated; statistics are gathered regarding the number of *valid*, *invalid*, and *not found* routes; but no special action is taken for *invalid* or *not found* routes—could be helpful, with respect to allowing organizations to determine the extent to which various potential policies that they may be considering using might affect routing.

- When configuring an RP, the trust anchor locator (TAL) of the five RIRs must be provided. In most VCs, four out of five TAL files are pre-loaded. The fifth TAL file, for ARIN, has to be downloaded. One should note that there are three TAL file formats: [RFC 7730], [RFC 6490], and RIPE NCC Validator format. It's important to be mindful of the TAL file format that the VC uses.

- On iBGP connections, we observed a slight increase in the number of BGP updates when the validation result was conveyed in iBGP using the extended community [RFC 8182]. The reason for this is that prefixes that originally could be incorporated into one update might not have been able to be incorporated into the same update anymore due to different validation results. Additionally, if selected updates change the validation result, then the router will resend the updates with the updated community string. In general, by turning on ROV, there will likely be a slight increase in the number of updates sent. An otherwise stable route whose configuration state changes will be re-signaled with the new extended community as its validation state changes.

<u>Delegated Model</u>

- Whether an address holder should use the hosted or delegated model for issuing ROAs depends on several factors. If the address holder is a large ISP that sub-allocates address space to various subscriber organizations, then it may well determine that it will be to its benefit to stand up its own CA infrastructure and to deploy the delegated model. The hosted model is likely preferable for smaller address holders that will not be sub-allocating their address space to other organizations and that do not necessarily have the resources to deploy, configure, operate, and maintain their own CA infrastructure and RPKI repository—and do so in a way that assures its accessibility, robustness, and responsiveness. Regardless of the model used, all address holders should create ROAs for their addresses in order to enable network operators and RPs to be able to verify the origin of route advertisements that are sent out advertising the address holder's prefixes.

- The documentation for the rpki.net toolkit, which implements the CA and repository, contains gaps. Moreover, we found that the rpki.net toolkit would benefit from additional debugging tools and guidance. It is, at times, unclear how the agents are interacting with each other. During set-up and for learning purposes, it may be beneficial to run a traffic scanner to see what is being passed between hosts. Through trial and error, we identified the steps needed to complete installation and configuration. We provide these steps in Volume C of this Practice Guide.

- It should be possible to declare an ROA with a time-out. It did not appear that the rpki.net tool could issue an ROA with an explicit time-out.

7   Functional and Robustness Results

We conducted a functional and robustness evaluation of the SIDR example implementation, as deployed in our laboratory, to verify that it worked as expected. The evaluation was intended to verify that the example implementation functioned as expected from several different perspectives:

- a resource holder (e.g., an ISP that sub-allocates the address space it holds and that provides addresses to its customers) setting up its own CA as a delegated RPKI participant and offering either a hosted model or a delegated model (or both) of RPKI support to its customers (i.e., obtaining CA certificates; creating EE certificates; creating, signing, and revoking ROAs; and uploading ROAs and other objects to the RPKI repository)

- an address holder protecting the addresses it holds, by creating and managing ROAs for those addresses by using either the hosted or delegated model

- an RP operating a BGP router and performing ROV on all of the route prefix advertisements that it receives to determine if they are *valid*, *invalid*, or *not found*, and applying configured policy based on the result

In all cases, the evaluation tested functionality, using both IPv4 and Internet Protocol Version 6 (IPv6) addresses. Both virtual and physical ROV-capable routers were used. Access to a live physical circuit was provided by CenturyLink. The circuit delivers full internet routes into the lab via live BGP peering and provides connectivity to the internet where the RIRs reside.

Some testing was performed using live and interactive full internet routes, while other testing was performed using static data injected via a predefined test harness created by NIST. The test harness provides a BGP traffic generation and collection framework—BGPSEC-IO (BIO) [NIST BGP-SRx]—as well as a mechanism for providing RPKI data by using an RPKI traffic generator, both part of the NIST Border Gateway Protocol Secure Routing Extension (BGP-SRx) Software Suite [NIST BGP-SRx]. The harness environment was used to ensure that the test scenarios performed can be regenerated using carefully manufactured static data that is pre-populated and controlled via traffic generators and measurement tools.

The VC used in both the functional and robustness tests was the RIPE NCC RPKI Validator Version 2.24. It was chosen because of its inherent flexibilities, including the ability to dynamically add local (white list) entries.

Whereas the RPKI delegated model that was developed in-house was used for preliminary functional tests, all of the documented functional tests were done using the hosted model with locally added entries for ROA data. These entries were added via web-interface/simplified local internet number resource management (SLURM) workload manager files, in the case of the Harness test environment for RIPEv2. We were able to install RIPEv3, on Linux systems by using the binary RPM Package Manager (originally Red Hat Package Manager) distribution. At the time of testing, RIPEv3 had some bugs that prevented us from using it. One issue was the incapability of processing large SLURM files (25-percent coverage of the routing table). This seems to be resolved in the latest binary version. An additional, more pressing issue was that RIPEv3 does not recognize ROA data if no TAL file is configured. The validator reports "no data" to the router. This issue has been reported and is expected to be resolved in a future release.

Figure 7-1 depicts the test bed using the test harness (BGP traffic generation and collection framework [BGPSEC-IO]). Figure 7-2 depicts the test bed using live traffic.

Note: The test bed using live traffic has a Palo Alto Next-Generation Firewall (PANW) that sits between the ISP and the internal environment to allow only the relevant traffic for this project.

Figure 7-1 SIDR Testbed Using the Test Harness

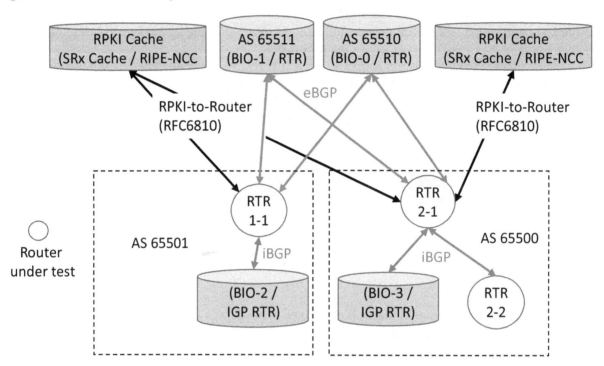

BGPSEC-IO (BIO) – BGP traffic generator & collector /   RTR – CISCO or Juniper Router

Figure 7-2 SIDR Testbed Using Live Traffic

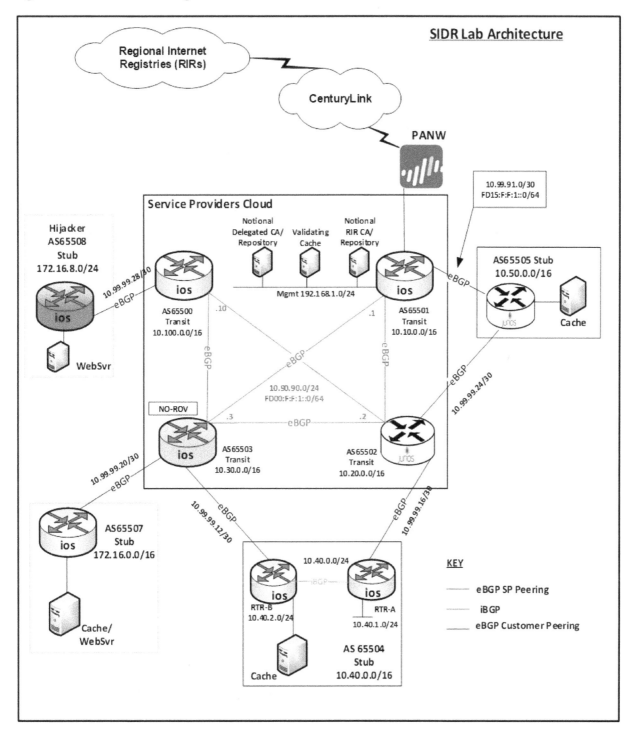

7.1 Assumptions and Limitations

This functional evaluation has the following limitations:

- It is neither a comprehensive test of all security components nor a red-team exercise.
- It cannot identify all weaknesses.
- The hardware components that were part of the demonstration build were typical of enterprise edge routers or small aggregation routers.
- The scaling tests that were performed included numbers of routers and peers that are typical of enterprise interconnectivity. In this context, we used routing tables of sizes similar to the full current internet routing table (approximately 700,000 routes).
- ISPs will require further testing, in terms of the number of routes, route changes, and sources of routes that are larger than the current global routing table, to handle future expected growth. In addition, carriers will need to test geographically distributed validators as well as anycast-capable validators. Testing of the impact of timing issues will also be required.

The functional evaluation also does not include the laboratory infrastructure security evaluation. It is assumed that its devices are hardened. Testing these devices would reveal only weaknesses in implementation that would not be relevant to those adopting this reference architecture. It is also important to note the need to harden the implementation if this Practice Guide is used by others, such as enterprise networking organizations or ISPs, as a roadmap for deployment. Although Section 4.4 and Section 4.5 describe [NIST SP 800-53] controls addressed by the demonstrated capabilities, they do not list the full set of [NIST SP 800-53] controls that apply to routers and routing systems. For example, issues such as signature validation and transfer protocol security must be addressed in any operational implementation.

Section 11 of the RPKI-to-router specification [RFC 6810] provides guidance regarding securing the protocol. The security considerations taken for our demonstration build (e.g., firewall rules) are documented in Volume C of this Practice Guide.

7.2 Functional Test Requirements

This section provides a summary of the functional requirements that were tested. A detailed table of functional test requirements and their corresponding tests is provided in Appendix E.

7.2.1 ROV Functional Requirements

The SIDR example implementation included a capability for BGP routers to perform ROV on all routes that they receive in BGP update messages. The router was capable of accurately establishing an initial validation state *(valid, invalid, or not found)* for a given route, and marking the route accordingly. The router was also capable of accurately reevaluating that route's validation state after RPKI test data has been perturbed and re-marking the route (where applicable). Tests were performed for the following cases:

- routes received through eBGP and iBGP updates
- local static routes redistributed into BGP
- routes redistributed into BGP from an interior gateway protocol (IGP)
- routes redistributed into BGP from an iBGP
- router cache synchronization

7.2.2 Delegated RPKI-Model Functional Requirements

The SIDR example implementation included the capability for a resource holder to set up its own delegated CA, create its own repository, and offer a hosted service to its customers, including the ability to publish customer ROAs to its repository, delete customer ROAs from its repository, and have customer ROAs expire from its repository. The ROAs in this delegated CA repository were included in the RPKI data that RPs downloaded to their VCs, and VRPs derived from these ROAs were provided to RP routers via the RPKI-to-router protocol.

7.3 Functional Test Findings

Securing the routing system is an important task for the internet. While RPKI-based ROV does not claim to solve all inherent security issues with the use of the BGP routing protocol, it provides significant progress in helping resolve some of the issues surrounding BGP route hijacks. To verify the maturity and effectiveness of RPKI technology, numerous functionality tests were performed using the prototype implementation in the NCCoE lab. It is important to note that most issues encountered during functional tests were quickly resolved either by installing an updated router OS provided by a vendor or by setting up some optional configuration.

Not all proposed test cases could be performed. The following observations resulted from completing the functional tests:

- Not all RIRs currently support RRDP.
- RIRs implement the hosted model differently from each other. RIRs offer different user interfaces and different RPKI support services.
- At the time of our testing, some interoperability issues were discovered in the iBGP signaling of the RPKI validation state between the various implementations under test.
  - During the course of the project, these issues were fixed in the affected implementations. Prerelease fixed versions of implementations were re-tested, and the interoperability issues were resolved.

- We expect that future full releases of the affected implementations will incorporate these fixes as well.

- Some versions of router software provided to this project did not correctly evaluate aggregated routes with the AS_SET attribute. Bug reports were filed with the implementors.

  - Users should verify support for proper BGP update validation in the presence of AS_SET.

- It was discovered that vendors evaluate locally learned routes (iBGP) differently. For example, some implementations default to *valid* for locally learned routes, while others determine the validity of locally learned routes via policy statements.

- There were router-to-VC interaction cases in which serial requests of delta ROA information did not completely conform with [RFC 6810]. Some VC versions do not support deltas in the RPKI-to-router protocol implementation [RFC 6810]. With the current scale of the deployed RPKI, it does not seem to produce issues; however, with a larger amount of RPKI coverage, this could cause unnecessary delays, especially for high poll frequencies.

  - Users should verify support for incremental updates in the RPKI-to-router protocol.

7.4 Robustness Findings

To test the impact of RPKI ROV on BGP routing convergence, we initially measured the convergence time of a router with one peer by using a full BGP table dump (approximately 700,000 BGP routes) without using ROV or any other policies to gather a baseline. We repeated the tests by adding RPKI origin validation by using 25%, 50%, 75%, and 100% ROA coverage. With no additional routing policies added, we observed an approximate increase of two percent to seven percent in convergence time across all tested platforms.

Note that this finding only provides a baseline from a single router standpoint. Scalability scenarios were not performed. Scalability of RPKI ROV would include other aspects of an enterprise or an ISP's network infrastructure design. Enterprises and ISPs should identify their own scalability requirements for further evaluation.

8 Recommendations for Follow-on Activities

8.1 Standards Initiatives

In the course of our testing, the SIDR Project identified clarifications that might be made to some ROV-related and RPKI-related IETF specifications to potentially reduce ambiguity and improve interoperability. The IETF is progressing with such clarifying specifications.

8.2 Future Demonstration Activities

As was discussed earlier in this document, while ROV can help detect when an ISP or enterprise originates an update for an address that it is not authorized to announce (route hijacking), it is not able to detect when an AS makes an unauthorized modification of routing path information in a BGP update that it forwards. Such path modification attacks can deny access to internet services, detour traffic, misdeliver traffic to malicious endpoints, undermine protection systems, and cause routing instability. The BGPsec protocol, which has recently been finalized within the IETF, is designed to protect against such path modification attacks. There are currently open-source prototype implementations of BGPsec available (e.g., NIST BGP-SRx Software Suite [NIST BGP-SRx], and the Parsons-enhanced BIRD implementation [Parsons BGPsec]).

As commercial implementations also become available, the NCCoE may consider further demonstration in support of resource certification in ISPs that have many customers with provider-independent prefixes. The NCCoE will also consider a project to build and demonstrate a BGPsec solution by using available protocols, products, and tools and publish a practice guide of lessons learned.

RPKI-based BGP ROV and BGPsec implemented together have the potential to greatly increase the security of the BGP routing protocol, enabling an entity that receives a BGP update to validate that the AS that is listed as the originating AS is, in fact, the AS that originated the update, that the path to that AS that is in the update has not been modified in an unauthorized manner, and that the AS that originated the update was authorized to do so.

BGPsec and ROV work hand-in-hand to secure internet routing. A follow-on project to promote the adoption of BGPsec can be expected to increase the adoption of not only BGPsec, but also of ROV. Organizations that implement one can be expected to be eager to implement the other.

8.3 Tool Development and Maintenance

As was mentioned earlier, commercial routers that support ROV are available from multiple vendors, and these products are supported and maintained. Some other key components, such as VCs, publication point software, and RPKI and CA tools, however, are not available with typical commercial support and backing. Ideally, commercial vendors will make this software available and will support and maintain these products.

Organizations wishing to use the delegated model for RPKI to host their own CA and repository should be aware that, to do so, they will have to either develop their own software or take responsibility for maintaining and supporting the open-source implementations.

8.4 Infrastructure Testing

Further testing on scalability and robustness issues with equipment and configurations with a scale similar to that of ISP networks should be considered.

The security of the infrastructure used to deploy either a hosted or delegated model will need to be tested. If carriers are using either model, then the integrity and availability of RIR implementations will directly affect the operation of the network. For example, a compromise of an RIR may lead to accepting incorrect routes or denying *valid* routes, or it may make the service unavailable. A DoS of the RIR may make updates of RPKI information unavailable. That may impact operations, due to stale routing data. In addition, the security and availability of the various communication paths will need to be tested. This includes transferring RPKI data from a repository to a VC and from a VC to routers.

8.5 Research Activities

Additional research is needed to determine how ROV-capable routers should best use the ROV evaluation state in the route selection policy. As was mentioned earlier, researchers affiliated with NIST and the IETF Working Group are investigating this question. Ideally, in the future, it will be possible to easily configure various policies based on this research in ROV-capable routers.

Appendix A   Application of Systems Security Engineering: Considerations for a Multidisciplinary Approach in the Engineering of Trustworthy Secure Systems (NIST SP 800-160) to the Secure Inter-Domain Routing Project

The Secure Inter-Domain Routing (SIDR) Project used [NIST SP 800-160] within a framework for planning and conducting the Internet Routing Security Project. [NIST SP 800-160] addresses the engineering-driven perspective and actions necessary to develop more defensible and survivable systems, inclusive of the machine, physical, and human components that compose the systems and the capabilities and services delivered by those systems. It starts with and builds upon a set of well-established international standards for systems and software engineering published by the International Organization for Standardization (ISO), the International Electrotechnical Commission (IEC), and the Institute of Electrical and Electronics Engineers (IEEE), and infuses systems security engineering methods, practices, and techniques into those systems and software engineering activities. The objective is to address security issues from a stakeholder's protection needs, concerns, and requirements, and to use established engineering processes to ensure that such needs, concerns, and requirements are addressed with appropriate fidelity and rigor early and in a sustainable manner throughout the life cycle of the system.

The full integration of the systems security engineering discipline into the systems and software engineering discipline involves fundamental changes in the traditional ways of doing business within organizations—breaking down institutional barriers that, over time, have isolated security activities from the mainstream organizational management and technical processes, including, for example, the system development life cycle, acquisition/procurement, and enterprise architecture. The integration of these interdisciplinary activities requires the strong support of senior leaders and executives, and increased levels of communication among all stakeholders who have an interest in, or are affected by, the systems being developed or enhanced.

The Internet Routing Security Project offered an opportunity to attempt to implement the principles underlying [NIST SP 800-160] at the project level and to uncover any issues associated with project-level application of those principles.

[NIST SP 800-160] defines systems security engineering as part of a multidisciplinary systems engineering effort that:

- defines stakeholder security objectives, protection needs and concerns, security requirements, and associated validation methods
- defines system security requirements and associated verification methods
- develops security views and viewpoints of the system architecture and design

- identifies and assesses vulnerabilities and susceptibility to life-cycle disruptions, hazards, and threats

- designs proactive and reactive security functions encompassed within a balanced strategy to control asset loss and associated loss consequences

- provides security considerations to inform systems engineering efforts with the objective to reduce errors, flaws, and weaknesses that may constitute security vulnerability leading to unacceptable asset loss and consequences

- identifies, quantifies, and evaluates the costs/benefits of security functions and considerations to inform the analysis of alternatives, engineering trade-offs, and risk treatment decisions [The term "risk treatment" as defined in [ISO 73] is used in [ISO/IEC/IEEE 15288:2015].

- performs system security analyses in support of decision making, risk management, and engineering trades

- demonstrates, through evidence-based reasoning, that security *claims* for the system have been satisfied

- provides evidence to substantiate claims for the trustworthiness of the system

- leverages multiple security and other specialties to address all feasible solutions to deliver a trustworthy, secure system

The *Systems Security Engineering Framework* [McEvilley15] provides a conceptual view of the key contexts within which systems security engineering activities are conducted. The framework defines, bounds, and focuses the systems security engineering activities and tasks, both technical and non-technical, toward the achievement of stakeholder *security objectives* and presents a coherent, well-formed, evidence-based case that those objectives have been achieved. The framework is independent of the system type and the engineering or acquisition process model and is not to be interpreted as a sequence of flows or process steps, but rather as a set of interacting contexts, each with its own checks and balances. The systems security engineering framework emphasizes an integrated, holistic security perspective across all stages of the system life cycle and is applied to satisfy the milestone objectives of each life-cycle stage. The framework defines three contexts within which the systems security engineering activities are conducted. These are the problem context, the solution context, and the trustworthiness context.

- The *problem* context defines the basis for an acceptably and adequately secure system, given the stakeholder's mission, capability, performance needs and concerns; the constraints imposed by stakeholder concerns related to cost, schedule, and risk and loss tolerance; and other constraints associated with life-cycle concepts for the system.

- The *solution* context transforms the stakeholder security requirements into design requirements for the system; addresses all security architecture, design, and related aspects necessary to realize a system that satisfies those requirements; and produces sufficient evidence to demonstrate that those requirements have been satisfied to the degree possible, practicable, and acceptable to stakeholders.

▪ The *trustworthiness* context is a decision-making context that provides an evidence-based demonstration, through reasoning, that the system-of-interest is deemed trustworthy based upon a set of claims derived from security objectives.

The systems security engineering framework also includes a closed-loop feedback for interactions among and between the three framework contexts, and the requisite system security analyses to continuously identify and address variances as they are introduced into the engineering effort. The feedback loop also helps achieve continuous process improvements for the system.

The SIDR Project was not the development of an operational system from scratch; rather, it was a demonstration of a proof-of-concept platform composed of off-the-shelf components in order to enable legacy systems to mitigate a defined set of cybersecurity threats. As such, many longer-term life-cycle processes (e.g., supply, human resource management, configuration management, transition) were primarily treated only in the Practice Guide in explaining how the platform might be used operationally. The SIDR Project was planned and conducted in six phases: Initiation, Planning, Design, Execution, Control, and Closing.

This project took the following (often recursive) steps in demonstrating the adaptation and use of [NIST SP 800-160] to provide a project planning framework for the internet routing project at the National Cybersecurity Center of Excellence (NCCoE):

▪ Develop, state, and support the value proposition of the candidate project for the following overlapping Communities of Interest:

  ▫ internet customers and users

  ▫ internet service providers (ISPs)

  ▫ routing product vendors

  ▫ security product vendors

▪ Define the project requirements:

  ▫ security objectives

  ▫ security requirements

  ▫ operational and design constraints

  ▫ success determination and/or measurement

  ▫ life-cycle security issues

▪ Describe, design, develop, and build the solution:

  ▫ specification of required components and component characteristics

- identify potential sources for components possessing the necessary characteristics
- define component-interface and related performance requirements
- solicit participation from sources of necessary components
- enter into collaboration agreements with sources of necessary components
- coordinate proof-of-concept architecture of composed security platform with collaborators
- build and demonstrate the security platform to realize the security aspects of the solution
- document the security platform's performance against project requirements as evidence for the security aspects of the solution

- Document project results:
  - demonstration of value proposition
  - demonstrated security improvements and residual risks
  - security platform build and integration details
  - how to use the security platform in a manner that achieves security objectives

From an [ISO/IEC/IEEE 15288:2015] life-cycle point of view, the Initiation phase of the project mapped to the following processes:

- Organization Project Enabling Process
  - Human Resource Management
- Technical Management Process
  - Portfolio Management
  - Project Assessment and Control
  - Decision Management
  - Risk Management
- Technical Process
  - Business or Mission Analysis
  - Stakeholder Needs and Requirements Definition
  - Project Planning
  - System Requirements Definition
  - Architecture Definition Processes

The Planning phase mapped to the following [ISO/IEC/IEEE 15288:2015] life-cycle processes:

- Agreement Process
    - Acquisition
    - Supply [*collaborator function*]
- Project Enabling Process
    - Risk Management
    - Human Resource Management
    - Quality Management
    - Knowledge Management
- Technical Management Process
    - Portfolio Management
    - Project Planning
    - Decision Management
    - Risk Management
    - Project Assessment and Control
    - Information Management
    - Measurement
    - Quality Assurance
- Technical Process
    - Business/Mission Analysis
    - Architecture Definition
    - Design Definition
    - System Analysis
    - Stakeholder Needs and Requirements Definition
    - System Requirements Definition
    - Implementation
    - Integration
    - Disposal

The Design phase mapped to the following [ISO/IEC/IEEE 15288:2015] life-cycle processes:

- Project Enabling Process
  - Infrastructure Management
- Technical Management Process
  - Portfolio Management
  - Project Planning
  - Decision Management
  - Configuration Management
  - Risk Management
  - Project Assessment and Control
- Technical Process
  - Business/Mission Analysis
  - Architecture Definition
  - Design Definition
  - System Analysis
  - Stakeholder Needs and Requirements Definition
  - Implementation
  - Integration
  - Verification

The Execution phase mapped to the following [ISO/IEC/IEEE 15288:2015] life-cycle processes:

- Agreement Process
  - Acquisition
  - Supply [*collaborator function*]
- Project Enabling Process
  - Infrastructure Management
  - Quality Management
  - Knowledge Management

- Technical Management Process
  - Project Assessment and Control
  - Configuration Management
  - Risk Management
  - Quality Assurance
- Technical Process
  - Implementation
  - Integration
  - Verification

The Control phase mapped to the following [ISO/IEC/IEEE 15288:2015] life-cycle processes:

- Project Enabling Process
  - Infrastructure Management
  - Quality Management
  - Knowledge Management
- Technical Management Process
  - Project Assessment and Control
  - Information Management
  - Risk Management
  - Quality Assurance
  - Measurement
- Technical Process
  - Implementation
  - Integration
  - Verification

The Closing phase mapped to the following [ISO/IEC/IEEE 15288:2015] life-cycle processes:

- Project Enabling Process
  - Infrastructure Management
  - Quality Management
  - Knowledge Management

- Technical Management Process
  - Project Planning
  - Information Management
  - Risk Management
  - Quality Assurance
  - Measurement
- Technical Process
  - Business or Mission Analysis
  - Implementation
  - Verification
  - Validation

Keeping the feedback aspect of the context framework in mind, we mapped the primary focus of each project phase to each of the context's component elements as follows:

- The *problem* context:
  - determining life-cycle security concepts – Initiation
  - defining security objectives – Initiation
  - defining security requirements – Initiation and Planning
  - determining measures of success – Initiation and Planning
- The *solution* context:
  - defining the security aspects of the solution – Planning and Design
  - realizing the security aspects of the solution – Design and Execution
  - producing evidence for the security aspects of the solution – Execution and Control
- The *trustworthiness* context:
  - developing and maintaining the assurance case – Execution and Control
  - demonstrating that the assurance case is satisfied – Control and Closing

Establishing the three contexts helped ensure that the engineering of the system was driven by a sufficiently complete understanding of the problem articulated in a set of stakeholder security objectives that reflected protection needs and security concerns—instead of by security solutions brought forth in the absence of consideration of the entire problem space and its associated constraints.

Moreover, the approach resulted in explicit focus and a set of activities to demonstrate the worthiness of the solution in providing adequate security across competing, and often conflicting, constraints.

One will note that, as we moved from Problem to Solution to Analysis elements of the [NIST SP 800-160] framework, the need for adaptation increased. This was partly due to the fact that the output of an NCCoE project is a proof-of-concept demonstration, not a finished commercial product or government system. Organizations adapting NCCoE security platforms to their own environments will necessarily alter the demonstrated solution as needed to fit their own physical, operational, and contractual environments and will perform trustworthiness analyses in the context of their own risk acceptance perceptions and constraints. In employing [NIST SP 800-160] in this Internet Routing Security Project, the project engineers recognized that the candidate project involved the composition of several security-dedicated and security-purposed components in demonstrating upgrades to fielded systems while continuing to sustain day-to-day operations. Internet routing was accomplished using constantly evolving systems of systems. While the motivation for the proposed upgrades was reactive, with respect to already realized attacks, the critical nature of internet routing systems is such that the planned security enhancements cannot be permitted to disrupt internet operations. Although current internet routing systems are generally built on operating systems that have both known and unknown security deficiencies, it is not currently practical to retire critical elements of the existing systems. Consequently, the security platform as demonstrated necessarily retained many existing vulnerabilities. The composition of the platform needed to be engineered in a manner that reduced the consequences of its flawed foundation.

The systems security engineering aspects of the project also accommodated context sensitive considerations. Among these were the private-sector ownership, operation, and use of key internet components and the need to support widely varying stakeholder assessments of asset value and risk tolerance. Context sensitivity addressed multiple contexts and perceptions of return on investment.

The following material explains the project life-cycle framework elements to which the [NIST SP 800-160] activities and tasks are mapped.

When mapped against the NCCoE's project management framework, the activities and tasks took place at each of the following project phases, as identified in the subsections below.

A.1 Project Initiation

Project initiation activities included initiation, concept, and business-case-review milestones.

A.1.1 Initiation

The initiation milestone involved identifying the business need, developing a Rough Order of Magnitude (ROM) cost and preliminary schedule, and identifying basic business and technical risks. The outcome of the initiation phase was the decision to invest in a full business case analysis and preliminary project management plan. In the case of the SIDR Project, meeting the initiation milestone involved both NIST's Information Technology Laboratory (ITL) Advanced Network Technology Division (ANTD) staff and NCCoE staff interactions with standards activities (e.g., the Internet Engineering Task Force [IETF]) and industry organizations (e.g., the North American Network Operators Group [NANOG]) to identify the business need and basic business and technical risks. Subsequently, ANTD and the NCCoE staff developed ROM cost information and a preliminary schedule as part of a business case that was submitted to the NCCoE Governance Team for approval to proceed with the project. Note that the project did not move to the next phase until following [NIST SP 800-160] guidelines (to the extent appropriate for this type of project) was added to the proposal.

The initiation activity was focused primarily on the following systems security engineering tasks described in Chapter 3 of [NIST SP 800-160]:

- Define and Authorize the Security Aspects of the Project (PM-1):
    - Portfolio Management (PM-1.2) – Prioritize, select, and establish new business opportunities, ventures, or undertakings with consideration for security objectives and concerns.
- Human Resources Management (HR-1):
    - HR-1.1 – Identify systems security engineering skills needed based on current and expected projects.
    - HR-1.2 – Identify existing systems security engineering skills of personnel.
- Business and Mission Analysis (BA-1):
    - BA-1.1 – Identify stakeholders who will contribute to the identification and assessment of any mission, business, or operational problems or opportunities.
    - BA-1.2 – Review organizational problems and opportunities with respect to desired security objectives.
    - BA-1.3 – Define the security aspects of the business or mission analysis strategy.
    - BA-1.4 – Identify, plan for, and obtain access to enabling systems or services to support the security aspects of the business or mission analysis process.
- Stakeholder Protection Needs and Security Requirements Definition (SN-1):
    - SN-1.1 – Identify the stakeholders who have a security interest in the system throughout its life cycle.

- SN-1.2 – Define the stakeholder protection needs and security requirements definition strategy.
- SN-1.3 – Identify, plan for, and obtain access to enabling systems or services to support the security aspects of the stakeholder needs and requirements definition process.

A.1.2 Concept

The concept milestone identified the high-level business and functional requirements to develop the full business case analysis and preliminary project management plan for the proposed project. The outcomes of the concept phase were the selection to the NCCoE cybersecurity project portfolio; approval of the initial project cost, schedule, and performance baselines; and issuance of a Project Charter. Meeting the concept milestone involved a two-step process. First, an initiative proposal that included an industry assessment report, a Community of Interest report, and a concept milestone plan was submitted to the NCCoE Governance Team. Following the approval of the initiative proposal, a project risk assessment, technology research report, standards report, outreach/engagement plan, communications plan, and high-level project plan were submitted to the NCCoE Governance Team as parts of a business case with a needs assessment summary.

The concept activity was focused primarily on the following systems security engineering tasks described in Chapter 3 of [NIST SP 800-160]:

- Define and Authorize Security Aspects of the Project (PM-1):
  - Portfolio Management (PM-1.2) – Prioritize, select, and establish new business opportunities, ventures, or undertakings with consideration for security objectives and concerns (continued from the initiation phase).
  - Portfolio Management (PM-1.3) – Define the security aspects of projects, accountabilities, and authorities.
  - Portfolio Management (PM-1.4) – Identify the security aspects of projects, accountabilities, and authorities.
- Human Resources Management (HR-2.1) – Establish a plan for systems security engineering skills and development.
- Project Planning (PL-1.1) – Identify the security objectives and security constraints for the project.
- Business and Mission Analysis (BA-1) – This was essentially a continuation of the tasks from the continuation phase.
- Define the Security Aspects of the Problem Space (BA-2):
  - BA-2.1 – Analyze the problems and opportunities in the context of the security objectives and measures of success to be achieved.

- BA-2.2 – Define the security aspects and considerations of the business or operational problem.
- Characterize the Security Aspects of the Solution Space (BA-3):
  - BA-3.1 – Define the security aspects of the preliminary operational concepts and other concepts in life-cycle stages.
  - BA-3.2 – Identify alternative solution classes that can achieve the security objectives within limitations, constraints, and other considerations.
- Define Stakeholder Protection Needs (SN-2):
  - SN-2.1 – Define the security context of use across all preliminary life-cycle concepts.
  - SN-2.2 – Identify stakeholder assets and asset classes.
  - SN-2.3 – Prioritize assets based on the adverse consequences of asset loss.
  - SN-2.4 – Determine the susceptibility to adversity and uncertainty.
  - SN-2.5 – Identify stakeholder protection needs.
  - SN-2.6 – Prioritize and down-select the stakeholder protection needs.
  - SN-2.7 – Define the stakeholder protection needs and rationale.
- Develop the Security Aspects of Operational and Other Life-Cycle Concepts (SN-3):
  - SN-3.1 – Define a representative set of scenarios to identify all required protection capabilities and security measures that correspond to anticipated operational and other life-cycle concepts.
  - SN-3.2 – Identify the security-relevant interaction between users and the system.

A.1.3 Business Case Review

A business case review was conducted by the NCCoE Governance Team after all requirements of the initiation phase were completed. The business case is a documented, structured proposal for a cybersecurity project that is prepared to facilitate a selection decision for the proposed project by the NCCoE Governance Team. The business case described the reasons and justification for the project in terms of cybersecurity performance, needs and/or problems, and expected benefits. It identified the high-level requirements that needed to be satisfied and an analysis of proposed alternative solutions. Based on the NCCoE Governance Team's review of the business case and needs assessment, the project was approved.

The business case review was focused primarily on the following systems security engineering tasks described in Chapter 3 of [NIST SP 800-160]:

- Define and Authorize the Security Aspects of Projects (PM-1):

- PM-1.8 – Authorize each project to commence execution with consideration of the security aspects of project plans.

- Define the Security Aspects of the Problem or Opportunity Space (BA-2) – This was essentially a continuation of the task from the concept phase.

A.2 Project Planning

Project planning activities include project management planning, project definition, team formation, and requirements analysis milestones.

A.2.1 Project Management Plan

Supporting the planning milestone, the NCCoE completed the development of a full project management plan and schedule. The preliminary plan was developed as part of the business case, but it was reviewed and refined in the course of weekly project review meetings. Project planning synthesized information from an analysis of capabilities requirements, resource requirements, risk information, and cost estimates, and developed a project baseline, a plan for laboratory setup and team formation, and a project management plan. It provided a structure and an implementation approach to ensure that the project could be successfully managed to completion.

The project management planning activity was focused primarily on the following systems security engineering tasks described in Chapter 3 of [NIST SP 800-160]:

- Prepare for Security Aspects of Acquisition (AQ-1):

  - AQ-1.1 – Define the security aspects for how acquisition will be conducted. [*for laboratory set-up and excludes collaborator and NCEP contributions*]

- Define and Authorize the Security Aspects of Projects (PM-1):

  - PM-1.5 – Identify and allocate resources for the achievement of the security aspects of project goals and objectives.

  - PM-1.7 – Specify the security aspects of project reporting requirements and review milestones that govern the execution of each project.

- Develop Systems Security Engineering Skills (HR-2) – This was a continuation of the task initiated in the concept development phase.

- Plan Security Quality Management (QM-1):

  - QM-1.1 – Establish security quality management objectives.

  - QM-1.2 – Establish security quality management policies, standards, and procedures.

  - QM-1.3 – Define responsibilities and authority for the implementation of security quality management.

- QM-1.4 – Define security quality evaluation criteria and methods.

- QM-1.5 – Provide resources, data, and information for security quality management.

- Plan Security Knowledge Management (KM-1):

  - KM-1.1 – Define the security aspects of the knowledge management strategy.

  - KM-1.2 – Identify the security knowledge, skills, and knowledge assets to be managed.

  - KM-1.3 – Identify projects that can benefit from the application of the security knowledge, skills, and knowledge assets.

- Define the Security Aspects of the Problem (PL-1):

  - PL-1.4 – Identify the security activities and tasks of the work breakdown structure.

- Plan the Security Aspects of the Project and Technical Management (PL-2):

  - PL-2.1 – Define and maintain the security aspects of a project schedule based on management and technical objectives and work estimates.

  - PL-2.2 – Define the security achievement criteria and major dependencies on external inputs and outputs for life-cycle-stage decision gates.

  - PL-2.3 – Define the security-related costs for the project and plan the budget informed by those projected costs.

  - PL-2.4 – Define the systems security engineering roles, responsibilities, accountabilities, and authorities.

  - PL-2.5 – Define the security aspects of infrastructure and services required.

  - PL-2.6 – Plan the security aspects of acquisition of materials and enabling systems and services supplied from outside the project.

  - PL-2.7 – Generate and communicate a plan for the project and technical management and execution, including reviews that address all security considerations.

- Plan for the Security Aspects of Project Assessment and Control (PA-1):

  - PA-1.1 – Define the security aspects of the project assessment strategy.

  - PA-1.2 – Define the security aspects of the project control strategy.

- Prepare for Decisions with Security Implications (DM-1):

  - DM-1.1 – Define the security aspects of the decision management strategy.

  - DM-1.2 – Identify the security aspects of the circumstances and need for a decision.

  - DM-1.3 – Involve stakeholders with relevant security expertise in the decision making in order to draw on their experience and knowledge.

- Prepare for the Security Aspects of Configuration Management (CM-1):

  - CM-1.1 – Define the security aspects of a configuration management strategy.

  - CM-1.2 – Define the approach for the secure archive and retrieval for configuration items, configuration management artifacts, data, and information.

- Prepare for the Security Aspects of Information Management (IM-1):

  - IM-1.1 – Define the security aspects of the information management strategy.

  - IM-1.2 – Define protections for information items that will be managed.

  - IM-1.3 – Designate authorities and responsibilities for the security aspects of information management.

  - IM-1.4 – Define protections for specific information item content, formats, and structure.

  - IM-1.5 – Define the security aspects of information maintenance actions.

- Prepare for Security Measurement (MS-1):

  - MS-1.1 – Define the security aspects of the measurement strategy.

  - MS-1.2 – Describe the characteristics of the organization that are relevant to security measurement.

  - MS-1.3 – Identify and prioritize the security-relevant information needs.

  - MS-1.4 – Select and specify measures that satisfy the security-relevant information needs.

  - MS-1.5 – Define procedures for the collection, analysis, access, and reporting of security-relevant data.

  - MS-1.6 – Define criteria for evaluating the security-relevant information items and the process used for the security aspects of measurement.

  - MS-1.7 – Identify, plan for, and obtain enabling systems or services to support the security aspects of measurement.

- Prepare for Security Quality Assurance (QA-1):

  - QA-1.1 – Define the security aspects of the quality assurance strategy.

  - QA-1.2 – Establish independence of security quality assurance from other life-cycle processes.

- Prepare for Stakeholder Protection Needs and Security Requirements Definition (SN-1):

  - SN-1.1 – Identify the stakeholders who have a security interest in the system throughout its life cycle.

  - SN-1.2 – Define the stakeholder protection needs and security requirements definition strategy.

- SN-1.3 – Identify, plan for, and obtain access to enabling systems or services to support the security aspects of the stakeholder needs and requirements definition process.
- Prepare for the Security Aspects of System Analysis (SA-1):
  - SA-1.1 – Identify the security aspects of the problem or question that requires system analysis.
  - SA-1.2 – Identify the stakeholders of the security aspects of system analysis.
  - SA-1.3 – Define the objectives, scope, level of fidelity, and level of assurance of the security aspects of system analysis.
  - SA-1.4 – Select the methods associated with the security aspects of system analysis.
  - SA-1.5 – Define the security aspects of the system analysis strategy.
  - SA-1.6 – Identify, plan for, and obtain access to enabling systems or services to support the security aspects of the system analysis process.
  - SA-1.7 – Collect the data and inputs needed for the security aspects of system analysis.
- Prepare for the Security Aspects of Implementation (IP-1):
  - IP-1.1 – Develop the security aspects of the implementation strategy.
  - IP-1.2 – Identify constraints from the security aspects of the implementation strategy and technology on the system requirements, architecture, design, or implementation techniques.
  - IP-1.3 – Identify, plan for, and obtain access to enabling systems or services to support the security aspects of implementation.
- Prepare for the Security Aspects of Disposal (DS-1) [*The focus is on the protection of government property and of collaborator intellectual property and components.*]:
  - DS-1.1 – Develop the security aspects of the disposal strategy.
  - DS-1.2 – Identify the system constraints resulting from the security aspects of disposal to be incorporated into the system requirements, architecture, and design.
  - DS-1.3 – Identify, plan for, and obtain the enabling systems or services to support the secure disposal of the system.
  - DS-1.4 – Specify secure storage criteria for the system if it is to be stored.
  - DS-1.5 – Identify and preclude terminated personnel or disposed system elements and materials from being returned to service.

A.2.2 Project Definition

The project definition milestone helped ensure that the requirements that are associated with the project result are specified as clearly as possible. This involved identifying the expectations that all of the involved parties had regarding the project result. The project definition activity took the form of a Project Description that documented a common understanding as to what was included in, and excluded from, the project. The scope element of the Project Description dealt only with the boundaries of the project and did not address cost or schedule. Because changes in scope are inevitable as project requirements become more refined, contingencies for scope management were built into the project management plan to accept only those significant scope changes that were approved by the NCCoE Governance Team. The Project Description was published on the NCCoE's website (https://nccoe.nist.gov/projects/building-blocks/secure-inter-domain-routing).

The project definition activity was focused primarily on the following systems security engineering tasks described in Chapter 3 of [NIST SP 800-160]:

- Prepare for Security Aspects of Supply (SP-1):
  - SP-1.1 – Identify the security aspects of the acquirer's need for a product or service.
  - SP-1.2 – Define the security aspects of the supply strategy. [*The focus is on the protection of government property and of collaborator intellectual property and components.*]
- Develop System Security Engineering Skills (HR-2) – This was a continuation of the task initiated in the concept development and project plan development phases.
- Define the Security Aspects of the Project (PL-1):
  - PL-1.5 – Define and maintain the security aspects of processes that will be applied on the project.
- Plan the Security Aspects of the Project and Technical Management (PL-2):
  - PL-2.5 – Define the security aspects of infrastructure and services required.
  - PL-2.6 – Plan the security aspects of acquisition of materials and enabling systems and services supplied from outside the project.
- Analyze the Security Aspects of Decision Information (DM-2):
  - DM-2.1 – Select and declare the security aspects of the decision management strategy for each decision.
  - DM-2.2 – Determine the desired security outcomes and measurable security selection criteria.
  - DM-2.3 – Identify the security aspects of the trade space and alternatives.
  - DM-2.4 – Evaluate each alternative against the security evaluation criteria.

- Plan Security Risk Management (RM-1):

    - RM-1.1 – Define the security aspects of the risk management strategy.

    - RM-1.2 – Define and record the security context of the risk management process.

- Evaluate and Select Solution Classes (BA-4):

    - BA-4.1 – Assess each alternative solution class, taking into account the security objectives, limitations, constraints, and other relevant security considerations.

    - BA-4.2 – Select the preferred alternative solution class (or classes) based on the identified security objectives, trade space factors, and other criteria defined by the organization.

- Define Stakeholder Protection Needs (SN-2) – This was a continuation of the task from the concept phase.

- Develop the Security Aspects of Operational and Other Life-Cycle Concepts (SN-3):

    - SN-3.1 – Define a representative set of scenarios to identify all required protection capabilities and security measures that correspond to anticipated operational and other life-cycle concepts.

    - SN-3.2 – Identify the security-relevant interaction between users and the system.

- Transform Stakeholder Protection Needs into Security Requirements (SN-4) – This was a continuation of the task from the concept phase.

- Prepare for System Security Requirements Definition (SR-1) – This is a continuation of the task from the concept phase.

- Define System Security Requirements (SR-2):

    - SR-2.1 – Define each security function that the system is required to perform.

    - SR-2.2 – Define system security requirements, security constraints on system requirements, and rationale.

    - SR-2.3 – Incorporate system security requirements and associated constraints into system requirements and define rationale.

- Analyze System Security in System Requirements (SR-3):

    - SR-3.1 – Analyze the complete set of system requirements in consideration of security concerns.

    - SR-3.2 – Define security-driven performance and assurance measures that enable the assessment of technical achievement.

    - SR-3.3 – Provide the analyzed system security requirements and security-driven constraints to applicable stakeholders for review.

    - SR-3.4 – Resolve system security requirements and security-driven constraints issues.

- Prepare for Architecture Definition from the Security Viewpoint (AR-1) – This a continuation of the activity from the initiation phase.

- Develop Security Aspects of the Architecture (AR-2):

  - AR-2.1 – Define the concept of secure function for the system at the architecture level.

  - AR-2.2 – Select, adapt, or develop the security viewpoints and model kinds based on stakeholder security concerns.

  - AR-2.3 – Identify the security architecture frameworks to be used in developing the security models and security views of the system architecture.

  - AR-2.4 – Record the rationale for the selection of architecture frameworks that address security concerns, security viewpoints, and security model types.

- Develop Security Models and Security Views of Candidate Architectures (AR-3):

  - AR-3.1 – Define the security context and boundaries of the system in terms of interfaces, interconnections, and interactions with external entities.

  - AR-3.2 – Identify architectural entities and relationships between entities that address key stakeholder security concerns and system security requirements.

  - AR-3.3 – Allocate security concepts, properties, characteristics, behavior, functions, or constraints to architectural entities.

  - AR-3.4 – Select, adapt, or develop security models of the candidate architectures.

  - AR-3.5 – Compose views in accordance with security viewpoints to express how the architecture addresses stakeholder security concerns and meets stakeholder and system security requirements.

  - AR-3.6 – Harmonize the security models and security views with each other and with the concept of secure function.

- Select Candidate Architecture (AR-5):

  - AR-5.1 – Assess each candidate architecture against the security requirements and security-related constraints.

  - AR-5.2 – Assess each candidate architecture against stakeholder security concerns using evaluation criteria.

  - AR-5.3 – Select the preferred architecture(s) and capture key security decisions and rationale for those decisions.

  - AR-5.4 – Establish the security aspects of the architecture baseline of the selected architecture.

- Prepare for Security Design Definition (DE-1):

    - DE-1.1 – Apply the concept of secure function for the system at the design level.

    - DE-1.2 – Determine the security technologies required for each system element composing the system.

    - DE-1.3 – Determine the types of security design characteristics.

    - DE-1.4 – Define the principles for secure evolution of the system design.

    - DE-1.5 – Define the security aspects of the design definition strategy.

    - DE-1.6 – Identify, plan for, and obtain access to enabling systems or services to support the security aspects of the design definition process.

- Establish Security Design Characteristics and Enablers for Each System Element (DE-2):

    - DE-2.1 – Allocate system security requirements to system elements.

    - DE-2.2 – Transform security architectural characteristics into security design characteristics.

    - DE-2.3 – Define the necessary security design enablers.

    - DE-2.4 – Examine security design alternatives.

    - DE-2.5 – Refine or define the security interfaces between the system elements and with external entities.

    - DE-2.6 – Develop the security design artifacts.

- Assess the Alternatives for Obtaining Security-Relevant System Elements (DE-3):

    - DE-3.1 – Identify security-relevant non-developmental items (NDI) that may be considered for use.

    - DE-3.2 – Assess each candidate NDI and new design alternative against the criteria developed from expected security design characteristics or system element security requirements to determine suitability for the intended application.

    - DE-3.3 – Determine the preferred alternative among candidate NDI solutions and new design alternatives for a system element.

- Prepare for the Security Aspects of Implementation (IP-1) – This is a continuation of the task from the project management planning phase.

- Prepare for the Security Aspects of Integration (IN-1):

    - IN-1.1 – Identify and define checkpoints for the trustworthy secure operation of the assembled interfaces and selected system functions.

- IN-1.3 – Identify, plan for, and obtain access to enabling systems or services to support the security aspects of integration.

- IN-1.4 – Identify the constraints resulting from the security aspects of integration to be incorporated into the system requirements, architecture, or design.

A.2.3 Team Formation

During the form collaborative team milestone, the NCCoE initiated a *Federal Register* Notice (FRN) process to announce the project and to request Letters of Interest (LOIs) from organizations desiring to participate in the project, linked the Project Description on the NCCoE's public website to the FRN, and worked with the NIST Technology Partnerships Office (TPO) to create the Cooperative Research and Development Agreements (CRADAs) needed to support the project. A CRADA is a written agreement between a private company and a government agency to work together on a project. To formally accept CRADA collaborators, we needed to receive LOIs from potential collaborators. LOIs were reviewed for consistency with the project requirements as stated in the FRN, and the NCCoE project staff supported the TPO negotiation of CRADAs with interested organizations. Once a CRADA was signed, the organizations that had entered into the agreement became part of the project team. Outcomes of this milestone were a published FRN, signed CRADAs, and a roster of collaborators.

The team formation activity was focused primarily on the following systems security engineering tasks described in Chapter 3 of [NIST SP 800-160]:

- Prepare for Security Aspects of the Acquisition (AQ-1) [*Here, AQ-2 is applied to the process employed to advertise for and acquire collaborators. Build components are provided by the collaborators.*]:

  - AQ-1.2 – Prepare a request for a product or service that includes the security requirements.

- Advertise the Acquisition and Select the Supplier to Conform with the Security Aspects of the Acquisition (AQ-2):

  - AQ-2.1 – Communicate the request for a product or service to potential suppliers consistent with security requirements.

  - AQ-2.2 – Select one or more suppliers that meet the security criteria.

- Establish and Maintain the Security Aspects of Agreements (AQ-3) [*The focus of AR-3 was on CRADAs for this project. NIST's Technology Partnerships Organization had the lead for CRADAs.*]:

  - AQ-3.1 – Develop an agreement with the supplier to satisfy the security aspects of acquiring the product or service and supplier acceptance criteria.

- AQ-3.2 – Identify and evaluate the security impact of necessary changes to the agreement.
- AQ-3.3 – Negotiate and institute changes to the agreement with the supplier to address identified security impacts.

- Prepare for Security Aspects of Supply (SP-1):
  - SP-1.1 – Identify the security aspects of the acquirer's need for a product or service.

- Response to a Solicitation (SP-2):
  - SP-2.1 – Evaluate a request for a product or service with respect to the feasibility of satisfying the security criteria.
  - SP-2.2 – Prepare a response that satisfies the security criteria expressed in the solicitation.

- Establish and Maintain the Security Aspects of Agreements (SP-3) [*SP-2 and SP-3 are collaborator functions.*]:
  - SP-3.1 – Develop an agreement with the acquirer to satisfy the security aspects of the product or service and security acceptance criteria.
  - SP-3.2 – Identify and evaluate the security impact of necessary changes to the agreement.
  - SP-3.3 – Negotiate and institute changes to the agreement with the acquirer to address identified security impacts.

- Acquire and Provide Systems Security Engineering Skills to Projects (HR-3):
  - HR-3.1 – Obtain qualified systems security engineering personnel to meet project needs.
  - HR-3.2 – Maintain and manage the pool of skilled systems security engineering personnel to staff ongoing projects.
  - HR-3.3 – Make personnel assignments based on the specific systems security engineering needs of the project and staff development needs.

- Define the Security Aspects of the Project (PL-1):
  - PL-1.2 – Define the security aspects of the project scope as established in agreements.

- Manage System Security Requirements (SR-4):
  - SR-4.1 – Obtain explicit agreement on the system security requirements and security-driven constraints.
  - SR-4.2 – Maintain traceability of system security requirements and security-driven constraints.
  - SR-4.3 – Provide security-relevant information items required for systems requirements definition to baselines.

- Perform the Security Aspects of Implementation (IP-2):

  - IP-2.1 – Realize or adapt system elements in accordance with the security aspects of the implementation strategy, defined implementation procedures, and security-driven constraints.

  - IP-2.2 – Develop initial training materials for users for operation, sustainment, and support.

  - IP-2.3 – Securely package and store system elements.

  - IP-2.4 – Record evidence that system elements meet the system security requirements.

- Prepare for the Security Aspects of Integration (IN-1):

  - IN-1.2 – Develop the security aspects of the integration strategy (continued from the project definition phase).

- Perform the Security Aspects of Integration (IN-2):

  - IN-2.1 – Obtain implemented system elements in accordance with security criteria and requirements established in agreements and schedules.

A.2.4 Requirements Analysis

During the requirements analysis milestone, the cybersecurity project requirements that were documented during the earlier phases were validated by project team members and were further analyzed and decomposed into functional and non-functional requirements that define the cybersecurity project in more detail regarding inputs, processes, outputs, and interfaces. A logical and physical depiction of the data entities, relationships, and attributes of the system/application were also created. During the requirements analysis milestone, the initial strategy for testing and implementation was considered. Updates were made, as required, to the Project Description and the project plan.

The requirements analysis activity was focused primarily on the following systems security engineering tasks described in Chapter 3 of [NIST SP 800-160]:

- Prepare for the Security Aspects of Supply (SP-1):

  - SP-1.2 – Define the security aspects of the supply strategy [*Verified that collaborator contributions met security requirements as stated in the FRN and the Project Description.*]

- Define and Authorize the Security Aspects of Projects (PM-1) [*Looked at functional interdependencies among NCCoE internet security projects.*]:

  - PM-1.6 – Identify the security aspects of any multi-project interfaces and dependencies to be managed or supported by each project.

- Evaluate the Security Aspects of the Portfolio of Projects (PM-2):

  - PM-2.1 – Evaluate the security aspects of projects to confirm ongoing viability.

- PM-2.2 – Continue or redirect projects that are satisfactorily progressing or can be expected to progress satisfactorily by appropriate redirection in consideration of project security aspects.
- Assess Security Quality Management (QM-2):
  - QM-2.1 – Obtain and analyze quality assurance evaluation results in accordance with the defined security quality evaluation criteria.
  - QM-2.2 – Assess customer security quality satisfaction.
  - QM-2.3 – Conduct periodic reviews of project quality assurance activities for compliance with the security quality management policies, standards, and procedures.
  - QM-2.4 – Monitor the status of security quality improvements on processes, products, and services.
- Activate the Security Aspects of the Project (PL-3):
  - PL-3.1 – Obtain authorization for the security aspects of the project.
  - PL-3.2 – Submit requests and obtain commitments for the resources required to perform the security aspects of the project.
  - PL-3.3 – Implement the security aspects of the project plan.
- Assess the Security Aspects of the Project (PA-2):
  - PA-2.1 – Assess the alignment of the security aspects of project objectives and plans with the project context.
  - PA-2.2 – Assess the security aspects of the management and technical plans against objectives to determine adequacy and feasibility.
  - PA-2.3 – Assess the security aspects of the project and its technical status against appropriate plans to determine actual and projected cost, schedule, and performance variances.
  - PA-2.4 – Assess the adequacy of the security roles, responsibilities, accountabilities, and authorities associated with the project.
  - PA-2.5 – Assess the adequacy and availability of resources allocated to the security aspects of the project.
- Prepare for Decisions with Security Implications (DM-1):
  - DM-1.3 – Involve stakeholders with relevant security expertise in the decision making in order to draw on their experience and knowledge (continued from project management planning).

- Manage the Security Aspects of the Risk Profile (RM-2) [*Conducted as part of the Practice Guide Volume B development.*]:

  - RM-2.1 – Define and record the security risk thresholds and conditions under which a level of risk may be accepted.

  - RM-2.2 – Establish and maintain the security aspects of the risk profile.

  - RM-2.3 – Provide the security aspects of the risk profile to stakeholders based on their needs.

- Perform Process Security Evaluations (QA-3):

  - QA-3.1 – Evaluate project life-cycle processes for conformance to established security criteria, contracts, standards, and regulations.

  - QA-3.2 – Evaluate tools and environments that support or automate the process for conformance to established security criteria, contracts, standards, and regulations.

  - QA-3.3 – Evaluate supplier processes for conformance to process security requirements.

- Analyze Stakeholder Security Requirements (SN-5):

  - SN-5.1 – Analyze the complete set of stakeholder security requirements.

  - SN-5.2 – Define critical security-relevant performance and assurance measures that enable the assessment of technical achievement.

  - SN-5.3 – Validate that stakeholder protection needs and expectations have been adequately captured and expressed by the analyzed security requirements.

  - SN-5.4 – Resolve stakeholder security requirements issues.

- Analyze System Security in System Requirements (SR-3) – Continued from project definition.

- Establish Security Design Characteristics and Enablers for Each System Element (DE-1) – Continued from project definition.

- Assess the Alternatives for Obtaining Security-Relevant System Elements (DE-3) – Continued from project definition.

- Perform the Security Aspects of System Analysis (SA-2):

  - SA-2.1 – Identify and validate the assumptions associated with the security aspects of system analysis.

  - SA-2.2 – Apply the selected security analysis methods to perform the security aspects of required system analysis.

  - SA-2.3 – Review the security aspects of the system analysis results for quality and validity.

- SA-2.4 – Establish conclusions, recommendations, and rationale based on the results of the security aspects of system analysis. [*Conducted as part of the Practice Guide Volume B development.*]

- SA-2.5 – Record the results of the security aspects of system analysis.

A.3 Build Design

Build design activities include design drafting, coordinating and refining the design to produce a final design, and conducting a successful detailed design review.

A.3.1 Draft Design

The draft design milestone sought to develop detailed specifications that emphasize the physical solution to cybersecurity needs. The system requirements and logical description of the entities, relationships, and attributes of the data that were documented during the requirements analysis phase were further refined and allocated in the Project Description, cybersecurity build design documentation, and design material included in *NIST Special Publication (SP) 1800-14B* and *NIST SP 1800-14C* that were organized in a way suitable for implementation within the constraints of the project's physical environment.

The draft design activity was focused primarily on the following systems security engineering tasks described in Chapter 3 of [NIST SP 800-160]:

- Establish the Secure Infrastructure (IF-1):
  - IF-1.1 – Define the infrastructure security requirements.
  - IF-1.2 – Identify, obtain, and provide the infrastructure resources and services that provide security functions and services that are adequate to securely implement and support projects.

- Make and Manage Security Decisions (DM-3):
  - DM-3.1 – Determine preferred alternative for each security-informed and security-based decision.
  - DM-3.2 – Record the security-informed or security-based resolution, decision rationale, and assumptions.
  - DM-3.3 – Record, track, evaluate, and report the security aspects of security-informed and security- based decisions.

- Analyze Security Risk (RM-3):
  - RM-3.1 – Identify security risks in the categories described in the security risk management context.

- RM-3.2 – Estimate the likelihood of occurrence and consequences of each identified security risk.

- RM-3.3 – Evaluate each security risk against its security risk thresholds.

- RM-3.4 – Define risk treatment strategies and measures for each security risk that does not meet its security risk threshold.

- Treat Security Risk (RM-4):

  - RM-4.1 – Identify recommended alternatives for security risk treatment.

  - RM-4.2 – Implement the security risk treatment alternatives selected by stakeholders.

  - RM-4.3 – Identify and monitor those security risks accepted by stakeholders to determine if any future risk treatment actions are necessary.

  - RM-4.4 – Coordinate management action for the identified security risk treatments.

- Perform the Security Aspects of Configuration Identification (CM-2):

  - CM-2.1 – Identify the security aspects of system elements and information items that are configuration items.

  - CM-2.2 – Identify the security aspects of the hierarchy and structure of system information.

  - CM-2.3 – Establish the security nomenclature for system, system element, and information item identifiers.

  - CM-2.4 – Define the security aspects of baseline identification throughout the system life cycle.

  - CM-2.5 – Obtain acquirer and supplier agreement for security aspects to establish a baseline.

- Develop the Security Aspects of Operational and Other Life-Cycle Concepts (SN-3) – Continued from project definition activity.

- Develop Security Models and Security Views of Candidate Architectures (AR-3) – Continued from project definition activity.

- Assess the Alternatives for Obtaining Security-Relevant System Elements (DE-2) – Continued from project definition activity.

- Manage the Security Design (DE-4):

  - DE-4.1 – Map the security design characteristics to the system elements.

  - DE-4.2 – Capture the security design and rationale.

- DE-4.3 – Maintain traceability of the security aspects of the system design.
- DE-4.4 – Provide security-relevant information items required for the system design definition to baselines.

- Manage the Security Aspects of System Analysis (SA-3):
  - SA-3.1 – Maintain traceability of the security aspects of the system analysis results.
  - SA-3.2 – Provide security-relevant system analysis information items that have been selected for baselines.

- Perform the Security Aspects of Implementation (IP-2) – Continued from team formation activity.

- Perform the Security Aspects of Integration (IN-2):
  - IN-2.1 – Obtain implemented system elements in accordance with security criteria and requirements established in agreements and schedules (continued from team formation activity).
  - IN-2.2 – Assemble the implemented systems elements to achieve secure configurations.
  - IN-2.3 – Perform checks of the security characteristics of interfaces, functional behavior, and behavior across interconnections.

- Prepare for the Security Aspects of Verification (VE-1):
  - VE-1.1 – Identify the security aspects within the verification scope and corresponding security-focused verification actions.
  - VE-1.2 – Identify the constraints that can potentially limit the feasibility of the security-focused verification actions.
  - VE-1.3 – Select the appropriate methods or techniques for the security aspects of verification and the associated security criteria for each security-focused verification action.
  - VE-1.4 – Define the security aspects of the verification strategy.
  - VE-1.5 – Identify the system constraints resulting from the security aspects of the verification strategy to be incorporated into the system requirements, architecture, or design.
  - VE-1.6 – Identify, plan for, and obtain access to enabling systems or services to support the security aspects of verification.

A.3.2 Final Design

During the final design milestone, the final architecture diagram and build design were completed and documented. The outcome of the design milestone was the successful completion of the detailed design reviews with the NCCoE Governance Team.

The final design activity was focused primarily on the following systems security engineering tasks described in Chapter 3 of [NIST SP 800-160]:

- Establish the Secure Infrastructure (IF-1):

    - IF-1.1 – Define the infrastructure security requirements (continued from design drafting activity).

- Make and Manage Security Decisions (DM-3) – Continued from design drafting activity.

- Analyze Security Risk (RM-3) – Continued from design drafting activity.

- Treat Security Risk (RM-4) – Continued from design drafting activity.

- Perform the Security Aspects of Configuration Identification (CM-2) – Continued from design drafting activity.

- Relate Security Views of the Architecture to the Design (AR-4):

    - AR-4.1 – Identify the security-relevant system elements that relate to architectural entities and the nature of these relationships.

    - AR-4.2 – Define the security interfaces, interconnections, and interactions between the system elements and with external entities.

    - AR-4.3 – Allocate system security requirements to architectural entities and system elements.

    - AR-4.4 – Map security-relevant system elements and architectural entities to security design characteristics.

    - AR-4.5 – Define the security design principles for the system design and evolution that reflect the concept of secure function.

- Select Candidate Architecture (AR-5):

    - AR-5.1 – Assess each candidate architecture against the security requirements and security-related constraints.

    - AR-5.2 – Assess each candidate architecture against stakeholder security concerns by using evaluation criteria.

- AR-5.3 – Select the preferred architecture(s) and capture key security decisions and rationale for those decisions.
- AR-5.4 – Establish the security aspects of the architecture baseline of the selected architecture.

- Manage the Security View of the Selected Architecture (AR-6):

  - AR-6.1 – Formalize the security aspects of the architecture governance approach and specify security governance-related roles and responsibilities, accountabilities, and authorities.

  - AR-6.2 – Obtain explicit acceptance of the security aspects of the architecture by stakeholders.

  - AR-6.3 – Maintain concordance and completeness of the security architectural entities and their security-related architectural characteristics.

  - AR-6.4 – Organize, assess, and control the evolution of the security models and security views of the architecture.

  - AR-6.5 – Maintain the security aspects of the architecture definition and evaluation strategy.

  - AR-6.6 – Maintain traceability of the security aspects of the architecture.

  - AR-6.7 – Provide security-relevant information items required for architecture definition to baselines.

- Manage the Security Aspects of System Analysis (SA-3) – Continued from design drafting activity.

- Perform the Security Aspects of Implementation (IP-2) – Continued from design drafting activity.

- Perform the Security Aspects of Integration (IN-2) – Continued from design drafting activity.

- Prepare for the Security Aspects of Verification (VE-1) – Continued from design drafting activity.

A.3.3 Detailed Design Review

The detailed design review is a formal inspection of the high-level architectural design of the project's cybersecurity solution and its internal and external interfaces. Following consensus by the project team regarding the build design, the final high-level architecture and build design were provided to the NCCoE Governance Team. This provided the NCCoE Governance Team with information necessary for a design review to achieve agreement and confidence that the design satisfied the functional and non-functional requirements and was in conformance with the solution architecture. The overall project status, proposed technical solutions, evolving software products, associated documentation, and capacity estimates were reviewed to determine completeness and consistency with design standards; to raise and resolve any technical and/or project-related issues; and to identify and mitigate project, technical, security, and/or business risks affecting continued detailed design and subsequent development, testing, implementation, and operations and maintenance activities.

The detailed design review activity was focused primarily on the following systems security engineering tasks described in Chapter 3 of [NIST SP 800-160]:

- Evaluate the Security Aspects of the Portfolio of Projects (PM-2):
    - PM-2.1 – Evaluate the security aspects of projects to confirm ongoing viability.
    - PM-2.2 – Continue or redirect projects that are satisfactorily progressing or can be expected to progress satisfactorily by appropriate redirection in consideration of project security aspects.

- Activate the Security Aspects of the Project (PL-3):
    - PL-3.1 – Obtain authorization for the security aspects of the project.
    - PL-3.2 – Submit requests and obtain commitments for the resources required to perform the security aspects of the project.
    - PL-3.3 – Implement the security aspects of the project plan.

- Assess the Security Aspects of the Project (PA-2):
    - PA-2.1 – Assess the alignment of the security aspects of project objectives and plans with the project context.
    - PA-2.2 – Assess the security aspects of the management and technical plans against objectives to determine adequacy and feasibility.
    - PA-2.3 – Assess the security aspects of the project and its technical status against appropriate plans to determine actual and projected cost, schedule, and performance variances.
    - PA-2.4 – Assess the adequacy of the security roles, responsibilities, accountabilities, and authorities associated with the project.
    - PA-2.5 – Assess the adequacy and availability of resources allocated to the security aspects of the project.
    - PA-2.6 – Assess progress using measured security achievement and milestone completion.
    - PA-2.7 – Conduct required management and technical reviews, audits, and inspections with full consideration for the security aspects of the project.
    - PA-2.9 – Analyze security measurement results and make recommendations.
    - PA-2.10 – Record and provide security status and security findings from the assessment tasks.

- Manage the Security View of the Selected Architecture (AR-6) – Continued from final design activity.

- Perform the Security Aspects of System Analysis (SA-2):

  - SA-2.1 – Identify and validate the assumptions associated with the security aspects of system analysis.

  - SA-2.2 – Apply the selected security analysis methods to perform the security aspects of required system analysis.

  - SA-2.3 – Review the security aspects of the system analysis results for quality and validity.

  - SA-2.4 – Establish conclusions, recommendations, and rationale based on the results of the security aspects of system analysis. [*Conducted as part of the Practice Guide Volume B development.*]

  - SA-2.5 – Record the results of the security aspects of system analysis.

- Perform Security-Focused Verification (VE-2):

  - Define the security aspects of the verification procedures, each supporting a security-focused verification action.

A.4 Build Execution

During the build milestone, the project team transformed any specifications for software harnesses (*glue* code) identified and documented in the detailed design phase into machine-executable form, and ensured that all of the individual components of the SIDR solution functioned correctly and interfaced properly with other components within the system/application. System hardware, networking and telecommunications equipment, and commercial off-the-shelf / government off-the-shelf software were acquired and configured (see Section 4.5).

The build activity was focused primarily on the following systems security engineering tasks described in Chapter 3 of [NIST SP 800-160]:

- Monitor the Security Aspects of Agreements (AQ-4): [*This task set focuses primarily on CRADAs with collaborators.*]

  - AQ-4.1 – Assess the execution of the security aspects of the agreement.

  - AQ-4.2 – Provide data needed by the supplier in a secure manner in order to achieve timely resolution of issues.

- Accept Products and Services (AQ-5):

  - AQ-5.1 – Confirm that the delivered product or service complies with the security aspects of the agreement.

- AQ-5.2 – Accept the product or service from the supplier or other party, as directed by the security criteria in the agreement.

- Execute the Security Aspects of Agreements (SP-4): [*SP-4 and SP-5 are primarily collaborator functions.*]

  - SP-4.1 – Execute the security aspects of the agreement according to the engineering project plans.

  - SP-4.2 – Assess the execution of the security aspects of the agreement.

- Deliver and Support the Security Aspects of Products and Services (SP-5):

  - SP-5.1 – Deliver the product or service in accordance with the security aspects and considerations.

  - SP-5.2 – Provide security assistance to the acquirer as stated in the agreement.

  - SP-5.3 – Transfer the responsibility for the product or service to the acquirer or other party, as directed by the security aspects and considerations in the agreement.

- Establish the Secure Infrastructure (IF-1):

  - IF-1.2 – Identify, obtain, and provide the infrastructure resources and services that provide security functions and services that are adequate to securely implement and support projects.

- Maintain the Secure Infrastructure (IF-2):

  - IF-2.1 – Evaluate the degree to which delivered infrastructure resources satisfy project protection needs.

  - IF-2.2 – Identify and provide security improvements or changes to the infrastructure resources as the project requirements change.

- Perform Security Quality Management Corrective and Preventive Actions (QM-3):

  - QM-3.1 – Plan corrective actions when security quality management objectives are not achieved.

  - QM-3.2 – Plan preventive actions when there is a sufficient risk that security quality management objectives will not be achieved.

  - QM-3.3 – Monitor security quality management corrective and preventive actions to completion and inform relevant stakeholders.

- Manage Security Knowledge, Skills, and Knowledge Assets (KM-4):

  - KM-4.1 – Maintain security knowledge, skills, and knowledge assets.

  - KM-4.2 – Monitor and record the use of security knowledge, skills, and knowledge assets.

- KM-4.3 – Periodically reassess the currency of the security aspects of technology and market needs of the security knowledge assets.

▪ Assess the Security Aspects of the Project (PA-2):

- PA-2.9 – Analyze security measurement results and make recommendations (continued from detailed design review).

▪ Control the Security Aspects of the Project (PA-3):

- PA-3.1 – Initiate the actions needed to address identified security issues.

- PA-3.2 – Initiate the security aspects of necessary project replanning.

- PA-3.3 – Initiate change actions when there is a contractual change to cost, time, or quality due to the security impact of an acquirer or supplier request.

- PA-3.4 – Recommend the project to proceed toward the next milestone or event, if justified, based on the achievement of security objectives and performance measures.

▪ Monitor Security Risks (RM-5):

- RM-5.1 – Continually monitor all risks and the security risk management context for changes and evaluate the security risks when their state has changed.

- RM-5.2 – Implement and monitor measures to evaluate the effectiveness of security risk treatment.

- RM-5.3 – Monitor, on an ongoing basis, the emergence of new security risks and sources of risk throughout the life cycle.

▪ Perform Security Configuration Change Management (CM-3):

- CM-3.1 – Identify security aspects of requests for change and requests for variance. to identify any security aspects. A request for variance is also referred to as a request for deviation, waiver, or concession.

- CM-3.2 – Determine the security aspects of action to coordinate, evaluate, and disposition requests for change or requests for variance.

- CM-3.3 – Incorporate security aspects in requests submitted for review and approval.

- CM-3.4 – Track and manage the security aspects of approved changes to the baseline, requests for change, and requests for variance.

▪ Perform Product/Service Security Evaluations (QA-2):

- QA-2.1 – Evaluate products and services for conformance to established security criteria, contracts, standards, and regulations.

- QA-2.2 – Perform the security aspects of verification and validation of the outputs of the life cycle processes to determine conformance to specified security requirements.

- Treat Security Incidents and Problems (QA-5):

    - QA-5.1 – The security aspects of incidents are recorded, analyzed, and classified.

    - QA-5.2 – The security aspects of incidents are resolved or elevated to problems.

    - QA-5.3 – The security aspects of problems are recorded, analyzed, and classified.

    - QA-5.4 – Treatments for the security aspects of problems are prioritized and implementation is tracked.

    - QA-5.6 – Stakeholders are informed of the status of the security aspects of incidents and problems.

    - QA-5.7 – The security aspects of incidents and problems are tracked to closure.

- Perform the Security Aspects of Implementation (IP-2) – Continued from detailed design review.

- Manage the Results of the Security Aspects of Implementation (IP-3):

    - IP-3.1 – Record the security aspects of implementation results and any security-related anomalies encountered.

    - IP-3.2 – Maintain traceability of the security aspects of implemented system elements.

    - IP-3.3 – Provide security-relevant information items required for implementation to baselines.

- Perform the Security Aspects of Integration (IN-2) – Continued from the design phase.

- Manage the Results of the Security Aspects of Integration (IN-3):

    - IN-3.1 – Record the security aspects of integration results and any security anomalies encountered.

    - IN-3.2 – Maintain traceability of the security aspects of integrated system elements.

    - IN-3.3 – Provide security-relevant information items required for integration to baselines.

- Prepare for the Security Aspects of Verification (VE-1) – Continued from the design phase.

- Perform Security-Focused Verification (VE-2):

    - VE-2.1 – Define the security aspects of the verification procedures, each supporting one or a set of security-focused verification actions (continued from detailed design review).

A.5 Control/Testing

The primary purpose of the test milestone was to determine that the cybersecurity solution developed and tested during the Execution phase was ready for publication. During the Control phase, formally controlled and focused testing was performed to uncover errors and bugs in the cybersecurity solution prior to publication that needed to be resolved. See Section 7 of this publication.

The Control/test activity was focused primarily on the following systems security engineering tasks described in Chapter 3 of [NIST SP 800-160]:

- Maintain the Secure Infrastructure (IF-2) – Continued from build phase.

- Perform Security Quality Management Corrective and Preventive Actions (QM-3) – Continued from build phase.

- Manage Security Knowledge, Skills, and Knowledge Assets (KM-4) – Continued from build phase.

- Assess the Security Aspects of the Project (PA-2):

    - PA-2.9 – Analyze security measurement results and make recommendations (continued from build phase).

    - PA-2.10 – Record and provide security status and security findings from the assessment tasks.

- Control the Security Aspects of the Project (PA-3) – Continued from build phase.

- Monitor Security Risks (RM-5) – Continued from build phase.

- Perform the Security Aspects of Information Management (IM-2):

    - IM-2.1 – Securely obtain, develop, or transform the identified information items.

    - IM-2.2 – Securely maintain information items and their storage records and record the security status of information. Perform Product and Service Security Evaluations (QA-2) (continued from build phase).

- Perform Process Security Evaluations (QA-3):

    - QA-3.1 – Evaluate project life-cycle processes for conformance to established security criteria, contracts, standards, and regulations.

    - QA-3.2 – Evaluate tools and environments that support or automate the process for conformance to established security criteria, contracts, standards, and regulations.

    - QA-3.3 – Evaluate supplier processes for conformance to process security requirements.

- Treat Security Incidents and Problems (QA-5) – Continued from build phase.

- Manage Results of the Security Aspects of Implementation (IP-3) – Continued from build phase.

- Manage Results of the Security Aspects of Integration (IN-3) – Continued from build phase.

- Perform Security-Focused Verification (VE-2):

    - VE-2.2 – Perform security verification procedures.

    - VE-2.3 – Analyze security-focused verification results against any established expectations and success criteria.

- Manage Results of Security-Focused Verification (VE-3):

- VE-3.1 – Record the security aspects of verification results and any security anomalies encountered.
- VE-3.2 – Record the security characteristics of operational incidents and problems and track their resolution.

A.6 Project Closing

Project closing activities included drafting and publishing the Practice Guide. Ongoing activities may continue to include additional capability demonstrations.

A.6.1 Draft Practice Guide

During the compose Practice Guide milestone, the cybersecurity solution operated in a full-scale demonstration environment to show readiness for sustained use and operations, and was ready for draft publication as a NIST 1800-series publication.

The draft Practice Guide activity was focused primarily on the following systems security engineering tasks described in Chapter 3 of [NIST SP 800-160]:

- Share Security Knowledge and Skills Throughout the Organization (KM-2):
    - KM-2.1 – Establish and maintain a classification for capturing and sharing security knowledge and skills.
    - KM-2.2 – Capture or acquire security knowledge and skills.
    - KM-2.3 – Share security knowledge and skills across the organization.
- Manage Security Knowledge, Skills, and Knowledge Assets (KM-4) – Continued from Control/test phase.
- Define the Security Aspects of the Problem (PL-1):
    - PL-1.3 – Define and maintain a security view of the life-cycle model and its constituent stages.
- Manage the Security Aspects of the Risk Profile (RM-2):
    - RM-2.1 – Define and record the security risk thresholds and conditions under which a level of risk may be accepted.
    - RM-2.2 – Establish and maintain the security aspects of the risk profile.
    - RM-2.3 – Provide the security aspects of the risk profile to stakeholders based on their needs.
- Analyze Security Risks (RM-3) – Revisited process employed during the design phase.
- Treat Security Risk (RM-4) – Revisited process employed during the design phase.

- Perform the Security Aspects of Information Management (IM-2):

  - IM-2.1 – Securely obtain, develop, or transform the identified information items (continued from Control/test phase).

  - IM-2.2 – Securely maintain information items and their storage records and record the security status of information (continued from Control/test phase).

  - IM-2.3 – Securely publish, distribute, or provide access to information and information items to designated stakeholders.

  - IM-2.4 – Securely archive designated information.

  - IM-2.5 – Securely dispose of unwanted or invalid information or information that has not been validated.

- Manage Quality Assurance Records and Reports (QA-4):

  - QA-4.1 – Create records and reports related to the security aspects of quality assurance activities.

  - QA-4.2 – Securely maintain, store, and distribute records and reports.

  - QA-4.3 – Identify the security aspects of incidents and problems associated with product, service, and process evaluations.

- Manage the Security Aspects of Business/Mission Analysis (BA-5):

  - BA-5.1 – Maintain traceability of the security aspects of business or mission analysis.

  - BA-5.2 – Provide security-relevant information items required for business or mission analysis to baselines.

- Manage the Security Aspects of System Analysis (SA-3) – Revisited process employed during the design phase.

- Manage Results of the Security Aspects of Implementation (IP-3) – Continued from build and Control/test phases.

- Manage Results of Security-Focused Verification (VE-3):

  - VE-3.3 – Obtain stakeholder agreement that the system or system element meets the specified system security requirements and characteristics.

- Prepare for the Security Aspects of Validation (VA-1):

  - VA-1.1 – Identify the security aspects of the validation scope and corresponding security-focused validation.

  - VA-1.2 – Identify the constraints that can potentially limit the feasibility of the security-focused validation actions.

- VA-1.3 – Select the appropriate methods or techniques for the security aspects of validation and the associated security criteria for each security-focused validation action.

- VA-1.4 – Develop the security aspects of the validation strategy.

- VA-1.5 – Identify system constraints resulting from the security aspects of validation to be incorporated into the stakeholder security requirements.

- VA-1.6 – Identify, plan for, and obtain access to enabling systems or services to support the security aspects of validation.

A.6.2 Special Publication Process

During the publish SP milestone, comments on the Cybersecurity Practice Guide were resolved, and it was published as a NIST SP.

The SP activity was focused primarily on the following systems security engineering tasks described in Chapter 3 of [NIST SP 800-160]:

- Share Security Knowledge Assets Throughout the Organization (KM-3):

  - KM-3.3 – Securely share knowledge assets across the organization.

- Define the Security Aspects of the Problem (PL-1) – Continued activity from the draft Practice Guide phase:

  - PL-1.3 – Define and maintain a security view of the life-cycle model and its constituent stages.

- Manage the Security Aspects of the Risk Profile (RM-2) – Continued activity from the draft Practice Guide phase.

- Analyze Security Risks (RM-3) – Continued activity from the draft Practice Guide phase.

- Treat Security Risk (RM-4) – Continued activity from the draft Practice Guide phase.

- Manage Quality Assurance Records and Reports (QA-4) – Continued activity from the draft Practice Guide phase.

- Manage the Security Aspects of Business/Mission Analysis (BA-5) – Continued activity from the draft Practice Guide phase.

- Manage Results of the Security Aspects of Implementation (IP-3) – Continued activity from the draft Practice Guide phase.

- Prepare for the Security Aspects of Validation (VA-1) – Continued activity from the draft Practice Guide phase.

Appendix B   Cybersecurity Education and Training

B.1 Assumptions and Limitations

Internet service provider (ISP) personnel have many duties related to operating a service provider network, of which cybersecurity is only one part. Likewise, enterprise personnel have many duties related to operating the enterprise's own network, of which cybersecurity is only one part. This appendix discusses only Resource Public Key Infrastructure (RPKI)-based route origin validation (ROV)-specific training that is recommended for enterprise and ISP personnel.

B.2 Staff Role Perspective

The perspective from which a staff member will need to be familiar with software, equipment, and procedures and to consult pertinent standards will differ depending on that staff member's role within the organization (regardless of whether the organization is an ISP or an enterprise):

- The procurement staff will need to understand ROV and RPKI standards to the extent that they are able to ensure that the standards are supported by the equipment being purchased.

- Managers will need to understand these standards to the extent that they are able to ensure that their organization has all software, equipment, personnel, and procedures in place to perform their RPKI-based ROV role(s) correctly and in a manner that is consistent with business policies and objectives.

- Operations and maintenance personnel will need to understand these standards to the extent that these personnel will enable the staff to support day-to-day RPKI-based ROV operations.

B.3 ISP Versus Enterprise Training Requirements

There is not necessarily a strict distinction between the type of RPKI-based ROV training that is needed at enterprises versus that which is needed at ISPs. Rather, the type of training that is required depends more on the roles that each organization assumes with respect to RPKI-based ROV.

All ISPs have dual RPKI-based ROV roles, in the sense that they serve as both network operators and address holders. In their capacity as network operators, they are concerned with obtaining and using RPKI information to perform ROV; in their capacity as address holders, they are concerned with creating route origin authorizations (ROAs) to help protect their addresses from being hijacked. Hence, the ISP staff need training in both the ROV-related and RPKI-related areas.

Unlike ISPs, enterprises do not necessarily need to perform ROV. Instead, an enterprise may rely on its service provider to perform ROV on its behalf. If an enterprise does not perform ROV, then its staff does not need training in ROV-related areas; however, if the enterprise does perform ROV, then its staff will need the same ROV training as the ISP staff.

Assuming that an enterprise is an address holder, it will need training in RPKI-related areas. One important difference between the RPKI training needed at ISPs versus enterprises stems from the fact that an ISP has a choice of deploying either the hosted or delegated model of RPKI, whereas an enterprise will always use the hosted model.

B.4 ROV Training Requirements

Organizations (whether they be ISPs or enterprises) that will perform ROV will need training in, and familiarity with, the following items:

- Border Gateway Protocol (BGP) routers
- RPKI validating caches (VCs)

B.5 ISP RPKI Training Requirements

ISPs will need training in, and familiarity with, the following areas:

- general RPKI information
- depending on which model the ISP chooses to use, either of the following two models:
  - RPKI hosted model
  - RPKI delegated model

Managers at the ISP who are responsible for choosing which model to use will need to be familiar with both the hosted and delegated models.

B.6 Enterprise RPKI Training Requirements

Enterprises that are address holders and that want to create ROAs to protect those addresses will need training in, and familiarity with, the following areas:

- general RPKI information
- RPKI hosted model

B.7 List of Standards and other Training Materials

The standards and other material with which the staff should be familiar under each topic area that is relevant to ROV and RPKI are as follows:

BGP Router Information:

- [RFC 6810], *The Resource Public Key Infrastructure (RPKI) to Router Protocol*
- [RFC 8210], *The Resource Public Key Infrastructure (RPKI) to Router Protocol, Version 1*

- [RFC 6811], *BGP Prefix Origin Validation*
- [RFC 8097], *BGP Prefix Origin Validation State Extended Community*
- Information regarding the configuration and use of the ROV-specific components of the border routers being used, including configuring routing policy based on the validation state

RPKI VC Information:

- [RFC 5781], *The rsync URI Scheme*
- [RFC 8182], *The RPKI Repository Delta Protocol (RRDP)*
- [RFC 6487], *A Profile for X.509 PKIX Resource Certificates*
- [RFC 6488], *Signed Object Template for the Resource Public Key Infrastructure (RPKI)*
- information regarding the installation and use of the specific VC software being used
- [RFC 6486], *Manifests for the Resource Public Key Infrastructure (RPKI)*

General RPKI Information:

- [RFC 6481], *A Profile for Resource Certificate Repository Structure*
- [RFC 7730], *Resource Public Key Infrastructure (RPKI) Trust Anchor Locator*

RPKI Hosted-Model Information:

The ISP staff should be familiar with the Regional Internet Registry (RIR) (or other authority) web interface that they will need to use to request the creation and storage of ROAs for their addresses. The ISP staff should receive training in both the mechanics of how to use the web interface and the meaning and ramifications of selecting various available options. (This information is of interest only to enterprises and to ISPs that plan to use the hosted model of RPKI for generating and storing ROAs for their addresses.)

RPKI Delegated-Model Information:

It is assumed that staff at these ISPs are already familiar with all standards related to running an X.509 certificate authority (CA), in general, independent of ROV. In addition, to be able to support the extensions to X.509 that are required for a delegated-model CA to support ROV, the ISP staff should be familiar with the following standards and other material:

- [RFC 3779], *X.509 Extensions for IP Addresses and AS Identifiers*
- [RFC 6480], *An Infrastructure to Support Secure Internet Routing*
- [RFC 6481], *A Profile for Resource Certification Repository Structure*
- [RFC 6482], *A Profile for Route Origin Authorizations (ROAs)*

- [RFC 7115], *Origin Validation Operation Based on the Resource Public Key Infrastructure (RPKI)* (operational considerations)

- [RFC 6492], *A Protocol for Provisioning Resource Certificates*

(This information is of interest only to ISPs that plan to set up their own CA and repository publication point.)

Appendix C Secure Inter-Domain Routing Project Mapping to the Cybersecurity Framework Core and Informative References

This appendix provides more detailed information regarding the security controls mapping of the Cybersecurity Framework categories and subcategories to the functionality supported by components of the secure inter-domain routing (SIDR) reference architecture solution, as well as a discussion of additional references, standards, and guidelines that informed the SIDR Project.

C.1 Cybersecurity Framework Functions, Categories, and Subcategories Addressed by the Secure Inter-Domain Routing Project

The following Cybersecurity Framework categories and subcategories are supported by the SIDR Project:

- The *Protect* function involves developing and implementing the appropriate safeguards needed to ensure the delivery of critical infrastructure services. The following SIDR platform capabilities support the *Protect* function:

  - The Integrity and Authenticity of Routing information (ensuring that Border Gateway Protocol [BGP] routes are originated from an authorized autonomous system [AS]) supports the *Data Security* (PR.DS) category under the *Protect* function. The *Data Security* (PR.DS) category includes managing information and data that are consistent with the organization's risk strategy to protect the confidentiality, integrity, and availability of information. The following subcategories are supported by the platform:

    - PR.DS-1 – Data-at-rest is protected.

    - PR.DS-2 – Data-in-transit is protected.

    - PR.DS-6 – Integrity checking mechanisms are used to verify information integrity.

  - System and Application Hardening (adjusting security controls on the server and/or software applications such that security is maximized ["hardened"] while maintaining the intended use) supports the *Information Protection Processes and Procedures* (PR.IP) category under the *Protect* function. The *Information Protection Processes and Procedures* category involves maintaining and using security policies, processes, and procedures to manage the protection of information systems and assets.

- Device Protection (ensuring the protection of devices, communications, and control networks) supports the *Access Control* and *Protective Technology* categories under the *Protect* function:

    ○ *Access Control* (PR.AC) includes the limiting of access to logical assets to authorized users and processes. The following subcategories are supported by the platform:

        – PR.AC-3 – Remote access is managed.

        – PR.AC-5 – Network integrity is protected, incorporating network segregation where appropriate.

    ○ *Protective Technology* (PR.PT) includes managing technical security solutions to ensure that the security and resilience of systems and assets are consistent with related policies, procedures, and agreements. A subcategory supported by the platform is as follows:

        – PR.PT-4 – Communications and control networks are protected.

- The *Detect* function involves developing and implementing the appropriate activities to identify the occurrence of a cybersecurity event. Protecting the authenticity of routing information and detecting anomalous routes support the following categories under the *Detect* function:

    - *Security Continuous Monitoring* (DE.CM) includes monitoring information systems and assets to identify cybersecurity events. The following subcategories are supported by the platform:

        ○ DE.CM-4 – Malicious code is detected.

        ○ DE.CM-7 – Monitoring for unauthorized personnel, connections, devices, and software is performed.

    - *Detection Processes* (DE.DP) include maintaining and testing detection processes and procedures to ensure timely and adequate awareness of anomalous events. The following subcategories are supported by the platform:

        ○ DE.DP-3 – Detection processes are tested.

        ○ DE.DP-4 – Event detection information is communicated to appropriate parties.

- The *Respond* function involves supporting the development and implementation of the appropriate activities that take action regarding a detected cybersecurity event. Platform capabilities that support the *Respond* function include ensuring the integrity of network connections in the case of incidents that result in a compromise. The effects of the compromise can be limited by the exclusion of systems and devices that have not implemented the integrity mechanisms. Also, when routes that originated from unauthorized ASes are received, these routes can be logged and reported. The platform supports the *Communications* and *Mitigation* categories under the *Response* function:

- *Communications* (RS.CO) includes the coordination of response activities with internal and external stakeholders. The following subcategories are supported by the platform:

  - RS.CO-2 – Events are reported consistent with response plans.

  - RS.CO-3—Information is shared consistent with response plans.

- *Mitigation* (RS.MI) includes preventing the expansion of events, mitigating their effects, and eradicating incidents. A subcategory supported by the platform is as follows:

  - RS.MI-1 – Incidents are contained.

C.2 Cybersecurity References Directly Tied to Those Cybersecurity Framework Categories and Subcategories Addressed by the Secure Inter-Domain Routing Project

The following references are mapped to the *Cybersecurity Framework* subcategories identified in Table 4-1 (Section 4.4.4) as being addressed by the SIDR security platform:

- *Information Technology – Security techniques – Information security management systems – Requirements* ([ISO/IEC 27001:2013]) Sections A.6.1.3, A.6.1.5, A.6.2.2, A.8.2.3, A.12.1.2, A.12.2.1, A.12.5.1, A.12.6.2, A.13.1.1, A.13.1.3, A.13.2.1, A.13.2.3, A.14.1.1, A.14.1.2, A.14.1.3, A.14.2.1, A.14.2.2, A.14.2.3, A.14.2.4, A.14.2.5, A.14.2.8, A.16.1.2, and A.16.1.5.

- *Security and Privacy Controls for Federal Information Systems and Organizations* ([NIST SP 800-53]) controls AC-4, AC-17, AC-18, AC-19, AC-20, AU-6, AU-12, CA-2, CA-7, CM-2, CM-3, CM-4, CM-5, CM-6, CM-7, CM-8, CM-9, CP-2, CP-8, IR-4, IR-6, IR-8, PE-3, PE-6, PE-20, PL-8, PM-14, RA-5, SA-3, SA-4, SA-8, SA-10, SA-11, SA-12, SA-15, SA-17, SC-7, SC-28, SI-3, and SI-4.

C.3 Other Security References Applied in the Design and Development of the Secure Inter-Domain Routing Project

The references, standards, and guidelines that informed the SIDR Project include federal policies and standards, National Institute of Standards and Technology (NIST) guidelines and recommendations, and Internet Engineering Task Force (IETF) standards (published as Requests for Comments [RFCs]). Relevant documents include [OMB A-130]; [FIPS 140-2]; [NIST SP 800-37] Rev. 1; [NIST SP 800-53] Rev. 4; [NIST SP 800-54]; [NIST SP 800-57 Part 1]; [NIST SP 800-130]; [NIST SP 800-152]; [NIST SP 800-160]; NIST *Framework for Improving Critical Infrastructure Cybersecurity*; and RFCs 3882, 4012, 4593, 5280, 5575, 6092, 6472, 6480, 6481, 6495, 6810, 6811, 6907, 7115, 7318, 7454, 7674, 7908, 7909, 8097, 8182, and 8205. The project was also informed by several internet drafts on BGP security and robustness (see Appendix D).

Appendix D   Assumptions Underlying the Build

This project was guided by the following assumptions.

D.1 Security and Performance

An underlying assumption was that the benefits of using the Resource Public Key Infrastructure (RPKI) and route origin validation (ROV) tools and protocols demonstrated in this project outweighed any additional performance risks that may be introduced by instantiating the security protocols. The assessment of the security of current systems and networks is out of scope for this project. A key assumption is that most potential adopters of the demonstrated builds, or of any build components, do not already have RPKI-based ROV protocols in place. We focused on what potential security impacts were being introduced to end users if they implement this solution. The goal of this solution was to provide RPKI-based ROV services without introducing additional performance or reliability risks into existing systems, but there is always an inherent risk of increased overhead and interoperability issues when adding systems and adding new features into an existing system.

D.2 Modularity

The modular approach taken in this project was based on one of the National Cybersecurity Center of Excellence (NCCoE) core operating tenets. It was assumed that organizations already have routing systems in place. Our philosophy is that a combination of certain components or a single component can improve routing security for an organization; the organization may not need to remove or replace most of its existing infrastructure. For example, some commercial routers already come with ROV/[RFC 6811] implemented. It is only a matter of turning it on. This guide provides a complete top-to-bottom solution and is also intended to provide various options based on need.

D.3 Technical Implementation

This Practice Guide is written from a "how-to" perspective, and its foremost purpose is to provide details on how to install, configure, and integrate the components. The NCCoE assumes that an organization has the technical resources to implement all or parts of the build or has access to companies that can perform the implementation on its behalf.

D.4 Operating System and Virtual Machine Environments

This project used commercially available routers and open-source software integrated into a VMware vCenter server Version 6.0.0 Build 3018523 virtual machine (VM) environment. It is assumed that user organizations will be able to use physical or virtual routers and will be able to install the demonstrated applications on cloud-hosted VMs, local VMs, or local native server client environments.

D.5 Address Holder Environments

It is assumed that address holders understand the usage of RPKI resources and have agreements in place with a Regional Internet Registry (RIR) or other authority that enables route origin authorizations (ROAs) for addresses that they hold to be created and signed. The address holder has two options for creating the ROAs: the hosted or delegated model.

D.5.1 Hosted

In the hosted model, the address holder assumes the responsibility of having the Internet Protocol (IP) addresses that it holds registered with the proper RIR to create end-entity (EE) certificates and ROAs. The RPKI infrastructure that is used to create the certificate authority (CA) certificates and store ROAs is managed by the RIR. Address holders should have ROAs only in the RPKI repository corresponding to the RIR or other authority that allocated or administers the address prefixes that are in the ROAs.

D.5.2 Delegated

Unlike the hosted environment, in the delegated environment, the RPKI infrastructure that is used to create the CA certificates and ROAs is managed by the address holder's organization. It is assumed that the address holder or their organization has the resources to design, configure, and operate the components of the RPKI infrastructure. The actual design and implementation of the RPKI infrastructure can be the responsibility of the address holder or can be assigned to the network operators or other information technology (IT) groups within the organization. In this model, a transit internet service provider (ISP) in the allocation hierarchy may offer the RPKI service of maintaining certificates, private keys, and ROAs to its customers.

D.6 Network Operator Environments

Network operators provide Border Gateway Protocol (BGP)-based routing services to route traffic to and from endpoints within their network and customer/peer networks in other autonomous systems (ASes). (Note that network operators may also be address holders, but whether they are or not does not impact their role as network operators.) For this document, the network operator is responsible for operating and managing the network environment, including monitoring and managing tools used for ROV, such as RPKI validating caches and RPKI-aware BGP routers. From an operational standpoint, when RPKI, ROAs, and ROV are being used, the network operator's role does not change depending on whether a hosted or delegated RPKI model is being used. In both cases, network operators are responsible for using ROA information to perform BGP ROV on routes that they receive.

D.7 Regional Internet Registry Environments

RIRs play vital roles in RPKI, both in terms of assisting with the creation of RPKI content by address holders and in terms of making that content available to relying parties. Regarding RPKI content creation for the hosted RPKI model, the RIRs provide an online hosting service to enable their customers to generate EE certificates and ROAs. For example, the Réseaux IP Européens Network Coordination Centre (RIPE NCC) provides a web-based portal for its customers to securely log into and manage their ROAs. For organizations that choose to use the delegated model and run their own CA, there is open-source software available to create the RPKI infrastructure and securely communicate with the RIR parent system.

RIRs also make the content of their RPKI repositories available to relying parties so that relying parties can use this information to perform ROV on the route advertisements that they receive. When a hosted model of RPKI has been used to cause the RIR to assist in the creation of an ROA, the RIR stores that ROA in its repository and makes the ROA directly available to all relying parties. When a delegated model of RPKI has been used to create an ROA, the RIR stores, in its repository, the Universal Resource Indicator (URI) that relying parties need to use to locate the publication point for the ROA.

D.8 Route Acceptance Decisions for Invalid and Not Found Routes

With the use of RPKI, BGP ROV results in BGP routes that are evaluated as either *valid*, *invalid*, or *not found*. While accepting the *valid* routes for usage is the default recommendation and non-controversial, organizations should use their local route selection policies for routes that are *invalid* or *not found*.

D.8.1 Decision Made by Service Provider

Service providers may have policies that are different due to their own local policies or the need to pass on routes to their customers. It is outside the scope of this project to consider incremental or partial deployment models that may be encountered by large commercial ISPs.

D.8.2 Decision Made by Enterprise

Enterprises that receive a default route from their service provider will not need to perform ROV because there is no need to use BGP ROV in this case. All traffic from the enterprise will always travel on the same single (default) route from the enterprise to its ISP. All traffic to the enterprise will travel on a static route from the ISP to the enterprise's public IP address range. On the other hand, enterprises that receive BGP routes from their peers will need to have a policy regarding how to address routes that are *invalid* or *not found*.

Appendix E   Functional Test Requirements and Results

E.1 Functional Test Plans

This test plan presents the functional requirements and associated test cases necessary to conduct the functional evaluation of the secure inter-domain routing (SIDR) example implementation. The SIDR example implementation is currently deployed in a lab at the National Cybersecurity Center of Excellence (NCCoE). The implementation tested is described in Section 7. The test cases are performed using the architectures shown in Figure E-1 and Figure E-2. Figure E-1 depicts the testbed using the test harness (Border Gateway Protocol [BGP] traffic generation and collection framework – BGPSEC-IO [BIO]). Figure E-2 depicts the testbed using live traffic.

Figure E-1 SIDR Testbed Using the Test Harness

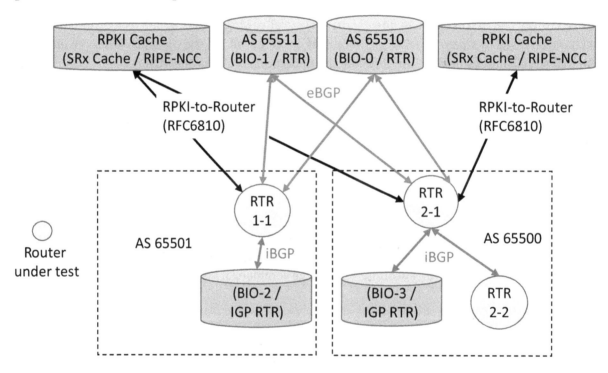

BGPSEC-IO (BIO) – BGP traffic generator & collector /   RTR – CISCO or Juniper Router

Figure E-2 SIDR Testbed Using Live Traffic

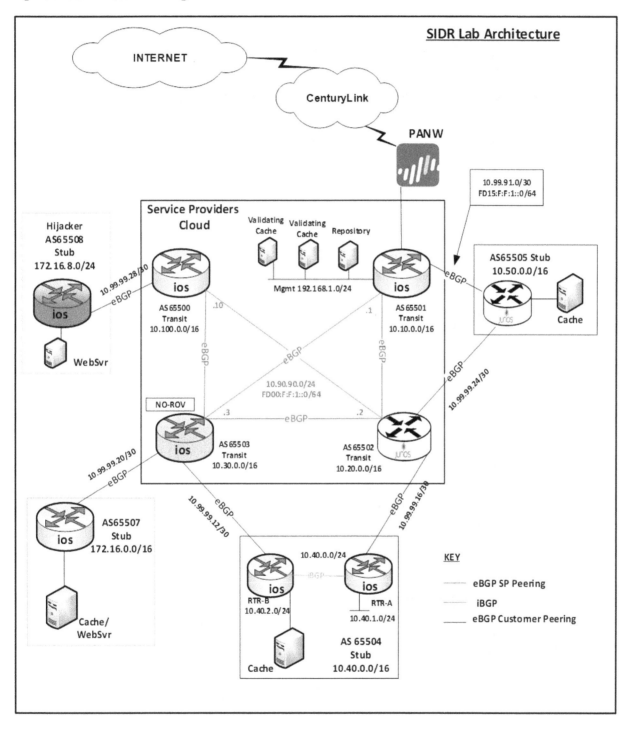

E.2 Requirements

Table E-1 identifies the SIDR functional evaluation requirements that are addressed in this test plan, and their associated test cases.

Table E-1 SIDR Functional Requirements

Capability Requirement (CR) Identifier (ID)	Parent Requirement	Sub-Requirement 1	Sub-Requirement 2	Test Case
CR-1	The SIDR example implementation shall include a capability for BGP routers to perform route origin validation (ROV) on all routes that they receive in BGP update messages. The router will be capable of accurately establishing an initial validation state (*valid*, *invalid*, or *not found*) for a given route and marking the route accordingly. The router will also be capable of accurately re-evaluating that route's validation state after Resource Public Key Infrastructure (RPKI) test data has been perturbed, re-marking the route (if applicable).			
CR-1.1		The advertised route is initially evaluated as *valid*. The single route origin authorization (ROA) that had made the route *valid* is removed from the RPKI;		

Capability Requirement (CR) Identifier (ID)	Parent Requirement	Sub-Requirement 1	Sub-Requirement 2	Test Case
		there is no ROA that covers the route, so the route is re-evaluated as *not found*.		
CR-1.1.1			IPv4 address type	SIDR-ROV-1.1.1
CR-1.1.2			IPv6 address type	SIDR-ROV-1.1.2
CR-1.2		The advertised route is initially evaluated as *valid*. The single ROA that had made the route *valid* is removed from the RPKI. There is another ROA that covers the route, but the autonomous system number (ASN) in this ROA does not match that of the route's origin, so the route is re-evaluated as *invalid*.		
CR-1.2.1			IPv4 address type	SIDR-ROV-1.2.1
CR-1.2.2			IPv6 address type	SIDR-ROV-1.2.2

Capability Requirement (CR) Identifier (ID)	Parent Requirement	Sub-Requirement 1	Sub-Requirement 2	Test Case
CR-1.3		The advertised route is initially evaluated as *valid*. The single ROA that had made the route *valid* is removed from the RPKI. There is another ROA that covers the route, but its maximum prefix length is less than the prefix length of the route, so the route is re-evaluated as *invalid*.		
CR-1.3.1			IPv4 address type	SIDR-ROV-1.3.1
CR-1.3.2			IPv6 address type	SIDR-ROV-1.3.2
CR-1.4		The advertised route is initially evaluated as *valid*. An ROA that had made the route *valid* is removed from the RPKI; there remains another ROA that matches the route, so the route still evaluates as *valid*.		
CR-1.4.1			IPv4 address type	SIDR-ROV-1.4.1
CR-1.4.2			IPv6 address type	SIDR-ROV-1.4.2

Capability Requirement (CR) Identifier (ID)	Parent Requirement	Sub-Requirement 1	Sub-Requirement 2	Test Case
CR-1.5		The advertised route is initially evaluated as *not found*. An ROA that matches the route is added to the RPKI, so the route is re-evaluated as *valid*.		
CR-1.5.1			IPv4 address type	SIDR-ROV-1.5.1
CR-1.5.2			IPv6 address type	SIDR-ROV-1.5.2
CR-1.6		The advertised route is initially evaluated as *not found*. An ROA that covers this route, but that has an ASN different from that of the route's origin, is added to the RPKI, so the route is re-evaluated as *invalid*.		
CR-1.6.1			IPv4 address type	SIDR-ROV-1.6.1
CR-1.6.2			IPv6 address type	SIDR-ROV-1.6.2
CR-1.7		The advertised route is initially evaluated as *invalid* due to an ROA that covers this route, but that has an ASN different from that of the route's origin. A second ROA that		

Capability Requirement (CR) Identifier (ID)	Parent Requirement	Sub-Requirement 1	Sub-Requirement 2	Test Case
		matches this route is added to the RPKI, so the route is re-evaluated as *valid*.		
CR-1.7.1			IPv4 address type	SIDR-ROV-1.7.1
CR-1.7.2			IPv6 address type	SIDR-ROV-1.7.2
CR-1.8		The advertised route is initially evaluated as *invalid* due to the presence of one ROA that covers this route, but that has an ASN different from that of the route's origin. This is the only ROA that covers the route. It is deleted from the RPKI, so the route is re-evaluated as *not found*.		
CR-1.8.1			IPv4 address type	SIDR-ROV-1.8.1
CR-1.8.2			IPv6 address type	SIDR-ROV-1.8.2
CR-1.9		The advertised route is initially evaluated as *invalid*. There are two ROAs that cover this route, both of which have ASNs different from the route's origin. Only one of these ROAs		

Capability Requirement (CR) Identifier (ID)	Parent Requirement	Sub-Requirement 1	Sub-Requirement 2	Test Case
		is deleted from the RPKI, so the route still evaluates as *invalid*.		
CR-1.9.1			IPv4 address type	SIDR-ROV-1.9.1
CR-1.9.2			IPv6 address type	SIDR-ROV-1.9.2
CR-1.10		The advertised route is initially evaluated to be *invalid* due to the fact that it contains AS_SET, even though there is an ROA that covers the route and that has a maximum length greater than the route's prefix. A second advertisement is received for this same route that does not contain AS_SET and that is matched by the ROA that is already in the RPKI. The route in this second advertisement is evaluated as *valid*.		
CR-1.10.1			IPv4 address type	SIDR-ROV-1.10.1
CR-1.10.2			IPv6 address type	SIDR-ROV-1.10.2

Capability Requirement (CR) Identifier (ID)	Parent Requirement	Sub-Requirement 1	Sub-Requirement 2	Test Case
CR-2	The SIDR example implementation shall include a capability for BGP routers to perform ROV on all routes that are redistributed into BGP from another source, such as another protocol or a locally defined static route. The router will be capable of accurately establishing an initial validation state (*valid*, *invalid*, or *not found*) for a given route, marking the route accordingly, and applying appropriate policy depending on the result. The router will also be capable of accurately re-evaluating that route's validation state after RPKI test data has been perturbed, re-marking the route (if applicable), and applying appropriate policy depending on the (possibly) new result.			
CR-2.1		A route is redistributed into BGP from a locally defined static route. This route is initially evaluated as *valid*. The single ROA that had made the route valid is		

Capability Requirement (CR) Identifier (ID)	Parent Requirement	Sub-Requirement 1	Sub-Requirement 2	Test Case
		removed from the RPKI. There is another ROA that covers the route, but the ASN in this ROA does not match that of the route's origin, so the route is re-evaluated as *invalid*.		
CR-2.1.1			IPv4 address type	SIDR-ROV-2.1.1
CR-2.1.2			IPv6 address type	SIDR-ROV-2.1.2
CR-2.1.3			IPv4 address type and virtual router instead of physical router	SIDR-ROV-2.1.3
CR-2.2		A route is redistributed into BGP from a locally defined static route. The route is initially evaluated as *not found*. An ROA that matches the route is added to the RPKI, so the route is re-evaluated as *valid*.		
CR-2.2.1			IPv4 address type	SIDR-ROV-2.2.1
CR-2.2.2			IPv6 address type	SIDR-ROV-2.2.2

Capability Requirement (CR) Identifier (ID)	Parent Requirement	Sub-Requirement 1	Sub-Requirement 2	Test Case
CR-2.3		A route is redistributed into BGP from a locally defined static route. The advertised route is initially evaluated as *not found*. An ROA that covers this route, but that has an ASN different from that of the route's origin, is added to the RPKI, so the route is re-evaluated as *invalid*.		
CR-2.3.1			IPv4 address type	SIDR-ROV-2.3.1
CR-2.3.2			IPv6 address type	SIDR-ROV-2.3.2
CR-3.1		A route is redistributed into BGP from an interior gateway protocol (IGP). This route is initially evaluated as *valid*. The single ROA that had made the route *valid* is removed from the RPKI; there is no ROA that covers the route, so the route is re-evaluated as *not found*.		
CR-3.1.1			IPv4 address type	SIDR-ROV-3.1.1

Capability Requirement (CR) Identifier (ID)	Parent Requirement	Sub-Requirement 1	Sub-Requirement 2	Test Case
CR-3.2		A route is redistributed into BGP from an IGP. This route is initially evaluated as *invalid* due to an ROA that covers this route, but that has an ASN different from that of the route's origin. A second ROA that matches this route is added to the RPKI, so the route is re-evaluated as *valid*.		
CR-3.2.1			IPv4 address type	SIDR-ROV-3.2.1
CR-3.3		A route is redistributed into BGP from an IGP. This route is initially evaluated as *invalid* due to the presence of one ROA that covers this route, but that has an ASN different from that of the route's origin. This is the only ROA that covers the route. It is deleted from the RPKI, so the route is re-evaluated as *not found*.		
CR-3.3.1			IPv4 address type	SIDR-ROV-3.3.1

Capability Requirement (CR) Identifier (ID)	Parent Requirement	Sub-Requirement 1	Sub-Requirement 2	Test Case
CR-4	The SIDR example implementation shall include a capability for BGP routers to be configured with a policy that treats locally defined interior border gateway protocol (iBGP) routes differently from other iBGP routes. In particular, it will be possible to configure router policy such that *invalid* locally generated iBGP routes and *invalid* locally defined static routes are not dropped, but other *invalid* iBGP routes are.			
CR-4.1		The router under test (RUT) implements its configured policy, which is to retain *invalid* routes if they are locally generated iBGP routes or locally defined static routes, but to drop all other *invalid* iBGP routes.		
CR-4.1.1			IPv4 address type	SIDR-ROV-4.1.1
			IPv6 address type	SIDR-ROV-4.1.1

Capability Requirement (CR) Identifier (ID)	Parent Requirement	Sub-Requirement 1	Sub-Requirement 2	Test Case
CR-4.2		ROV-capable routers can evaluate routes correctly within an iBGP network by using a single, but shared, VC for the iBGP peers, whether the routes are received via an exterior border gateway protocol (eBGP), IGP, static, or from a local network.		
CR-4.2.1			IPv4 address type with Router A	SIDR-ROV-4.2.1
			IPv6 address type with Router A	SIDR-ROV-4.2.1
CR-4.2.2			IPv4 address type with Router B	SIDR-ROV-4.2.2
			IPv6 address type with Router B	SIDR-ROV-4.2.2
CR-4.3		ROV-capable routers can evaluate routes correctly using eBGP, IGP, static, and local network routes within an iBGP network using one shared VC within iBGP peers without Extended Community Strings.		
CR-4.3.1			IPv4 address type with Router A	SIDR-ROV-4.3.1

Capability Requirement (CR) Identifier (ID)	Parent Requirement	Sub-Requirement 1	Sub-Requirement 2	Test Case
			IPv6 address type with Router A	SIDR-ROV-4.3.1
CR-4.3.2			IPv4 address type with Router B	SIDR-ROV-4.3.2
			IPv6 address type with Router B	SIDR-ROV-4.3.2
CR-4.4		ROV-capable routers can evaluate routes correctly using eBGP, IGP, static, and local network routes within an iBGP network using one shared VC within iBGP peers with Extended Community Strings.		
CR-4.4.1			IPv4 address type with Router A	SIDR-ROV-4.4.1
			IPv6 address type with Router A	SIDR-ROV-4.4.1
CR-4.4.2			IPv4 address type with Router B	SIDR-ROV-4.4.2
			IPv6 address type with Router B	SIDR-ROV-4.4.2
CR-4.5		ROV-capable routers can evaluate routes correctly using eBGP, IGP, static, and local network routes within		

Capability Requirement (CR) Identifier (ID)	Parent Requirement	Sub-Requirement 1	Sub-Requirement 2	Test Case
		an iBGP network using two distinct VCs for the iBGP peers while enabling Extended Community Strings.		
CR-4.5.1			IPv4 address type with Router A	SIDR-ROV-4.5.1
			IPv6 address type with Router A	SIDR-ROV-4.5.1
CR-4.6		ROV-capable routers can evaluate routes correctly using eBGP, IGP, static, and local network routes within an iBGP network using two distinct VCs with conflicting records for the iBGP peers while enabling Extended Community String.		
CR-4.6.1			IPv4 address type with Router A	SIDR-ROV-4.6.1
			IPv6 address type with Router A	SIDR-ROV-4.6.1
CR-5	The SIDR example implementation shall be capable of applying policies to the ROV-route selection process.			

Capability Requirement (CR) Identifier (ID)	Parent Requirement	Sub-Requirement 1	Sub-Requirement 2	Test Case
CR-5.1		The router can be configured such that *invalid* routes are discarded and *not found* routes are installed with a low local preference (LP) value.		
CR-5.1.1			IPv4 address type	SIDR-ROV-5.1.1
			IPv6 address type	SIDR-ROV-5.1.1
CR-5.1.1		The router can be configured such that *invalid* routes are installed with the lowest LP value, *valid* routes are installed with the highest LP value, and *not found* routes are installed with an LP value in between.		
CR-5.1.2			IPv4 address type	SIDR-ROV-5.1.2
			IPv6 address type	SIDR-ROV-5.1.2
CR-6	The SIDR example implementation shall be capable of having the router and VC synchronize properly such that the correct			

Capability Requirement (CR) Identifier (ID)	Parent Requirement	Sub-Requirement 1	Sub-Requirement 2	Test Case
	RPKI information is received at the router following a disruption to the connectivity between a router and its VC.			
CR-6.1		The router and the VC get re-synchronized properly after a loss of connectivity.		
CR-6.1.1			IPv4 address type	SIDR-ROV-6.1.1
			IPv6 address type	SIDR-ROV-6.1.1
CR-6.2		The router and the VC get re-synchronized properly after the VC loses power.		
CR-6.2.1			IPv4 address type	SIDR-ROV-6.2.1
			IPv6 address type	SIDR-ROV-6.2.1
CR-6.3		The router and the VC get re-synchronized properly after the router loses power.		
CR-6.3.1			IPv4 address type	SIDR-ROV-6.3.1
			IPv6 address type	SIDR-ROV-6.3.1

Capability Requirement (CR) Identifier (ID)	Parent Requirement	Sub-Requirement 1	Sub-Requirement 2	Test Case
CR-6.4		The router synchronizes to a different VC after disconnecting from a previous VC.		
CR-6.4.1			IPv4 address type	SIDR-ROV-6.4.1
			IPv6 address type	SIDR-ROV-6.4.1
CR-6.5		The router is connected to two VC with identical RPKI information, and then one of those VC is shut down.		
CR-6.5.1			IPv4 address type	SIDR-ROV-6.5.1
			IPv6 address type	SIDR-ROV-6.5.1
CR-6.6		The router is connected to two VCs that have different RPKI information, and then one of those VCs is shut down.		
CR-6.6.1			IPv4 address type	SIDR-ROV-6.6.1
			IPv6 address type	SIDR-ROV-6.6.1
CR-7	The SIDR example implementation shall include the capability			

Capability Requirement (CR) Identifier (ID)	Parent Requirement	Sub-Requirement 1	Sub-Requirement 2	Test Case
	for a resource holder to set up its own delegated certificate authority (CA), create its own repository, and offer a hosted service to its customers, including the ability to publish customer ROAs to its repository, delete customer ROAs from its repository, and have customer ROAs expire from its repository. The ROAs in this delegated CA repository will be included in the RPKI data that relying parties download to their VCs, and validated ROA payloads (VRPs) derived from these ROAs will be provided to relying-party routers via the RPKI-to-router protocol.			
CR-7.1		A resource holder is able to set up its own delegated CA, create its own repository, create ROAs for the addresses that it holds, and store these ROAs in its own repository.		
CR-7.1.1			IPv4 address type	SIDR-DM-7.1.1

Capability Requirement (CR) Identifier (ID)	Parent Requirement	Sub-Requirement 1	Sub-Requirement 2	Test Case
CR-7.2		A delegated CA is able to create ROAs on behalf of its customers and store them in its repository.		
CR-7.2.1			IPv4 address type	SIDR-DM-7.2.1
CR-7.3		A delegated CA is able to delete/revoke an ROA, from its own repository, that it has created for addresses that it holds.		
CR-7.3.1			IPv4 address type	SIDR-DM-7.1.1
CR-7.4		A delegated CA is able to delete/revoke an ROA, from its own repository, that it has created and is storing on behalf of its customers.		
CR-7.4.1			IPv4 address type	SIDR-DM-7.2.1
CR-7.5		A delegated CA is able to create ROAs, for addresses that it holds, that will expire as designed.		
CR-7.5.1			IPv4 address type	SIDR-DM-7.1.1

Capability Requirement (CR) Identifier (ID)	Parent Requirement	Sub-Requirement 1	Sub-Requirement 2	Test Case
CR-7.6		A delegated CA is able to create ROAs, on behalf of its customers, that will expire as designed.		
CR-7.6.1			IPv4 address type	SIDR-DM-7.2.1
CR-7.7		ROAs that are stored in the delegated CA's repository are downloaded to the VCs that relying parties construct, validate, and maintain.		
CR-7.7.1			IPv4 address type	SIDR-DM-7.1.1 and 7.2.1
CR-7.8		The VRP information that is downloaded by routers from VCs using the RPKI-to-router protocol includes information derived from ROAs that are stored in the delegated CA's repository.		
CR-7.8.1			IPv4 address type	SIDR-DM-7.1.1 and 7.2.1

E.3 Tests

The remaining subsections provide the tests that have been designed to validate that the SIDR example implementation meets each of the SIDR functional requirements specified in Table E-1 above. Each test consists of multiple fields that collectively identify the objective of the test, the steps required to implement the test, and how to assess the results of the test. Table E-2 provides a template of a test case, including a description of each field in the test case.

Unless otherwise specified, these tests are written under the assumption that the amount of time that elapses between any test step and the next is sufficient to allow modifications that are made to the global RPKI to propagate down to the VC and then to the RUT. This means that if an ROA is updated in one step of the test, then the effects that this ROA has on the validation state of routes in the RUT's router information base will be evident in the next step of the test.

Table E-2 Test Case Fields

Test Case Field	Description		
Test Objective	Lists the requirement being tested (as identified in the table of SIDR functional test requirements). Describes the objective of the test case.		
Preconditions	The starting state of the test case. Preconditions indicate various starting state items, such as a specific capability configuration required or specific protocol and content.		
IPv4 or IPv6?	States which type of addresses are being used.	**Test Harness or Hardware with Live RPKI?**	Indicates the source of the test data.
Test Procedure	The step-by-step actions required to implement the test case. A procedure may consist of a single sequence of steps or multiple sequences of steps (with delineation) to indicate variations in the test procedure.		
Expected Results	The expected results for each variation in the test procedure, assuming that the test functions as intended.		
Actual Results	As expected or the observed results.		
Additional Comments (If Needed)	None.		

E.3.1 SIDR ROV Test Cases —Routes Received in BGP Updates

During all harness tests, the RUT communicates the validation result of selected routes to an iBGP peer by using the Extended Community String specified in [RFC 8097] or via the regular community string using the type 0x4300 and values 0–2, as specified in [RFC 8097], only in 4-octet notation, rather than

8-octet notation. However, visual verification was used with appropriate show commands to verify the expected results with tests performed using hardware with a live RPKI data stream.

The route validation results, as well as the RPKI table within the RUT, will be retrieved and logged. For all tests, the commands used are as follows:

- Cisco:
  - To "Verify that this route is installed in the routing table" and "Verify that the RUT evaluates this route advertisement as valid, invalid, or not found," use: `show ip bgp`.
  - To "Verify that the RUT receives VRP information," use: `show ip bgp rpki table`.
- Juniper:
  - To "Verify that this route is installed in the routing table" and "Verify that the RUT evaluates this route advertisement as valid, invalid, or not found," use: `show table`.
  - To "Verify that the RUT receives VRP information," use: `show validation database`.

E.3.1.1   Test Case: SIDR-ROV-1.1.1 and 1.1.2

Test Objective	**Test SIDR Requirement CR-1.1. Show that the ROV-capable router correctly evaluates received routes in the following situation: The advertised route is initially evaluated as *valid*. The single ROA that had made the route *valid* is removed from the RPKI; there is no ROA that covers the route, so the route is re-evaluated as *not found*.** **(*valid* → *not found*)**		
Preconditions	The testbed is configured with the topology and ASNs as depicted in the Testbed Architecture in <u>Figure E-1</u> and <u>Figure E-2</u>. The router is set up to accept every BGP route, regardless of the validation state. No ROAs have been published that cover 10.100.0.0/16. RUT is Router AS 65501. The following configuration for Router AS65501 has been added: **Test 1-1-1 Config.txt**		
IPv4 or IPv6?	Both	**Test Harness or Hardware with Live RPKI?**	Both
Test Procedure	1. AS 65511 publishes an ROA for its address space: (10.100.0.0/16, 16, AS65511). 2. AS 65511 originates a BGP route advertisement for 10.100.0.0/16. 3. Verify that the RUT receives VRP information. 4. Verify that the RUT evaluates this route advertisement as *valid*.		

	5. Verify that this route is installed in the routing table.
	6. AS 65511 removes the ROA published in Step 1 from the RPKI.
	7. Verify that the RUT evaluates this route advertisement as *not found*.
	For IPv6, use IP address FD10:100:100:1::/64 in place of 10.100.0.0/16.
Expected Results	IPv4 Results: Each of the expected results in Steps 3, 4, 5, and 7 above are verified.
Actual Results	Test completed and functions as intended in Steps 3, 4, 5, and 7.
Additional Comments (If Needed)	Changes in the validation state of selected routes are also observed via iBGP traffic. Step 5 is observed by monitoring the incoming traffic on its iBGP peer.

Test case SIDR-ROV-1.1.2 is identical to test case SIDR-ROV-1.1.1, except that IPv6 addresses are used instead of IPv4 addresses.

Note: Test case SIDR-ROV-1.1.1 was also completed using the Cisco IOS-XR image running on VMware. Using the same procedures, AS65501 was replaced by this Cisco IOS-XR router with the configuration of the attached file:

Test 1-1-1
Config-IOS-XR.txt

E.3.1.2   Test Case: SIDR-ROV-1.2.1 and 1.2.2

Test Objective	**Test SIDR Requirement CR-1.2. Show that the ROV-capable router correctly evaluates received routes in the following situation: The advertised route is initially evaluated as *valid*. The single ROA that had made the route *valid* is removed from the RPKI. There is another ROA that covers the route, but the ASN in this ROA does not match that of the route's origin, so the route is re-evaluated as *invalid*.** **(*valid → invalid*)**
Preconditions	The testbed is configured with the topology, IP addressing scheme, and ASNs as depicted in the Testbed Architecture in Figure E-1 and Figure E-2. The router is set up to accept every BGP route, regardless of the validation state. RUT is Router AS65501. The attached file shows the configuration for Router AS65501 that has been added. **Test 2-1-1** **Config.txt**

IPv4 or IPv6?	Both	Test Harness or Hardware with Live RPKI?	Both
Procedure	1. AS 65511 publishes an ROA for its address space: (10.100.0.0/16, 16, AS65511). 2. AS 65511 publishes a second ROA for the same address space that authorizes a different AS to originate addresses for it (10.100.0.0/16, 16, AS65510). 3. AS 65511 originates a BGP route advertisement for 10.100.0.0/16. 4. Verify that the RUT receives VRP information. 5. Verify that the RUT evaluates this route advertisement as *valid*. 6. Verify that this route is installed in the routing table. 7. AS 65511 removes the ROA published in Step 1 from the RPKI. 8. Verify that the RUT now evaluates the route advertisement for 10.100.0.0/16 that originated from 65511 as *invalid*. **For IPv6, use IP address FD10:100:100:1::/64 in place of 10.100.0.0/16.**		
Expected Results	Each of the expected results in Steps 4, 5, 6, and 8 above are verified.		
Actual Results	Test completed and functions as intended in Steps 4, 5, 6, and 8.		
Additional Comments (If Needed)	Changes in the validation state of selected routes are also observed via iBGP traffic. Step 6 is validated by monitoring the incoming traffic on its iBGP peer.		

Test case SIDR-ROV-1.2.2 is identical to test case SIDR-ROV-1.2.1, except that IPv6 addresses are used instead of IPv4 addresses.

E.3.1.3   Test Case: SIDR-ROV-1.3.1 and 1.3.2

Test Objective	Test SIDR Requirement CR-1.3.1. Show that the ROV-capable router correctly evaluates received routes in the following situation: The advertised route is initially evaluated as *valid*. The single ROA that had made the route *valid* is removed from the RPKI. There is another ROA that covers the route, but its maximum prefix length is less than the prefix length of the route, so the route is re-evaluated as *invalid*. (*valid* → *invalid*)		
Preconditions	The testbed is configured with the topology, IP addressing scheme, and ASNs as depicted in the Testbed Architecture in Figure E-1 and Figure E-2. The router is set up to accept every BGP route, regardless of the validation state.		
IPv4 or IPv6?	Both	Test Harness or Hardware with Live RPKI?	Both

Procedure	1. AS 65511 publishes an ROA for its address space: (10.100.0.0/16, 16, AS65511).
	2. AS 65511 publishes a second ROA for the same address space, but with a larger maximum length: (10.100.0.0/16, 24, AS65511).
	3. AS 65511 originates a BGP route advertisement for 10.100.8.0/24.
	4. Verify that the RUT receives VRP information.
	5. Verify that the RUT evaluates this route advertisement as *valid*.
	6. Verify that this route is installed in the routing table.
	7. AS 65511 removes the ROA published in Step 2 from the RPKI.
	8. Verify that the RUT evaluates the route to 10.100.8.0/24 that was originated by AS 65511 as *invalid*.
	For IPv6, use IP address FD10:100:100:1::/64 in place of 10.100.0.0/16.
Expected Results	Each of the expected results in Steps 4, 5, 6, and 8 above are verified.
Actual Results	Test completed and functions as intended in Steps 4, 5, 6, and 8.
Additional Comments (If Needed)	Changes in the validation state of selected routes are also observed via iBGP traffic. Step 6 is validated by monitoring the incoming traffic on its iBGP peer.

Test case SIDR-ROV-1.3.2 is identical to test case SIDR-ROV-1.3.1, except that IPv6 addresses are used instead of IPv4 addresses.

E.3.1.4   Test Case: SIDR-ROV-1.4.1 and 1.4.2

Test Objective	**Test SIDR Requirement CR-1.4.1. Show that the ROV-capable router correctly evaluates received routes in the following situation: The advertised route is initially evaluated as *valid*. An ROA that had made the route *valid* is removed from the RPKI; there remains another ROA that matches the route, so the route still evaluates as *valid*.**
	(*valid* → *valid*)
Preconditions	The testbed is configured with the topology, IP addressing scheme, and ASNs as depicted in the Testbed Architecture in Figure E-1 and Figure E-2. The router is set up to accept every BGP route, regardless of the validation state.

IPv4 or IPv6?	Both	**Test Harness or Hardware with Live RPKI?**	Both

| **Procedure** | 1. AS 65511 publishes an ROA for its address space: (10.100.0.0/16, 16, AS65511). |
| | 2. AS 65511 publishes a second ROA for the same address space, but with a larger maximum length: (10.100.0.0/16, 24, AS65511). |

3. AS 65511 originates a BGP route advertisement for 10.100.0.0/16.
4. Verify that the RUT receives VRP information.
5. Verify that the RUT evaluates this route advertisement as *valid*.
6. Verify that this route is installed in the routing table.
7. AS 65511 removes the ROA published in Step 1 from the RPKI.
8. Verify that the RUT still evaluates the route to 10.100.0.0/16 that AS 65511 originated as *valid*.
9. Verify that this route is still in the routing table.

For IPv6, use IP address FD10:100:100:1::/64 in place of 10.100.0.0/16.

Expected Results	Each of the expected results in Steps 4, 5, 6, 8, and 9 above are verified.
Actual Results	Test completed and functions as intended in Steps 4, 5, 6, 8, and 9.
Additional Comments (If Needed)	Changes in the validation state of selected routes are also observed via iBGP traffic. Steps 6 and 9 are validated by monitoring the incoming traffic on its iBGP peer.

Test case SIDR-ROV-1.4.2 is identical to test case SIDR-ROV-1.4.1, except that IPv6 addresses are used instead of IPv4 addresses.

E.3.1.5 Test Case: SIDR-ROV-1.5.1 and 1.5.2

Test Objective	**Test SIDR Requirement CR-1.5.1. Show that the ROV-capable router correctly evaluates received routes in the following situation: The advertised route is initially evaluated as *not found*. An ROA that matches the route is added to the RPKI, so the route is re-evaluated as *valid*.** **(*not found* → *valid*)**		
Preconditions	The testbed is configured with the topology, IP addressing scheme, and ASNs as depicted in the Testbed Architecture in Figure E-1 and Figure E-2. The router is set up to accept every BGP route, regardless of the validation state. No ROAs have been published that cover 10.100.0.0/16.		
IPv4 or IPv6?	Both	**Test Harness or Hardware with Live RPKI?**	Both
Procedure	1. Verify that there are no published ROAs that cover the route 10.100.0.0/16. 2. AS 65511 originates a BGP route advertisement for 10.100.0.0/16. 3. Verify that the RUT evaluates this route advertisement as *not found*. 4. Verify that this route is installed in the routing table. 5. AS 65511 publishes an ROA for its address space: (10.100.0.0/16, 16, AS65511). 6. Verify that the RUT now evaluates the route to 10.100.0.0/16 that AS 65511 originated as *valid*.		

	7. Verify that this route is still in the routing table.
	For IPv6, use IP address FD10:100:100:1::/64 in place of 10.100.0.0/16.
Expected Results	Each of the expected results in Steps 1, 3, 4, 6, and 7 above are verified.
Actual Results	Test completed and functions as intended in Steps 1, 3, 4, 6, and 7.
Additional Comments (If Needed)	Changes in the validation state of selected routes are also observed via iBGP traffic. Steps 1 and 3 are verified combined. Steps 4 and 7 are verified monitoring the incoming traffic via iBGP peer.

Test case SIDR-ROV-1.5.2 is identical to test case SIDR-ROV-1.5.1, except that IPv6 addresses are used instead of IPv4 addresses.

E.3.1.6   Test Case: SIDR-ROV-1.6.1 and 1.6.2

Test Objective	**Test SIDR Requirement CR-1.6.1. Show that the ROV-capable router correctly evaluates received routes in the following situation: The advertised route is initially evaluated as *not found*. An ROA that covers this route, but that has an ASN different from that of the route's origin, is added to the RPKI, so the route is re-evaluated as *invalid*.** **(*not found → invalid*)**		
Preconditions	The testbed is configured with the topology, IP addressing scheme, and ASNs as depicted in the Testbed Architecture in Figure E-1 and Figure E-2. The router is set up to accept every BGP route, regardless of the validation state. No ROAs have been published that cover 10.100.0.0/16.		
IPv4 or IPv6?	Both	**Test Harness or Hardware with Live RPKI?**	Both
Procedure	1. Verify that there are no published ROAs that cover the route 10.100.0.0/16. 2. AS 65511 originates a BGP route advertisement for 10.100.0.0/16. 3. Verify that the RUT evaluates this route advertisement as *not found*. 4. Verify that this route is installed in the routing table. 5. AS 65511 publishes an ROA for its address space authorizing a different AS to originate addresses for it: (10.100.0.0/16, 16, AS65510). 6. Verify that the RUT now evaluates the route to 10.100.0.0/16 that AS 65511 originated as *invalid*. 7. Verify that this route is still in the routing table. **For IPv6, use IP address FD10:100:100:1::/64 in place of 10.100.0.0/16.**		
Expected Results	Each of the expected results in Steps 1, 3, 4, 6, and 7 above are verified.		

Actual Results	Test completed and functions as intended in Steps 1, 3, 4, 6, and 7.
Additional Comments (If Needed)	Changes in the validation state of selected routes are also observed via iBGP traffic. Steps 1 and 3 are verified combined. Steps 4 and 7 are verified monitoring the incoming traffic via iBGP peer.

Test case SIDR-ROV-1.6.2 is identical to test case SIDR-ROV-1.6.1, except that IPv6 addresses are used instead of IPv4 addresses.

E.3.1.7 Test Case: SIDR-ROV-1.7.1 and 1.7.2

Test Description	**Test SIDR Requirement CR-1.7.1. Show that the ROV-capable router correctly evaluates received routes in the following situation: The advertised route is initially evaluated as invalid due to an ROA that covers this route, but that has an ASN different from that of the route's origin. A second ROA that matches this route is added to the RPKI, so the route is re-evaluated as *valid*.** (*invalid → valid*)
Preconditions	The testbed is configured with the topology, IP addressing scheme, and ASNs as depicted in the Testbed Architecture in Figure E-1 and Figure E-2. The router is set up to accept every BGP route, regardless of the validation state.
IPv4 or IPv6?	Both **Test Harness or Hardware with Live RPKI?** Both
Procedure	1. AS 65511 publishes an ROA for its address space that authorizes a different AS to originate addresses for it: (10.100.0.0/16, 16, AS65510). 2. AS 65511 originates a BGP route advertisement for 10.100.0.0/16. 3. Verify that the RUT receives VRP information. 4. Verify that the RUT evaluates this route advertisement as *invalid*. 5. Verify that this route is installed in the routing table. 6. AS 65511 publishes an ROA for its address space: (10.100.0.0/16, 16, AS65511). 7. Verify that the RUT now evaluates the route to 10.100.0.0/16 that AS 65511 originated as *valid*. 8. Verify that this route is still in the routing table. **For IPv6, use IP address FD10:100:100:1::/64 in place of 10.100.0.0/16.**
Expected Results	Each of the expected results in Steps 3, 4, 5, 7, and 8 above are verified.
Actual Results	Test completed and functions as intended in Steps 3, 4, 5, 7, and 8.
Additional Comments (If Needed)	Changes in the validation state of selected routes are also observed via iBGP traffic. Steps 5 and 8 are verified monitoring the incoming traffic via iBGP peer.

Test case SIDR-ROV-1.7.2 is identical to test case SIDR-ROV-1.7.1, except that IPv6 addresses are used instead of IPv4 addresses.

E.3.1.8 Test Case: SIDR-ROV-1.8.1 and 1.8.2

Test Objective	**Test SIDR Requirement CR-1.8.1. Show that the ROV-capable router correctly evaluates received routes in the following situation: The advertised route is initially evaluated as *invalid* due to the presence of one ROA that covers this route, but that has an ASN different from that of the route's origin. This is the only ROA that covers the route. It is deleted from the RPKI, so the route is re-evaluated as *not found*. (*invalid* → *not found*)**		
Preconditions	The testbed is configured with the topology, IP addressing scheme, and ASNs as depicted in the Testbed Architecture in Figure E-1 and Figure E-2. The router is set up to accept every BGP route, regardless of the validation state. No ROAs have been published that cover 10.100.0.0/16.		
IPv4 or IPv6?	Both	**Test Harness or Hardware with Live RPKI?**	Both
Procedure	1. AS 65511 publishes an ROA for its address space that authorizes a different AS to originate addresses for it: (10.100.0.0/16, 16, AS65510). 2. AS 65511 originates a BGP route advertisement for 10.100.0.0/16. 3. Verify that the RUT receives VRP information. 4. Verify that the RUT evaluates this route advertisement as *invalid*. 5. Verify that this route is installed in the routing table. 6. AS 65511 removes the ROA that it published in Step 1 from the RPKI. 7. Verify that the RUT now evaluates the route to 10.100.0.0/16 that AS65511 originated as *not found*. 8. Verify that this route is still in the routing table. **For IPv6, use IP address FD10:100:100:1::/64 in place of 10.100.0.0/16.**		
Expected Results	Each of the expected results in Steps 3, 4, 5, 7, and 8 above are verified.		
Actual Results	Test completed and functions as intended in Steps 3, 4, 5, 7, and 8.		
Additional Comments (If Needed)	Changes in the validation state of selected routes are also observed via iBGP traffic. Steps 5 and 8 are verified monitoring the incoming traffic via iBGP peer.		

Test case SIDR-ROV-1.8.2 is identical to test case SIDR-ROV-1.8.1, except that IPv6 addresses are used instead of IPv4 addresses.

Test Objective	**Test SIDR Requirement CR-1.9.1. Show that the ROV-capable router correctly evaluates received routes in the following situation: The advertised route is initially evaluated as *invalid*. There are two ROAs that cover this route, both of which have ASNs different from that of the route's origin. Only one of these ROAs is deleted from the RPKI, so the route still evaluates as *invalid*.** **(*invalid* → *invalid*)**
Preconditions	The testbed is configured with the topology, IP addressing scheme, and ASNs as depicted in the Testbed Architecture in <u>Figure E-1</u> and <u>Figure E-2</u>. The router is set up to accept every BGP route, regardless of the validation state.

IPv4 or IPv6?	Both	**Test Harness or Hardware with Live RPKI?**	Both

Procedure	1. AS 65511 publishes an ROA for its address space that authorizes a different AS to originate addresses for it: (10.100.0.0/16, 16, AS65510). 2. AS 65511 publishes a second ROA for its address space that authorizes a second AS to originate addresses for it: (10.100.0.0/16, 16, AS65509). 3. AS 65511 originates a BGP route advertisement for 10.100.0.0/16. 4. Verify that the RUT receives VRP information. 5. Verify that the RUT evaluates this route advertisement as *invalid*. 6. Verify that this route is installed in the routing table. 7. AS 65511 removes the ROA that it published in Step 1 from the RPKI. 8. Verify that the RUT still evaluates the route to 10.100.0.0/16 that AS 65511 had originated as *invalid*. 9. Verify that this route is still in the routing table. **For IPv6, use IP address FD10:100:100:1::/64 in place of 10.100.0.0/16.**
Expected Results	Each of the expected results in Steps 4, 5, 6, 8, and 9 above are verified.
Actual Results	Test completed and functions as intended in Steps 4, 5, 6, 8, and 9.
Additional Comments (If Needed)	Changes in the validation state of selected routes are also observed via iBGP traffic. Steps 6 and 9 are verified monitoring the incoming traffic via iBGP peer.

Test case SIDR-ROV-1.9.2 is identical to test case SIDR-ROV-1.9.1, except that IPv6 addresses are used instead of IPv4 addresses.

E.3.1.10 Test Case: SIDR-ROV-1.10.1 and 1.10.2

Test Objective	**Test SIDR Requirement CR-1.4.1. Show that the ROV-capable router correctly evaluates received routes in the following situation: The advertised route is initially evaluated to be** *invalid* **due to the fact that it contains AS_SET, even though there is an ROA that covers the route and that has a maximum length greater than the route's prefix. The route is re-announced, this time without the AS_SET in the path. The route in the second advertisement is evaluated as** *valid*. (*invalid* → *valid*)
Preconditions	The testbed is configured with the topology, IP addressing scheme, and ASNs as depicted in the Testbed Architecture in Figure E-1 and Figure E-2. The router is set up to accept every BGP route, regardless of the validation state. The following configuration for Routers AS65501, AS65504, AS65507, and AS65511 has been added: **Test1 1-10-1.txt**

IPv4 or IPv6?	Both	**Test Harness or Hardware with Live RPKI?**	Both

Procedure	1. AS 65511 publishes an ROA for (10.0.0.0/8, 8, AS65511). 2. AS 65507 publishes an ROA for its address space: (10.60.0.0/16, 16, AS65507). 3. AS 65504 publishes an ROA for its address space: (10.40.0.0/16, 16, AS65504). 4. The router in AS 65511 is configured to aggregate routes from AS 65504 and AS 65507 and advertise the aggregate route with the AS_SET segment. 5. AS 65507 originates a BGP route advertisement for 10.60.0.0/16, and AS 65504 originates a BGP route advertisement for 10.40.0.0/16, causing AS 65511 to aggregate these two announcements and send out a BGP route advertisement for 10.0.0.0/8 that contains AS_SET (AS65507, AS65504) as its origin. 6. Verify that the RUT evaluates this route to 10.0.0.0/8 as *invalid*. 7. Verify that this route is installed into the routing table. 8. Now change the configuration on AS 65511 so that it will no longer advertise the AS_SET segment. 9. AS 65511 originates a BGP route advertisement for 10.0.0.0/8. 10. Verify that the RUT evaluates this route advertisement as *valid*. 11. Verify that that this route is still in the routing table.

	For IPv6, use IP address FD40:40:40:40::68/64, FD60:6060:6060:60::1/64, FD10:100:100:1::1/64.
Expected Results	Each of the expected results in Steps 6, 7, 10, and 11 above are verified.
Actual Results	In a few cases, Step 6 did not have the expected result. We found that, in some implementations, the aggregated route/prefix 10.0.0.0/8, 65511 (65504, 65507) was evaluated as *not found* instead of *invalid*, as stipulated in [RFC 8210].
Additional Comments (If Needed)	Most commercially provided platforms did validate routes containing AS_SET as *not found*, whether covering ROAs exist or not.

Test case SIDR-ROV-1.10.2 is identical to test case SIDR-ROV-1.10.1, except that IPv6 addresses are used instead of IPv4 addresses.

E.3.2 SIDR ROV Test Cases – Local Static Routes Redistributed into BGP

E.3.2.1 Test Case: SIDR-ROV-2.1.1, 2.1.2, and 2.1.3

Test Objective	**Test SIDR Requirement CR-2.1.1. Show that the ROV-capable router correctly evaluates received routes in the following situation: A route is redistributed into BGP from a locally defined static route. This route is initially evaluated as *valid*. The single ROA that had made the route *valid* is removed from the RPKI. There is another ROA that covers the route, but the ASN in this ROA does not match that of the route's origin, so the route is re-evaluated as *invalid*. (valid → invalid)**
	(This test case is analogous to test case SIDR-ROV-1.2.1, but this test case evaluates a route that has been redistributed into BGP from a static route, rather than a route that was received as a BGP update.)
Preconditions	The testbed is configured with the topology, IP addressing scheme, and ASNs as depicted in the Testbed Architecture in Figure E-2. The router is set up to accept every BGP route, regardless of the validation state. No ROAs have been published that cover 10.10.0.0/16. The following configuration for Router AS65501 has been added: **Test 2-1-1 Config.txt**

IPv4 or IPv6?	Both	**Test Harness or Hardware with Live RPKI?**	Hardware with Live RPKI

Procedure	1. Configure the AS 65501 router to redistribute static routes into BGP.

	2. AS 65501 publishes an ROA for its address space: (10.10.0.0/16, 16, AS65501).
	3. AS 65501 publishes a second ROA for the same address space that authorizes a different AS to originate addresses for it: (10.10.0.0/16, 16, AS65505).
	4. At the AS 65501 router, configure a static route 10.10.1.0/16.
	5. Verify that the RUT (i.e., the AS 65501 router) evaluates the 10.10.1.0/16 route as *valid*. (show ip bgp)
	6. Verify that this route is installed in the routing table. (show ip route)
	7. AS 65501 removes the ROA published in Step 2 from the RPKI.
	8. Verify that the RUT now evaluates the 10.10.1.0/16 route as *invalid*.
	9. Verify that this route is still in the routing table.
	For IPv6, use IP address FD10:10:10:10::/64 in place of 10.10.0.0/16.
Expected Results	Each of the expected results in Steps 5, 6, 8, and 9 above are verified.
Actual Results	Test completed and functions as expected.
Additional Comments (If Needed)	We noticed that, while some vendors' implementation evaluates local routes (e.g., prefixes learned from static, IGP, and connected routes) as *valid*, others assess the same routes as *unverified*.

Test case SIDR-ROV-2.1.2 is identical to test case SIDR-ROV-2.1.1, except that IPv6 addresses are used instead of IPv4 addresses. The following configuration for Routers AS65501 and AS65505 was added prior to running the test:

Test 2-1-1B Config.txt

Test case SIDR-ROV-2.1.3 is identical to test case SIDR-ROV-2.1.1, except that the Cisco IOS XR virtual router was used instead of the Cisco 7206 physical router. The following configuration for the Cisco IOS XR virtual router was added prior to running the test:

Test 2-1-1 XR Config.txt

Test Objective	**Test SIDR Requirement CR-2.2.1. Show that the ROV-capable router correctly evaluates received routes in the following situation: A route is redistributed into BGP from a locally defined static route. This route is initially evaluated as *not found*. An ROA that matches the route is added to the RPKI, so the route is re-evaluated as *valid*. (*not found → valid*)**
	(This test case is analogous to test case SIDR-ROV-1.5.1, but this test case evaluates a route that has been redistributed into BGP from a static route, rather than a route that was received as a BGP update.)
Preconditions	The testbed is configured with the topology, IP addressing scheme, and ASNs as depicted in the Testbed Architecture in Figure E-1. The router is set up to accept every BGP route, regardless of the validation state. No ROAs have been published that cover the route 10.10.1.0/16. The following configuration for Routers AS65501 and AS65505 has been added: **Test 2-2-1 Config.txt**

IPv4 or IPv6?	Both	**Test Harness or Hardware with Live RPKI?**	Hardware with Live RPKI

Procedure	1. Configure the AS 65501 router to redistribute static routes into BGP.
	2. Verify that there are no published ROAs that cover the route 10.10.1.0/16.
	3. At the AS 65501 router, configure a static route 10.10.1.0/16.
	4. Verify that the RUT (i.e., the AS 65501 router) evaluates this route as *not found*. (show ip bgp)
	5. Verify that this route is installed in the routing table. (show ip route)
	6. AS 65501 publishes an ROA for its address space: (10.10.0.0/16, 16, AS 65501).
	7. Verify that the RUT (i.e., the AS65501 router) re-evaluates its static route 10.10.1.0/16 as *valid*.
	8. Verify that this route is still in the routing table.
	For IPv6, use IP address FD10:10:10:10::/64 in place of 10.10.0.0/16.
Expected Results	Each of the expected results in Steps 4, 5, 7, and 8 above are verified.
Actual Results	Test completed and functions as expected.
Additional Comments (If Needed)	None

Test case SIDR-ROV-2.2.2 is identical to test case SIDR-ROV-2.2.1, except that IPv6 addresses are used instead of IPv4 addresses. The following configuration for Router AS65505 was updated prior to running the test:

**Test 2-2-1B
Config.txt**

E.3.2.3   Test Case: SIDR-ROV-2.3.1 and 2.3.2

Test Objective	**Test SIDR Requirement CR-2.3.1. Show that the ROV-capable router correctly evaluates received routes in the following situation: A route is redistributed into BGP from a locally defined static route. This route is initially evaluated as *not found*. An ROA that covers this route, but that has an ASN different from that of the route's origin, is added to the RPKI, so the route is re-evaluated as *invalid*. (*not found* → *invalid*)** **(This test case is analogous to test case SIDR-ROV-1.6.1, but this test case evaluates a route that has been redistributed into BGP from a static route, rather than a route that was received as a BGP update.)**
Preconditions	The testbed is configured with the topology, IP addressing scheme, and ASNs as depicted in the Testbed Architecture in Figure E-1 and Figure E-2. The router is set up to accept every BGP route, regardless of the validation state. No ROAs have been published that cover the route 10.10.1.0/16. The following configuration for Routers AS65501 and AS65505 has been added: **Test 2-3-1 Config.txt**

IPv4 or IPv6?	Both	**Test Harness or Hardware with Live RPKI?**	Both

Procedure	1. Configure the AS 65501 router to redistribute static routes into BGP. 2. Verify that there are no published ROAs that cover the route 10.10.1.0/16. 3. At the AS 65501 router, configure a static route 10.10.1.0/16. 4. Verify that the RUT (i.e., the BGP router at AS 65501) evaluates this route as *not found*. (show ip bgp) 5. Verify that this route is installed in the routing table. (show ip route) 6. AS 65501 publishes an ROA for its address space authorizing a different AS to originate addresses for it: (10.10.0.0/16, 16, AS65505).

	7. Verify that the RUT (i.e., the BGP router at AS 65501) re-evaluates this route 10.10.1.0/16 as *invalid*.
	8. Verify that this route is still in the BGP routing table.
	For IPv6, use IP address FD10:10:10:10::/64 in place of 10.10.0.0/16.
Expected Results	Each of the expected results in Steps 4, 5, 7, and 8 above are verified.
Actual Results	Test completed and functions as expected.
Additional Comments (If Needed)	None

Test case SIDR-ROV-2.3.2 is identical to test case SIDR-ROV-2.3.1, except that IPv6 addresses are used instead of IPv4 addresses. The following configuration for Router AS65505 was updated prior to running the test:

**Test 2-3-1B
Config.txt**

E.3.3   SIDR ROV Test Cases — Routes Redistributed into BGP from an IGP

E.3.3.1   Test Case: SIDR-ROV-3.1.1

Test Objective	**Test SIDR Requirement CR-3.1.1. Show that the ROV-capable router correctly evaluates received routes in the following situation: A route is redistributed into BGP from an IGP. This route is initially evaluated as *valid*. The single ROA that had made the route *valid* is removed from the RPKI; there is no ROA that covers the route, so the route is re-evaluated as *not found*. (valid → not found)**
	(This test case is analogous to test case SIDR-ROV-1.1.1, but this test case evaluates a route that has been redistributed into BGP from an IGP, rather than a route that was received as a BGP update.)
Preconditions	The testbed is configured with the topology, IP addressing scheme, and ASNs as depicted in the Testbed Architecture in Figure E-1 and Figure E-2. The router is set up to accept every BGP route, regardless of the validation state. No ROAs have been published that cover the route 10.10.0.0/16. The following configuration for Routers AS65501 and AS65505 has been added:
	**Test 3-1-1
Config.txt**

IPv4 or IPv6?	IPv4	Test Harness or Hardware with Live RPKI?	Both
Procedure	1. Configure the AS 65501 router to redistribute routes from an IGP that is in use in AS 65501 into BGP. 2. AS 65501 publishes an ROA for its address space: (10.10.0.0/16, 16, AS 65501). 3. Create route 10.10.2.0/16 in the IGP that is running on AS 65501. This route should get redistributed into BGP. 4. Verify that the RUT (i.e., the BGP router in AS 65501) evaluates this route as *valid*. (show ip bgp) 5. Verify that this route is installed in the routing table. (show ip route) 6. AS 65501 removes the ROA published in Step 2 from the RPKI. 7. Verify that the RUT (i.e., the BGP router in AS 65501) re-evaluates this route 10.10.2.0/16 as *not found*. 8. Verify that this route is still in the BGP routing table. **For IPv6, use IP address FD10:10:10:10::/64 in place of 10.10.0.0/16.**		
Expected Results	Each of the expected results in Steps 4, 5, 7, and 8 above are verified.		
Actual Results	Test completed and functions as expected.		
Additional Comments (If Needed)	None		

E.3.3.2 Test Case: SIDR-ROV-3.2.1

Test Objective	Test SIDR Requirement CR-3.2.1. Show that the ROV-capable router correctly evaluates received routes in the following situation: A route is redistributed into BGP from an IGP. This route is initially evaluated as *invalid* due to an ROA that covers this route, but that has an ASN different from that of the route's origin. A second ROA that matches this route is added to the RPKI, so the route is re-evaluated as *valid*. (*invalid* → *valid*) (This test case is analogous to test case SIDR-ROV-1.7.1, but this test case evaluates a route that has been redistributed into BGP from an IGP, rather than a route that was received as a BGP update.)

Preconditions	The testbed is configured with the topology, IP addressing scheme, and ASNs as depicted in the Testbed Architecture in Figure E-1 and Figure E-2. The router is set up to accept every BGP route, regardless of the validation state. The following configuration for Routers AS65501 and AS65505 has been added: **Test 3-2-1 Config.txt**		
IPv4 or IPv6?	IPv4	**Test Harness or Hardware with Live RPKI?**	Both
Procedure	1. Configure the AS 65501 router to redistribute routes from an IGP that is in use in AS 65501 into BGP. 2. AS 65501 publishes an ROA for its address space that authorizes a different AS to originate addresses for it: (10.10.0.0/16, 16, AS65505). 3. Create route 10.10.2.0/16 in the IGP that is running on AS 65501. This route should get redistributed into BGP. 4. Verify that the RUT (i.e., the BGP router in AS 65501) evaluates this route as *invalid*. (show ip bgp) 5. Verify that this route is installed in the routing table. (show ip route) 6. AS 65501 publishes an ROA for its address space: (10.10.0.0/16, 16, AS65501). 7. Verify that the RUT (i.e., the BGP router in AS 65501) re-evaluates this route 10.10.2.0/16 as *valid*. 8. Verify that this route is still in the routing table. **For IPv6, use IP address FD10:10:10:10::/64 in place of 10.10.0.0/16.**		
Expected Results	Each of the expected results in Steps 4, 5, 7, and 8 above are verified.		
Actual Results	Test completed and functions as expected.		
Additional Comments (If Needed)	None		

E.3.3.3 Test Case: SIDR-ROV-3.3.1

Test Objective	**Test SIDR Requirement CR-3.3.1. Show that the ROV-capable router correctly evaluates received routes in the following situation: A route is redistributed into BGP from an IGP. This route is initially evaluated as *invalid* due to the presence of one ROA that covers this route, but that has an ASN different from that of the route's origin. This is the only ROA that covers the route. It is deleted from the RPKI, so the route is re-evaluated as *not found*. (*invalid → not found*)** **(This test case is analogous to test case SIDR-ROV-1.8.1, but this test case evaluates a route that has been redistributed into BGP from an IGP, rather than a route that was received as a BGP update.)**
Preconditions	The testbed is configured with the topology, IP addressing scheme, and ASNs as depicted in the Testbed Architecture in Figure E-1 and Figure E-2. The router is set up to accept every BGP route, regardless of the validation state. No ROAs have been published that cover 10.10.0.0/16. The following configuration for Routers AS65501 and AS65505 has been added: **Test 3-3-1 Config.txt**
IPv4 or IPv6?	IPv4 **Test Harness or Hardware with Live RPKI?** Both

IPv4 or IPv6?	IPv4
Test Harness or Hardware with Live RPKI?	Both

Procedure	1. Configure the AS 65501 router to redistribute routes from an IGP that is in use in AS 65501 into BGP. 2. AS 65501 publishes an ROA for its address space that authorizes a different AS to originate addresses for it: (10.10.0.0/16, 16, AS65505). There are no other published ROAs that cover the route 10.10.0.0/16. 3. Create route 10.10.2.0/16 in the IGP that is running on AS 65501. This route should get redistributed into BGP. 4. Verify that the RUT (i.e., the BGP router in AS 65501) evaluates this route as *invalid*. (show ip bgp) 5. Verify that this route is installed in the routing table. (show ip route) 6. AS 65501 removes the ROA that it published in Step 2 from the RPKI. 7. Verify that the RUT (i.e., the BGP router in AS 65501) re-evaluates this route 10.10.2.0/16 as *not found*. 8. Verify that this route is still in the routing table. **For IPv6, use IP address FD10:10:10:10::/64 in place of 10.10.0.0/16.**
Expected Results	Each of the expected results in Steps 4, 5, 7, and 8 above are verified.

Actual Results	Test completed and functions as expected.
Additional Comments (If Needed)	None

E.3.4 iBGP Testing

E.3.4.1 Test Case: SIDR-ROV-4.1.1

| Test Objective | Test SIDR Requirement CR-4.1. Show that the ROV-capable router correctly implements its policy to treat locally defined iBGP routes differently from other iBGP routes. In particular, show that the router can be configured to drop *invalid* routes, unless the route is a locally generated iBGP or a locally defined static route. Define two route prefixes in iBGP: Prefix A, which is locally generated, and Prefix B, which is not. Define Prefix C, which is an eBGP route. Define a static route, D. Ensure that all four routes will be evaluated and marked as *invalid* due to having exactly one ROA that covers each route, but that ROA has an ASN different from that of the route's origin. Configure routing policy such that Prefixes A and D (which are locally generated) will not be dropped. Validate that Prefixes A and D are inserted into the routing table, whereas Prefixes B and C are not.

This test case is similar to test case SIDR-ROV-2.3.1, but, in this test case, the invalid non-locally defined static route that evaluates as *invalid* is dropped. It is also similar to test case SIDR-ROV-2.5.1, but, in this test case, the invalid non-locally generated iBGP route that evaluates as *invalid* is dropped. |
|---|---|
| Preconditions | The testbed is configured with the topology, IP addressing scheme, and ASNs as depicted in the Testbed Architecture in Figure E-2. The RUT is configured with a policy of discarding invalid routes unless those invalid routes are locally generated iBGP or locally defined static routes. There is at least one iBGP route that is not locally generated. The following configuration for Routers AS65501 and AS65501i has been added:

Test 4-1-1 Config.txt |

IPv4 or IPv6?	Both	**Test Harness or Hardware with Live RPKI?**	Hardware with Live RPKI

Procedure	1. Configure the AS 65501 router to redistribute routes from an IGP that is in use in AS 65501 into BGP.
	
	2. Configure the AS 65501 router to redistribute static routes into BGP.
	
	3. Verify that there are no published ROAs that cover the prefix 10.10.0.0/16.
	
	4. AS 65501 publishes an ROA for its address space that authorizes AS 65505 to originate addresses for it: (10.10.0.0/16, 16, AS65505).
	
	5. Assume that route 10.10.2.0/16 is a route that was not locally generated, but ensure that it is being advertised in the IGP. (This route should get redistributed into BGP.)
	
	6. AS 65503 originates a BGP update for route 10.10.3.0/16.
	
	7. Generate local route 10.10.4.0/16 in the IGP that is running on AS 65501. (This route should get redistributed into BGP.)
	
	8. At the AS 65501 router, configure a static route 10.10.5.0/16. (This route should get redistributed into BGP.)
	
	9. Verify that the RUT (i.e., the BGP router in AS 65501) evaluates all four of the above routes as *invalid* (show ip bgp):
	   a. 10.10.0.0/16 = Static
	   b. 10.20.0.0/16 = eBGP
	   c. 10.30.0.0/16 = IGP (RIPv2)
	   d. 10.40.0.0/16 = Local (Connected)
	
	10. Verify that the first two of the above routes are not installed in the routing table and that the invalid routes are logged. (show ip route):
	   a. 10.20.0.0/16
	   b. 10.30.0.0/16
	
	11. Verify that the last two routes above are installed in the routing table:
	   c. 10.10.40.0/16
	   d. 10.10.5.0/16
	
	For IPv6, use FD10:10:10:10::/64, FD20:20:20:1::1/64, FD30:30:30:1::1/64, FD40:40:40:1::1/64.

Expected Results	Each of the expected results in Steps 3, 9, 10, and 11 above are verified.
Actual Results	Vendor implementation varies. Certain vendors present all local routes and prefixes as *valid*, while others show them as *unverified*.
Additional Comments (If Needed)	Whereas [RFC 6810] stipulates that routes or prefixes learned locally (IGP, static and connected) should be designated as *not found*, vendor implementation variables interpret them as either *unverified* or *valid*.

E.3.4.2   Test Case: SIDR-ROV-4.2.1

Test Objective	Examine RPKI validation by using eBGP, IGP, static, and local network routes within an iBGP network by using a single, but shared, VC within the iBGP peers.
Preconditions	The testbed is configured with the topology, IP addressing scheme, and ASNs as depicted in the Testbed Architecture in <u>Figure E-2</u>.
	AS 65511 is connected to AS 65501, and AS 65501 consists of two routers speaking iBGP. The edge router is connected to AS 65511 via eBGP and labeled AS65501-R1-1 and the iBGP peer AS65501i-R1-2.
	The RPKI VC 1 contains all used IP prefixes (10.10.0.0/16, 10.20.0.0/16, 10.30.0.0/16, and 10.40.0.0/16), but is assigned to origin AS 65509. The outcome should result in *invalid* based on the validation algorithm.
	Note: All routers are configured to NOT drop *invalid*.
	Traffic A: 10.20.0.0/16 is a route originated by AS 65511.
	Traffic B: There are three routes: one learned via IGP (10.30.0.0/16), another via static (10.10.0.0/16), and the third via local (10.40.0.0/16) network.
	AS65501-R1-1: Configure connection to RPKI VC 1, NO Extended Community String. AS65501i-R1-2: Configure router as plain BGP (no RPKI).
	The following configuration for Routers AS65501 and AS65501i was added:
	Test 4-2-1 Config.txt

IPv4 or IPv6?	Both	**Test Harness or Hardware with Live RPKI?**	Hardware with Live RPKI

Procedure	1. Configure the AS 65511 router to forward Traffic A to AS 65501.
	2. Configure AS 65501 to redistribute Traffic B into BGP.
	3. AS65501-R1-1: Verify that the router contains Traffic A and B.
	4. AS65501-R1-1: Verify that the router contains VRPs in the RPKI table.
	5. AS65501-R1-1: Verify that the router validated Traffic A as *invalid*.
	6. AS65501-R1-1: Verify that the router validated Traffic B as either *invalid* or *not found*.
	7. AS65501-R1-1: Send Traffic A and B to AS65501i-R1-2.
	8. AS65501i-R1-2: Verify that the router does not contain the RPKI table or that the table is empty.
	9. AS65501i-R1-2: Verify the receipt of Traffic A and B and that NO validation state is assigned.
	For IPv6, use FD10:10:10:10::/64, FD20:20:20:1::1/64, FD30:30:30:1::1/64, FD40:40:40:1::1/64.

Expected Results	Each of the expected results in Steps 3, 4, 5, 6, 8, and 9 above are verified.
Actual Results	Vendor implementation varies. Certain vendors present all local routes and prefixes as *valid*, while others show them as *unverified*.
Additional Comments (If Needed)	Whereas [RFC 6810] stipulates that routes or prefixes learned locally (IGP, static, and connected) should be designated as *not found*, vendor implementation variable interprets them as either *unverified* or *valid*.

Test case SIDR-ROV-4.2.2 is identical to test case SIDR-ROV-4.2.1, except that a Juniper router was used instead of a Cisco router for Router AS65501i. The following configuration for Routers AS65501 and AS65501i was updated prior to running the test:

Test 4-2-1 Juniper Config.txt

E.3.4.3   Test Case: SIDR-ROV-4.3.1

Test Objective	**Examine RPKI validation by using eBGP, IGP, static, and local network routes within an iBGP network using one shared VC within the iBGP peers without the Extended Community Strings configuration.**
Preconditions	The testbed is configured with the topology, IP addressing scheme, and ASNs as depicted in the Testbed Architecture in Figure E-2.
	AS 65511 is connected to AS 65501, and AS 65501 consists of two routers speaking iBGP. The edge router is connected to AS 65511 via eBGP and labeled as AS65501-R1-1, and the iBGP peer labeled as. AS65501i-R1-2.
	The RPKI VC 1 contains all used IP prefixes (10.10.0.0/16, 10.20.0.0/16, 10.30.0.0/16, and 10.40.0.0/16), but is assigned to origin AS 65509. The outcome should result in *invalid* based on the validation algorithm.
	All routers are configured to NOT drop *invalid*.
	Traffic A is a route originated by AS 65501.
	Traffic B has three routes: one learned via IBGP network, one via static network, and one via local network.
	R1-1: Configure connection to RPKI VC 1, NO Extended Community String. R1-2: Configure connection to RPKI VC 1.
	The following configuration for Routers AS65501 and AS65501i was added:

Test 4-3-1 Config.txt

IPv4 or IPv6?	Both	Test Harness or Hardware with Live RPKI?	Hardware with Live RPKI
Procedure	1. Configure the AS 65505 router to redistribute Traffic A to AS 65501.		
	2. Configure AS 65501 to redistribute Traffic B.		
	3. R1-1: Verify that the router contains Traffic A and B.		
	4. R1-1: Verify that the router contains RVPs in the RPKI table.		
	5. R1-1: Verify that the router validated Traffic A as *invalid*.		
	6. R1-1: Verify that the router validated Traffic B as either *invalid* or *not found*.		
	7. R1-1: Send Traffic A and B to R1-2 WITHOUT Extended Community String.		
	8. R1-2: Verify that the router contains RVPs in the RPKI table.		
	9. R1-2: Verify the receipt of Traffic A and B and that the validation state is assigned to either *invalid* or *not found*.		
	For IPv6, use FD10:10:10:10::/64, FD20:20:20:1::1/64, FD30:30:30:1::1/64, FD40:40:40:1::1/64.		
Expected Results	Each of the expected results in Steps 3, 4, 5, 6, and 8 above are verified.		
Actual Results	Vendor implementation varies. Certain vendors present all local routes and prefixes as *valid*, while others show them as *unverified*.		
Additional Comments (If Needed)	Whereas [RFC 6810] stipulates that routes or prefixes learned locally (IGP, static, and connected) should be designated as *not found*, vendor implementation differ and designate them as either *unverified* or *valid*.		

Test case SIDR-ROV-4.3.2 is identical to test case SIDR-ROV-4.3.1, except that a Juniper router was used instead of a Cisco router for Router AS65501i. The following configuration for Routers AS65501 and AS65501i was updated prior to running the test:

Test 4-3-1 Juniper Config.txt

E.3.4.4   Test Case: SIDR-ROV-4.4.1

Test Objective	**Examine RPKI validation by using eBGP, IGP, static, and local network routes within an iBGP network using one shared VC within the iBGP peers. (With Extended Community Strings)**
Preconditions	The testbed is configured with the topology, IP addressing scheme, and ASNs as depicted in the Testbed Architecture in Figure E-2.

AS 65511 is connected to AS 65501, and AS 65501 consists of two routers speaking iBGP. The edge router is connected to AS 65511 via eBGP and labeled AS65501-R1-1 and the iBGP peer as AS65501i-R1-2.

The RPKI VC 1 contains all used IP prefixes (10.10.0.0/16, 10.20.0.0/16, 10.30.0.0/16, and 10.40.0.0/16) but is assigned to origin AS 65509. The outcome should result in *invalid* based on the validation algorithm.

All routers are configured to NOT drop *invalid*.

Traffic A is a route originated by AS 65501.

Traffic B has three routes: one learned via IBGP network, one via static network, and one via local network.

R1-1: Configure connection to RPKI VC 1, enable Extended Community String.
R1-2: Configure router as plain BGP (no RPKI).

The following configuration for Routers AS65501 and AS65501i was added:

**Test 4-4-1
Config.txt**

IPv4 or IPv6?	Both		**Test Harness or Hardware with Live RPKI?**	Hardware with Live RPKI

Procedure	1. Configure the AS 65511 router to send eBGP Traffic A to AS 65501.
	2. Configure AS 65501 to redistribute Traffic B.
	3. R1-1: Verify that the router contains Traffic A and B.
	4. R1-1: Verify that R1-1 contains RVPs in the RPKI table.
	5. R1-1: Verify that the router validated Traffic A as *invalid*.
	6. R1-1: Verify that the router validated Traffic B as either *invalid* or *not found*.
	7. R1-1: Send Traffic A and B to R1-2 with Extended Community String.
	8. R1-2: Verify that the router does not contain the RPKI RVP table or that the table is empty.
	9. R1-2: Verify the receipt of Traffic A and B and that no validation state is assigned.
	For IPv6, use FD10:10:10:10::/64, FD20:20:20:1::1/64, FD30:30:30:1::1/64, FD40:40:40:1::1/64.

Expected Results	Each of the expected results in Steps 3, 4, 5, 6, 8, and 9 above are verified.
Actual Results	Vendor implementation varies. Certain vendors present all local routes and prefixes as *valid*, while others show them as *unverified*.
Additional Comments (If Needed)	Whereas [RFC 6810] stipulates that routes or prefixes learned locally (IGP, static, and connected) should be designated as *not found*, vendor implementation differ and designate them as either *unverified* or *valid*.

Test case SIDR-ROV-4.4.2 is identical to test case SIDR-ROV-4.4.1, except that a Juniper router was used instead of a Cisco router for Router AS65501i. The following configuration for Router AS65501i was updated prior to running the test:

**Test 4-4-1 Juniper
Config.txt**

E.3.4.5   Test Case: SIDR-ROV-4.5.1

Test Objective	**Examine RPKI validation by using eBGP, IGB, static, and local network routes within an iBGP network using two distinct VCs (VCs 1 and 2) within the iBGP peers while enabling Extended Community String.**
Preconditions	The testbed is configured with the topology, IP addressing scheme, and ASNs as depicted in the Testbed Architecture in Figure E-2.
	AS 65511 is connected to AS 65501, and AS 65501 consists of two routers speaking iBGP.
	The edge router connected to AS 65511 is labeled R1-1, and the iBGP peer to AS65501-R1-1 is labeled AS65501i-R1-2.
	The RPKI VC 1 contains all used IP prefixes, but for origin 65509. The RPKI VC 2 contains all used IP prefixes of Traffic A with origin 65511, and IP prefixes of Traffic B with origin 65501.
	VC 1 should result in *invalid* for all routes in R1-1, and VC 2 will result in *valid* for all routes in R1-2 if validated using the RPKI validation algorithm.
	All routers are configured to NOT drop *invalid*.
	Traffic A is a route originated by AS 65511.
	Traffic B has three routes: one learned via IBGP network, one via static network, and one via local network.
	R1-1: Configure the connection to RPKI VC 1 and enable Extended Community String. R1-2: Configure the connection to RPKI VC 2 and enable Extended Community String.
	The following configuration for Routers AS65501 and AS65501i has been added:
	**Test 4-5-1
Config.txt**
IPv4 or IPv6?	Both

IPv4 or IPv6?	Both	**Test Harness or Hardware with Live RPKI?**	Hardware with Live RPKI
Procedure	1. Configure the AS 65511 router to redistribute Traffic A to AS 65501.		
	2. Configure AS 65501 to redistribute Traffic B.		

	3. R1-1: Verify that the router contains Traffic A and B.
	4. R1-1: Verify that the router contains RVPs in the RPKI table.
	5. R1-1: Verify that the router validated Traffic A as *invalid*.
	6. R1-1: Verify that the router validated Traffic B as either *invalid* or *not found*.
	7. R1-1: Send Traffic A and B to R1-2 with Extended Community String.
	8. R1-2: Verify that the router contains RVPs in the RPKI table.
	9. R1-2: Verify the receipt of Traffic A and B and that a validation state of *valid* is assigned to all routes.
	For IPv6, use FD10:10:10:10::/64, FD20:20:20:1::/64, FD30:30:30:1::/64, FD40:40:40:1::/64.
Expected Results	Each of the expected results in Steps 3, 4, 5, 6, 8, and 9 above will be verified.
Actual Results	Vendor implementation varies. Certain vendors present all local routes and prefixes as *valid*, while others show them as *unverified*.
Additional Comments (If Needed)	Whereas [RFC 6810] stipulates that routes or prefixes learned locally (IGP, static, and connected) should be designated as *not found*, vendor implementation differ and designate them as either *unverified* or *valid*.

E.3.4.6   Test Case: SIDR-ROV-4.6.1

Test Objective	**Examine RPKI validation by using eBGP, IGP, static, and local network routes within an iBGP network using two distinct VCs with conflicting records within the iBGP peers while enabling Extended Community String. Verify the validation state of the RUT.**
Preconditions	The testbed is configured with the topology, IP addressing scheme, and ASNs as depicted in the Testbed Architecture in Figure E-2.
	AS 65511 is connected to AS 65501, and AS 65501 consists of two routers speaking iBGP.
	The edge router connected to AS 65511 is labeled R1-1, and the iBGP peer to AS65501-R1-1 is labeled AS65501i-R1-2.
	The RPKI VC 1 contains all used IP prefixes, except for origin 65509. The RPKI VC 2 contains all used IP prefixes of Traffic A with origin 65511, and IP prefixes of Traffic B with origin 65501.
	VC 1 should result in *invalid* for all routes in R1-1, and VC 2 will result in *valid* for all routes in R1-2, if validated using the RPKI validation algorithm.
	All routers are configured to NOT drop *invalid*.

Traffic A is a route originated by AS 65511.

Traffic B has three routes: one learned via IGP, one via static network, and one via local network.

R1-1: Configure the connection to RPKI VC 1 and enable Extended Community String.

R1-2: Configure the connection to RPKI VC 2 and enable Extended Community String.

The following configuration for Routers AS65501 and AS65501i has been added:

Test 4-6-1 Config.txt

IPv4 or IPv6?	Both	**Test Harness or Hardware with Live RPKI?**	Hardware with Live RPKI
Procedure	1. Configure the AS 65511 router to redistribute Traffic A to AS 65501. 2. Configure AS 65501 to redistribute Traffic B. 3. R1-1: Verify that the router contains Traffic A and B. 4. R1-1: Verify that the router contains RVPs in the RPKI table. 5. R1-1: Verify that the router validated Traffic A as *invalid*. 6. R1-1: Verify that the router validated Traffic B as either *invalid* or *not found*. 7. R1-1: Send Traffic A and B to R1-2 with Extended Community String. 8. R1-2: Verify that the router contains RVPs in the RPKI table. 9. R1-2: Verify the receipt of Traffic A and B and that a validation state of *valid* is assigned to all routes. **For IPv6, use FD10:10:10:10::/64, FD20:20:20:1::/64, FD30:30:30:1::/64, FD40:40:40:1::/64.**		
Expected Results	Each of the expected results in Steps 3, 4, 5, 6, 8, and 9 above will be verified.		
Actual Results	Vendor implementation varies. Certain vendors present all local routes and prefixes as *valid*, while others show them as *unverified*.		
Additional Comments (If Needed)	Whereas [RFC 6810] stipulates that routes or prefixes learned locally (IGP, static, and connected) should be designated as *not found*, vendor implementation differ and designate them as either *unverified* or *valid*.		

E.3.5 Applying Policies to ROV – Route Selection Process

E.3.5.1 Test Case: SIDR-ROV-5.1.1

Test Objective	**RUT: If the route is *invalid*, discard the route; if the route is *not found*, install the route with a low local preference (LP) value.**

Preconditions	The testbed is configured with the topology, IP addressing scheme, and ASNs as depicted in the Testbed Architecture in Figure E-1 and Figure E-2.		
IPv4 or IPv6?	Both	**Test Harness or Hardware with Live RPKI?**	Both

Procedure	1. Configure AS 65510 and AS65511 to send traffic to RUT AS65501.
	
	2. AS65510 and AS65511 send the following prefixes:
	   a. 10.10.0.0/16, AS65510 and AS65511
	   b. 10.20.0.0/16, AS65510 and AS65511
	   c. 10.30.0.0/16, AS65510 and AS65511
	   d. 10.40.0.0/16, AS65511 *(not found)*
	   e. 10.50.0.0/16, AS65510, but has ROV in AS65507 *(invalid)*
	
	3. Configure AS 65501 with a single policy to:
	   a. Discard the prefix with *invalid*.
	   b. Apply "Local Preference = 90" for the prefix with *not found*.
	   c. Accept prefixes that are *valid*.
	
	4. Verify that the RUT contains appropriate policies.
	
	For IPv6, use FD10:10:10:0::/64, FD20:20:20::/64, FD30:30:30::/64, FD40:40:40::/64.		

Expected Results	*Invalid* routes will be discarded. *Not found* routes will have an LP of 90. *Valid* routes will be inserted in the routing table with a default LP.		
Actual Results	All implemented polices performed as expected.		
Additional Comments (If Needed)	Note that one vendor (e.g., Cisco) discards *invalid* routes by default, while another vendor leaves the decision to discard to its customer.		

E.3.5.2 Test Case: SIDR-ROV-5.1.2

Test Objective	**RUT: Allow the installation of *invalid* routes and configure policies such that:** **If the route is *invalid*, install the route with LP=70.** **If the route is *not found*, install the route with LP=80.** **If the route is *valid*, install the route with LP=110.**		
Preconditions	The testbed is configured with the topology, IP addressing scheme, and ASNs as depicted in the Testbed Architecture in Figure E-1 and Figure E-2.		
IPv4 or IPv6?	Both	**Test Harness or Hardware with Live RPKI?**	Both

Procedure	1. Configure AS 65510 and AS65511 to send traffic to RUT AS65501.
	2. AS65510 and AS65511 send the following prefixes:
	   a. 10.10.0.0/16, AS65510 and AS65511
	   b. 10.20.0.0/16, AS65510 and AS65511
	   c. 10.30.0.0/16, AS65510 and AS65511
	   d. 10.40.0.0/16, AS65511 *(not found)*
	   e. 10.50.0.0/16, AS65510, but has ROV in AS65507 *(invalid)*
	3. Configure AS 65501 with a single policy:
	   a. If the route is *invalid*, install the route with LP=70.
	   b. If the route is *not found*, install the route with LP=80.
	   c. If the route is *valid*, install the route with LP=110.
	4. Verify that the RUT contains appropriate policies.
	For IPv6, use FD10:10:10:0::/64, FD20:20:20::/64, FD30:30:30::/64, FD40:40:40::/64.

Expected Results	*Invalid* routes with LP=70 *Not found* routes with LP=80 *Valid* routes with LP=110
Actual Results	All implemented policies performed as expected.
Additional Comments (If Needed)	Note that one vendor (e.g., Cisco) discards *invalid* routes by default, while another vendor leaves the decision to discard to its customer.

E.3.6 Router Cache Synchronization

E.3.6.1 Test Case: SIDR-ROV-6.1.1

Test Objective	**Test SIDR Requirements CR-6.1.1, when working with IPv4/6 addresses. Show that the RUT receives and installs VRPs into the RPKI database properly after a loss of connectivity to the RPKI validator.**
Preconditions	The testbed is configured with the topology, IP addressing scheme, and ASNs as depicted in the Testbed Architecture in Figure E-1 and Figure E-2. The RUT's VC is empty, and the RPKI validator/cache is empty. The following configuration for the Cisco IOS XR router is used as the baseline for this test: **Test 6-1-1 Config.txt**

IPv4 or IPv6?	Both	Test Harness or Hardware with Live RPKI?	Both

Procedure	1. Verify that the RUT has an empty RPKI database. 2. From the RPKI cache, there are four ROAs:
	    a. 10.100.0.0/16 16 65500
	    b. 10.100.0.0/16 20 65500
	    c. 10.100.0.0/16 24 65500
	    d. FD00:10:100::/64 64 65500
	3. Configure the RUT with the VC by using the following file:
	
	6-1-1 Cache Config.txt
	
	4. Verify that the RUT received and installs all VRPs in Step 2 into the database.
	5. Disconnect the RUT from the cache by disconnecting the Transmission Control Protocol (TCP) connection (i.e., via the firewall).
	6. Remove the ROAs from Steps 2a and 2d from the RPKI validator.
	7. Add ROAs to the RPKI validator:
	    a. 10.100.0.0/16 16 65510
	    b. FD00:10:100::/64 64 65510
	8. Reenable the TCP connection between the RUT and the RPKI validator.
	9. Verify that the RUT received and installed VRPs in the RPKI database and that it contains only VRPs in Steps 2b, 2c, and 7.		

Expected Results	Each of the expected results in Steps 1, 3, and 8 above will be verified.		
Actual Results	The test completed and the functions were as intended in Steps 1, 3, and 8.		
Additional Comments (If Needed)	The TCP connection was disrupted by shutting down the TCP interface. After reenabling the interface, a new TCP session was established.		

E.3.6.2   Test Case: SIDR-ROV-6.2.1

Test Objective	**Test SIDR Requirements CR-6.2.1 when working with IPv4/6 addresses. Show that the RUT and the RPKI validator function properly when the RPKI validator loses power, causing it to lose state.**
Preconditions	The testbed is configured with the topology, IP addressing scheme, and ASNs as depicted in the Testbed Architecture in Figure E-1 and Figure E-2.

	The RUT's cache is empty, and the RPKI validator/cache is empty. The following configuration for the Cisco IOS XR router is used as the baseline for this test:		
	Test 6-2-1 Config.txt		
IPv4 or IPv6?	Both	**Test Harness or Hardware with Live RPKI?**	Both

Procedure	1. Verify that the RUT has an empty RPKI database.
	2. From the RPKI cache, there are four ROAs:
	   a. 10.100.0.0/16 16 65500
	   b. 10.100.0.0/16 20 65500
	   c. 10.100.0.0/16 24 65500
	   d. FD00:10:100::/64 64 65500
	3. Configure the RUT with the VC by using the following file:
	 Test 6-2-1 Cache Config.txt
	4. Verify that the RUT received the cache and installed all VRPs in Step 2 into the database.
	5. Perform a hard reset of the RPKI validator (reboot the RPKI validator server).
	6. Once the RPKI validator is restarted, it contains the following ROAs:
	   a. 10.100.0.0/16 16 65510
	   b. 10.100.0.0/16 20 65500
	   c. 10.100.0.0/16 24 65500
	   d. FD00:10:100::/64 64 65501
	7. Verify that the RUT received and installed VRPs in the RPKI database from Step 5.		

Expected Results	Each of the expected results in Steps 1, 3, and 6 above will be verified.		
Actual Results	The test was completed, and the functions were as intended in Steps 1, 3, and 6, but only if the VC presented a new session ID [RFC 6810] for the newly created session.		
Additional Comments (If Needed)	In cases where the cache presented the router erroneously with a re-used session ID, not all router implementations cleared the previous validation state correctly and immediately. This problem was resolved, after a configurable time period of one minute up to one hour.		

E.3.6.3   Test Case: SIDR-ROV-6.3.1

Test Objective	**Test SIDR Requirements CR-6.3.1 when working with IPv4/6 addresses. Show that the RUT receives and installs VRPs into the RPKI database properly after the RUT experienced a loss of power.**
Preconditions	The testbed is configured with the topology, IP addressing scheme, and ASNs as depicted in the Testbed Architecture in Figure E-1 and Figure E-2. The RUT's cache is empty, and the RPKI validator/cache is empty. The following configuration for the Cisco IOS XR router is used as the baseline for this test: **Test 6-3-1 Config.txt**

IPv4 or IPv6?	Both	Test Harness or Hardware with Live RPKI?	Both

Procedure	1. Verify that the RUT has an empty RPKI database.
	2. From the RPKI cache, receive four ROAs:
	    a. 10.100.0.0/16 16 65500
	    b. 10.100.0.0/16 20 65500
	    c. 10.100.0.0/16 24 65500
	    d. FD00:10:100::/64 64 65500
	3. Configure the RUT with the VC by using the following file:
	
	Test 6-3-1 Cache Config.txt
	
	4. Verify that the RUT received and installed all VRPs in Step 2 into the database.
	5. Disconnect the RUT from the cache by going through a power cycle on the RUT.
	6. Remove the ROAs from the RPKI validator in Steps 2a and 2d.
	7. Add two ROAs:
	    a. 10.100.0.0/16 16 65510
	    b. FD00:10:100::/64 64 65510
	8. Reenable the TCP connection between the RUT and the RPKI validator.
	9. Verify that the RUT received and installed VRPs in the RPKI database and that the RUT contains only VRPs in Steps 2b, 2c, 7a, and 7b.

Expected Results	Each of the expected results in Steps 1, 3, and 8 above will be verified.

Actual Results	The results were as expected.
Additional Comments (If Needed)	None

E.3.6.4   Test Case: SIDR-ROV-6.4.1

Test Objective	**Test SIDR Requirements CR-6.4.1 when working with IPv4/6 addresses. Show that the RUT receives and installs VRPs into the RPKI database properly when switching to a cache with a different RPKI state.**		
Preconditions	The testbed is configured with the topology, IP addressing scheme, and ASNs as depicted in the Testbed Architecture in Figure E-1 and Figure E-2. The RUT's cache is empty, and RPKI validator/Caches 1 and 2 are empty. The following configuration for the Cisco IOS XR router is used as the baseline for this test: **Test 6-4-1 Config.txt**		
IPv4 or IPv6?	Both	**Test Harness or Hardware with Live RPKI?**	Both

Procedure	1. Verify that the RUT has an empty RPKI database.
	2. Connect the RUT to RPKI Cache 1 and receive four ROAs:
	   a. 10.100.0.0/16 16 65500
	   b. 10.100.0.0/16 20 65500
	   c. 10.100.0.0/16 24 65500
	   d. FD00::10.100.0.0/64 64 65500
	3. Configure the RUT with the VC by using the following file:
	
	Test 6-4-1 Cache Config.txt
	
	4. Verify that the RUT received and installed all VRPs in Step 2 into the database.
	5. Disconnect the RUT from the cache by using RUT configuration commands to remove the cache from the RUT.
	6. Connect the RUT to RPKI Cache 2 and receive three ROAs:
	   a. 10.100.0.0/16 16 65510		

	b. 10.100.0.0/16 20 65500
	c. FD00::10.100.0.0/64 64 65510
	7. Verify that the RUT received all VRPs in the RPKI database coming from Cache 2 and that no VRP is left from Cache 1.
	Only the VRPs of Steps 6a, 6b, and 6c must reside in the RUT's RPKI database.
Expected Results	Each of the expected results in Steps 1, 3, and 6 above will be verified.
Actual Results	The results were as expected.
Additional Comments (If Needed)	This experiment included operator involvement. In our test cases, we did not encounter any issues with the remaining stale data, but, even if we had, clearing the table would resolve the issue.
	Also, all vendor systems that we used perform a union on the validation databases. Therefore, it will be good practice to add the new cache and retrieve the VRP data prior to removing the old cache, to keep churn in the routing table to a minimum.

E.3.6.5 Test Case: SIDR-ROV-6.5.1

Test Objective	**Test SIDR Requirements CR-6.5.1 when working with IPv4/6 addresses. Show that the RUT receives and installs VRPs of two identical RPKI caches into the RPKI database properly. Then, Cache 1 disappears.**
Preconditions	The testbed is configured with the topology, IP addressing scheme, and ASNs as depicted in the Testbed Architecture in Figure E-1 and Figure E-2.
	The RUT's cache is empty, and RPKI validator/Caches 1 and 2 are empty. The following configuration for the Cisco IOS XR router is used as the baseline for this test:
	Test 6-5-1 Config.txt

IPv4 or IPv6?	Both	Test Harness or Hardware with Live RPKI?	Both

Procedure	1. Verify that the RUT has an empty RPKI database.
	2. Connect the RUT to RPKI Cache 1 and receive three ROAs:
	a. 10.100.0.0/16 16 65510
	b. 10.100.0.0/16 20 65510
	c. FD00::10.100.0.0/64 64 65510
	3. Connect the RUT to RPKI Cache 2 and receive three ROAs:
	a. 10.100.0.0/16 16 65510

     b.   10.100.0.0/16 20 65510

     c.   FD00::10.100.0.0/64 64 65510

4. Configure the RUT with the VCs by using the following file:

**Test 6-5-1 Cache
Config.txt**

5. Verify that the RUT received all VRPs in the RPKI database coming from Caches 1 and 2.

6. The RUT receives Update 10.100.0.0/16 65510.

7. Verify that the RUT received the update from Step 6 and validated it as *valid*.

8. The RUT receives Update 10.100.0.0/16 65511.

9. Verify that the RUT received the update from Step 8 and validated it as *invalid*.

10. Shut down Cache 1.

11. Verify that the validation state of both updates did not change.

Expected Results	Each of the expected results in Steps 1, 4, 6, 8, and 10 above will be verified.
Actual Results	Results were as expected.
Additional Comments (If Needed)	The vendor implementations act differently, mainly controlled by their configurations. This means that one implementation identified the loss of the cache faster than the other. We determined that the router that kept data longer cleared stale data after a configured time span between one minute and one hour.

E.3.6.6   *Test Case: SIDR-ROV-6.6.1*

Test Objective	**Test SIDR Requirements CR-6.6.1 when working with IPv4/6 addresses. Show that the RUT receives and installs VRPs of two RPKI caches with a slightly different view on the RPKI into the RPKI database properly. Then, Cache 1 disappears.**		
Preconditions	The testbed is configured with the topology, IP addressing scheme, and ASNs as depicted in the Testbed Architecture in Figure E-1 and Figure E-2. The RUT's cache is empty, and RPKI validator/Caches 1 and 2 are empty. **Test 6-6-1 Config.txt**		
IPv4 or IPv6?	Both	**Test Harness or Hardware with Live RPKI?**	Both
Procedure	1. Verify that the RUT has an empty RPKI database.		

2. Connect the RUT to RPKI Cache 1 and receive three ROAs:
   a. 10.100.0.0/16 16 65510
   b. 10.100.0.0/16 20 65510
   c. FD00::10.100.0.0/64 64 65510
3. Connect the RUT to RPKI Cache 2 and receive three ROAs:
   a. 10.100.0.0/16 16 65511
   b. 10.100.0.0/16 20 65511
   c. FD00::10.100.0.0/64 64 65511
4. Configure the RUT with the VCs by using the following file:

**Test 6-6-1 Cache
Config.txt**

5. Verify that the RUT received all VRPs in the RPKI database coming from Caches 1 and 2.
6. The RUT receives Update 10.100.0.0/16 65510.
7. Verify that the RUT received the update from Step 6 and validated it as *valid*.
8. The RUT receives Update 10.100.0.0/16 65511.
9. Verify that the RUT received the update from Step 8 and validated it as *valid* or *invalid*, depending on if both caches are active or only Cache 1 is active.
10. The RUT receives Update 10.100.0.0/15 65510.
11. Verify that the RUT validates the received update from Step 10 as *not found*.
12. Shut down Cache 1.
13. Verify that the RUT contains only VRP values of 3.
14. Verify that update from step 6 is *invalid*, the update from step 8 is *valid*, and the update from step 10 is *not found*.

Expected Results	Each of the expected results in Steps 1, 4, 6, 8, 10, 12, and 13 above will be verified.
Actual Results	Results were as expected.
Additional Comments (If Needed)	The vendor implementations act differently, mainly controlled by their configurations. This means that one implementation identified the loss of the cache faster than the other. We determined that the router that kept data longer cleared stale data after a configured time span between one minute and one hour.
	Also, all router implementations that were tested take a union of the connected caches.

E.3.7 SIDR Delegated Model Test Cases

Test case SIDR-ROV-2.7.2 is identical to test case SIDR-ROV-2.7.1, except that IPv6 addresses are used instead of IPv4 addresses.

The following tests are designed to verify capabilities related to the implementation of a delegated CA.

E.3.7.1 Test Case: SIDR-DM-7.1.1

Test Objective	Test SIDR Requirements CR-7.1.1 when working with IPv4 addresses. Show that a resource holder can set up its own CA as a delegated RPKI participant and create, store, and manage ROAs for its own addresses in its own repository, and that this ROA information will be downloaded to local VCs and provided to routers that are performing ROV. Furthermore, show that ROAs will be removed from the RPKI upon expiration.		
	(In this test case, a resource holder sets up its own delegated CA and repository and demonstrates the ability to create, manage, and store ROAs for itself. The resource holder demonstrates the ability to create, manage, and store ROAs for its customers.)		
Preconditions	The testbed is configured with the topology, IP addressing scheme, and ASNs as depicted in the Testbed Architecture in Figure E-2.		
	1. The resource holder that is going to set up the delegated CA (AS 65501) holds IPv4 address space 10.10.0.0/16.		
	2. AS 65501 is in possession of the CA certificate for this IPv4 address space.		
	3. There are no ROAs in the RPKI that cover these addresses:		
	a. 10.10.128.128/19		
	b. 10.10.128.192/19		
	c. 10.10.128.224/19		
	4. Select any router, other than the AS 65501 router, that has an associated VC to be the RUT.		
IPv4 or IPv6?	IPv4	Test Harness or Hardware?	Hardware
Procedure	1. Examine the VC attached to the RUT to verify that it is not storing any ROAs that cover the following three addresses:		
	a. 10.10.128.128/19		
	b. 10.10.128.192/19		
	c. 10.10.128.224/19		
	2. Use the **show ip bgp rpki table** command at the RUT to list the VRP information that it has received from its VC. Verify that the RUT has not received any VRPs that cover the addresses listed in the previous step.		

3. AS 65501 sets up a CA and a repository within its own AS as a child of the test RIR.
4. AS 65501 creates three ROAs:
   a. (10.10.128.128/19, 19, AS 65501)
   b. (10.10.128.192/19, 19, AS 65501)
   c. (10.10.128.224/19, 19, AS 65501)

   The first two ROAs are created with default expiration time values (i.e., their end-entity [EE] certificates have the default expiration value, which, in the case of the tool that we are using, is one year from creation). The third ROA's corresponding EE certificate is given an expiration time of 24 hours from creation.
5. Verify, by looking in AS 65501's repository, that these three ROAs have been created and are stored in the repository.
6. Wait for an amount of time to elapse that is greater than the RPKI-to-VC content update interval, but less than 12 hours (i.e., within the expiration time set for the third ROA created in Step 4 above). (Or, alternatively, force the VC to be updated with the latest RPKI repository information.)
7. Verify that all three of the ROAs that were created in Step 4 above have been received by the VC that is attached to the RUT.
8. Wait for an amount of time to elapse that is greater than the VC-to-router refresh interval, but less than 12 hours (i.e., still within the expiration time set for the third ROA created in Step 4 above).
9. Verify that VRPs for all three of these ROAs have been received by the RUT that is attached to this VC. (Use the **show ip bgp rpki table** command at the RUT to list the VRP information that it has received from its VC.)
10. Wait for an amount of time to elapse so that the 24-hour expiration time set in Step 4 above will have passed.
11. Verify, by looking in AS 65501's repository, that only the first two ROAs that were created in Step 4 remain in the repository (i.e., that the third ROA is no longer in the repository):
    a. (10.10.128.128/19, 19, AS 65501) is present.
    b. (10.10.128.192/19, 19, AS 65501) is present.
    c. (10.10.128.224/19, 19, AS 65501) is absent.
12. Wait for an amount of time to elapse that is greater than the RPKI-to-VC content update interval, or, alternatively, force the validator/VC to be updated with the latest RPKI repository information.
13. Verify that VRPs for only the first two ROAs created in Step 4 above have been received by the VC that is attached to the RUT.

14. Wait for an amount of time to elapse that is greater than the VC-to-router refresh interval.

15. Verify that VRPs for only the first two ROAs created in Step 4 are received by the RUT (i.e., no VRP for the third ROA is received by the router). (Use the **show ip bgp rpki table** command at the RUT to list the VRP information that it has received from its VC.)

16. Remove ROA 10.10.128.192/19 AS 65501.

17. Verify, by looking in AS 65501's repository, that only the first ROA that was created in Step 4 remains in the repository (i.e., that the second and third ROAs are no longer in the repository):
    a. (10.10.128.128/19, 19, AS 65501) is present.
    b. (10.10.128.192/19, 19, AS 65501) is absent.
    c. (10.10.128.224/19, 19, AS 65501) is absent.

18. Wait for an amount of time to elapse that is greater than the RPKI-to-VC content update interval, or, alternatively, force the validator/VC to be updated with the latest RPKI repository information.

19. Verify that a VRP for only the first ROA created in Step 4 above has been received by the VC that is attached to the RUT.

20. Wait for an amount of time to elapse that is greater than the VC-to-router refresh interval.

21. Verify that a VRP for only the first ROA created in Step 4 is received by the RUT (i.e., no VRP for the second or third ROA is received by the router). (Use the **show ip bgp rpki table** command at the RUT to list the VRP information that it has received from its VC.)

Expected Results	Each of the expected results in Steps 5, 7, 9, 11, 13, 15, 17, 19, and 21 are be verified.
Actual Results	Unable to complete certain steps. See comments below.
Additional Comments (If Needed)	Observations (with comments). Steps 6 through 10 cannot be met because the Dragon Research Labs rpki.net toolkit does not permit specifying an expiration date of an EE certificate. According to the creators of the only documented delegated RPKI toolkit, the toolkit was designed under the assumption that all ROAs in the repository should have current EE certificates. If their EE certificate is expired, then it shouldn't be in the repository. There is debate as to whether this is a sound model. For example, the American Registry for Internet Numbers' (ARIN's) hosted RPKI model permits the specification of EE certificate expiration dates. All test procedures are possible, with the exception of the specification of an EE certificate expiration date.

Test Objective	**Test SIDR Requirements CR-7.2.1 when working with IPv4 addresses. Show that a resource holder can set up its own CA as a delegated RPKI participant and create, store, and manage ROAs on behalf of its customers in its own repository, and that this ROA information will be downloaded to local VCs and provided to routers that are performing ROV. Furthermore, show that these ROAs will be removed from the RPKI upon expiration.** **(In this test case, a resource holder sets up its own delegated CA and repository and demonstrates the ability to create, manage, and store ROAs on behalf of its customers.)**

Preconditions	1. The resource holder, depicted as "Repository" in <u>Figure E-2</u>, that is going to set up the delegated CA (AS 65501) holds IPv4 address space 10.10.0.0/16.
	2. AS 65501 is in possession of the CA certificate for this IPv4 address space.
	3. There are no ROAs in the RPKI that cover these addresses:
	   a. 10.10.240.128/20
	   b. 10.10.240.192/19
	   c. 10.10.240.224/19
	4. Select any router, other than the AS 65501 router, that has an associated VC to be the RUT.

IPv4 or IPv6?	IPv4	**Test Harness or Hardware?**	Hardware

Procedure	1. Examine the VC attached to the RUT to verify that it is not storing any ROAs that cover the following three addresses:
	   a. 10.10.240.128/20
	   b. 10.10.240.192/19
	   c. 10.10.240.224/19
	2. Use the **show ip bgp rpki table** command at the RUT to list the VRP information that it has received from its VC. Verify that the RUT has not received any VRPs that cover the addresses listed in the previous step.
	3. AS 65501 sets up a CA and a repository within its own AS as a child of the test RIR.
	4. AS 65501 creates three ROAs for portions of its own address space that it is delegating to AS 65505, thereby authorizing AS 65505 to originate BGP updates for these addresses:
	   a. (10.10.240.128/20, 20, AS 65505)
	   b. (10.10.240.192/19, 19, AS 65505)
	   c. (10.10.240.224/19, 19, AS 65505)

The first two ROAs are created with default expiration time values (i.e., their EE certificates have the default expiration value, which, in the case of the tool that we are using, is one year from creation). The third ROA's corresponding EE certificate is given an expiration time of 24 hours from creation.

5. Verify, by looking in AS 65501's repository, that these three ROAs have been created and are stored in the repository.

6. Wait for an amount of time to elapse that is greater than the RPKI-to-VC content update interval, but less than 12 hours (i.e., prior to the expiration time set for the third ROA created in Step 4 above). (Or, alternatively, force the VC to be updated with the latest RPKI repository information.)

7. Verify that all three of the ROAs that were created in Step 4 above have been received by the VC that is attached to the RUT.

8. Wait for an amount of time to elapse that is greater than the VC-to-router refresh interval, but less than 12 hours (i.e., still prior to the expiration time set for the third ROA created in Step 4 above).

9. Verify that VRPs for all three of these ROAs have been received by the RUT that is attached to this VC. (Use the **show ip bgp rpki table** command at the RUT to list the VRP information that it has received from its VC.)

10. Wait for an amount of time to elapse so that the 24-hour expiration time set in Step 4 above will have passed.

11. Verify, by looking in AS 65501's repository, that only the first two ROAs that were created in Step 4 remain in the repository (i.e., the third ROA is no longer in the repository):

    a. (10.10.240.128/19, 19, AS 65501) is present.

    b. (10.10.240.192/19, 19, AS 65501) is present.

    c. (10.10.240.224/19, 19, AS 65501) is absent.

12. Wait for an amount of time to elapse that is greater than the RPKI-to-VC content update interval, or, alternatively, force the validator/VC to be updated with the latest RPKI repository information.

13. Verify that VRPs for only the first two ROAs created in Step 4 above have been received by the VC that is attached to the RUT.

14. Wait for an amount of time to elapse that is greater than the VC-to-router refresh interval.

15. Verify that VRPs for only the first two ROAs created in Step 4 are received by the RUT (i.e., no VRP for the third ROA is received by the router). (Use the **show ip bgp rpki table** command at the RUT to list the VRP information that it has received from its VC.)

16. AS 65501 revokes the second ROA that was created in Step 4 above.

17. Verify, by looking in AS 65501's repository, that only the first ROA that was created in Step 4 remains in the repository (i.e., that the second and third ROAs are no longer in the repository):
    a. (10.10.240.128/19, 19, AS 65501) is present.
    b. (10.10.240.192/19, 19, AS 65501) is absent.
    c. (10.10.240.224/19, 19, AS 65501) is absent.
18. Wait for an amount of time to elapse that is greater than the RPKI-to-VC content update interval, or, alternatively, force the validator/VC to be updated with the latest RPKI repository information.
19. Verify that a VRP for only the first ROA created in Step 4 above has been received by the VC that is attached to the RUT.
20. Wait for an amount of time to elapse that is greater than the VC-to-router refresh interval.
21. Verify that a VRP for only the first ROA created in Step 4 is received by the RUT (i.e., no VRP for the second or third ROA is received by the router). (Use the **show ip bgp rpki table** command at the RUT to list the VRP information that it has received from its VC.)

Expected Results	Each of the expected results in Steps 4, 6, 8, 10, 12, and 14 above will be verified.
Actual Results	Unable to complete certain steps. See the comments below.
Additional Comments (If Needed)	Observations (with comments).
	Similar to Appendix E.3.7.1, Steps 6 through 10 cannot be met because the Dragon Research Labs rpki.net toolkit does not permit specifying an expiration date of an EE certificate. According to the creators of the only documented delegated RPKI toolkit, the toolkit was designed under the assumption that all ROAs in the repository should have current EE certificates. If their EE certificate is expired, then it shouldn't be in the repository. There is debate as to whether this is a sound model. For example, ARIN's hosted RPKI model permits the specification of EE certificate expiration dates. All test procedures are possible, with the exception of the specification of an EE certificate expiration date.

1 Appendix F   Acronyms

ANTD	Advanced Network Technology Division
ARIN	American Registry for Internet Numbers
AS	Autonomous System
ASN	Autonomous System Number
BGP	Border Gateway Protocol
BGP-4	Border Gateway Protocol 4
BGPsec	Border Gateway Protocol Security
BGP-SRx	Border Gateway Protocol Secure Routing Extension
BIO	BGPSEC-IO
CA	Certificate Authority
COI	Community of Interest
COTS	Commercial Off-The-Shelf
CR	Capability Requirement
CRADA	Cooperative Research and Development Agreement
CVE	Common Vulnerability and Exposures
DE	Detect
DoS	Denial of Service
eBGP	Exterior Border Gateway Protocol
EE	End-Entity
FIB	Forwarding Information Base
FIPS	Federal Information Processing Standards
FOIA	Freedom of Information Act
FRN	Federal Register Notice
GbE	Gigabit(s) Ethernet
Gbps	Gigabit(s) per Second (Billions of Bits per Second)

iBGP	Interior Border Gateway Protocol
ID	Identifier
ID	Identify
IEC	International Electrotechnical Commission
IEEE	Institute of Electrical and Electronics Engineers
IETF	Internet Engineering Task Force
IGP	Interior Gateway Protocol
INR	Internet Number Resource
IP	Internet Protocol
IPv4	Internet Protocol Version 4
IPv6	Internet Protocol Version 6
ISO	International Organization for Standardization
ISP	Internet Service Provider
IT	Information Technology
ITL	Information Technology Lab
LOI	Letter of Interest
LP	Local Preference
maxLength	Maximum Prefix Length
NANOG	North American Network Operators Group
NCCoE	National Cybersecurity Center of Excellence
NCEP	National Cybersecurity Excellence Partnership
NDI	Non-Developmental Items
NIST	National Institute of Standards and Technology
OS	Operating System
PANW	Palo Alto Next-Generation Firewall
PKI	Public Key Infrastructure

PR	Protect
RFC	Request for Comments
RIPE NCC	Réseaux IP Européens Network Coordination Centre
RIR	Regional Internet Registry
RMF	Risk Management Framework
ROA	Route Origin Authorization
ROM	Rough Order of Magnitude
ROV	Route Origin Validation
RP	Relying Party
RPKI	Resource Public Key Infrastructure
RRDP	RPKI Repository Delta Protocol
RS	Respond
rsync	Remote Synchronization
RUT	Router Under Test
SIDR	Secure Inter-Domain Routing
SLURM	Simplified Local Internet Number Resource Management
SONET	Synchronous Optical Network
SP	Special Publication
SQL	Structured Query Language
TAL	Trust Anchor Locator
TCP	Transmission Control Protocol
TPO	Technology Partnerships Office
U.S.	United States
URI	Uniform Resource Identifier
VC	Validating Cache

| **VM** | Virtual Machine |
| **VRP** | Validated ROA Payload |

Appendix G   References

[A_Greenberg]	A. Greenberg, *Wired.com Security*, "Hacker Redirects Traffic from 19 Internet Providers to Steal Bitcoins," August 7, 2014.
[Cybersecurity Framework]	*Framework for Improving Critical Infrastructure Cybersecurity*, National Institute of Standards and Technology, [website]. Available: http://www.nist.gov/cyberframework/.
[FIPS 140-2]	*Security Requirements for Cryptographic Modules*, FIPS 140-2 (including change notices as of 12-03-2002), National Institute of Standards and Technology, May 2001. Available: http://csrc.nist.gov/publications/fips/fips140-2/fips1402.pdf.
[ISO/IEC 27001:2013]	*Information Technology – Security techniques – Information security management systems – Requirements*, ISO/IEC 27001:2013, International Organization for Standards, October 2013. Available: https://www.iso.org/standard/54534.html.
[ISO/IEC/IEEE 15288:2015]	*Systems and software engineering — System life cycle processes*, ISO/IEC/IEEE 15288:2015, International Organization for Standards, May 2015. Available: https://www.iso.org/standard/63711.html.
[McEvilley15]	M. McEvilley, *Towards a Notional Framework for Systems Security Engineering*, The MITRE Corporation, NDIA 18th Annual Systems Engineering Conference, October 2015.
[N Anderson]	N. Anderson, *Ars Technica*, "How China swallowed 15% of 'Net traffic for 18 minutes," November 17, 2010. Available: https://arstechnica.com/information-technology/2010/11/how-china-swallowed-15-of-net-traffic-for-18-minutes/.
[NANOG69]	M. Adalier, K. Sriram, O. Borchert, K. Lee, and D. Montgomery, "High Performance BGP Security: Algorithms and Architectures," *North American Network Operators Group (NANOG69)*, February 2017. Available: https://nanog.org/meetings/abstract?id=3043.
[NIST BGP-SRx]	*BGP Secure Routing Extension (BGP SRx) Prototype*, National Institute of Standards and Technology, [website]. Available: https://www.nist.gov/services-resources/software/bgp-secure-routing-extension-bgp-srx-prototype.
[NIST SP 800-130]	E. Barker, M. Smid, D. Branstad, and S. Chokhani, *A Framework for Designing Cryptographic Key Management Systems*, NIST SP 800-130, National Institute of Standards and Technology, August 2013. Available: http://dx.doi.org/10.6028/NIST.SP.800-130.

[NIST SP 800-152]	E. Barker, M. Smid, and D. Branstad, A Profile for U.S. Federal Cryptographic Key Management Systems, NIST SP 800-152, National Institute of Standards and Technology, October 2015. Available: http://dx.doi.org/10.6028/NIST.SP.800-152.
[NIST SP 800-160]	*Systems Security Engineering: An Integrated Approach to Building Trustworthy Resilient Systems*, NIST SP 800-160 Second Public Draft, National Institute of Standards and Technology, November 2016. Available: https://doi.org/10.6028/NIST.SP.800-160.
[NIST SP 800-30]	*Guide for Conducting Risk Assessments*, NIST SP 800-30 Revision 1, National Institute of Standards and Technology, September 2012. Available: https://nvlpubs.nist.gov/nistpubs/Legacy/SP/nistspecialpublication800-30r1.pdf.
[NIST SP 800-37]	*Guide for Applying the Risk Management Framework to Federal Information Systems: A Security Life Cycle Approach*, NIST SP 800-37 Revision 1, National Institute of Standards and Technology, February 2010. Available: http://dx.doi.org/10.6028/NIST.SP.800-37r1.
[NIST SP 800-53]	*Security and Privacy Controls for Federal Information Systems and Organizations*, NIST SP 800-53 Revision 4, Joint Task Force Transformation Initiative, National Institute of Standards and Technology, April 2013. Available: http://dx.doi.org/10.6028/NIST.SP.800-53r4.
[NIST SP 800-54]	D. R. Kuhn, K. Sriram, and D. Montgomery, *Border Gateway Protocol Security*, NIST SP 800-54, July 2007. Available: https://doi.org/10.6028/NIST.SP.800-54.
[NIST SP 800-57 Part 1]	*Recommendation for Key Management — Part 1: General,* NIST SP 800-57 Part 1 Revision 3 and Draft Revision 4, National Institute of Standards and Technology, January 2016. Available: https://doi.org/10.6028/NIST.SP.800-57p1r3 http://dx.doi.org/10.6028/NIST.SP.800-57pt1r4.
[NIST SP 800-57 Part 2]	*Recommendation for Key Management — Part 2: Best Practices for Key Management Organization,* NIST SP 800-57 Part 2, National Institute of Standards and Technology, August 2005. Available: https://doi.org/10.6028/NIST.SP.800-57pt2r1f.
[OMB A-130]	*Managing Federal Information as a Strategic Resource*, OMB Circular A-130, Executive Office of the President, Office of Management and Budget, July 28, 2016. Available: https://www.whitehouse.gov/sites/whitehouse.gov/files/omb/circulars/A130/a130revised.pdf.

[Parsons BGPSec]	*The BGPsec enabled Bird Routing Daemon*, Secure Routing, [website]. Available: http://www.securerouting.net/tools/bird/
[RFC 3779]	C. Lynn, S. Kent, and K. Seo, *X.509 Extensions for IP Addresses and AS Identifiers*, RFC 3779, June 2004. Available: https://www.ietf.org/rfc/rfc3779.txt.
[RFC 3882]	D. Turk, *Configuring BGP to Block Denial-of-Service Attacks*, RFC 3882, September 2004. Available: https://tools.ietf.org/rfc/rfc3882.txt.
[RFC 4012]	L. Blunk, J. Damas, F. Parent, and A. Robachevsky, *Routing Policy Specification Language next generation (RPSLng)*, RFC 4012, March 2005. Available: https://tools.ietf.org/html/rfc4012.
[RFC 4271]	Y. Rekhter, T. Li, and S. Hares, *A Border Gateway Protocol 4 (BGP-4)*, RFC 4271, January 2006. Available: https://www.ietf.org/rfc/rfc4271.txt.
[RFC 4272]	S. Murphy, *BGP Security Vulnerabilities Analysis*, RFC 4272, January 2006. Available: https://www.ietf.org/rfc/rfc4272.txt.
[RFC 4593]	A. Babir, S. Murphy, and Y. Yang, *Generic Threats to Routing Protocols*, RFC 4593, October 2006. Available: https://www.ietf.org/rfc/rfc4593.txt.
[RFC 5280]	D. Cooper, S. Santesson, S. Farrell, S. Boeyen, R. Housley, and W. Polk, *Internet X.509 Public Key Infrastructure Certification and Certificate Revocation List (CRL) Profile*, RFC 5280, May 2008. Available: https://www.ietf.org/rfc/rfc5280.txt.
[RFC 5575]	P. Marques et al., *Dissemination of Flow Specification Rules*, RFC 5575, August 2009. Available: https://tools.ietf.org/html/rfc5575.
[RFC 5781]	S. Weiler, D. Ward, and R. Housley, *The rsync URI Scheme*, RFC 5781, February 2010. Available: https://tools.ietf.org/html/rfc5781.
[RFC 6092]	J. Woodyatt, *Recommended Simple Security Capabilities in Customer Premises Equipment (CPE) for Providing Residential IPv6 Internet Service*, RFC 6092, January 2011. Available: https://tools.ietf.org/html/rfc6092.
[RFC 6472]	W. Kumari and K. Sriram, *Recommendation for Not Using AS_SET and AS_CONFED_SET in BGP*, RFC 6472, December 2011. Available: https://tools.ietf.org/html/rfc6472.
[RFC 6480]	M. Lepinski and S. Kent, *An Infrastructure to Support Secure Internet Routing*, RFC 6480, February 2012. Available: https://tools.ietf.org/html/rfc6480.
[RFC 6481]	G. Huston, R. Loomans, and G. Michaelson, *A Profile for Resource Certificate Repository Structure*, RFC 6481, February 2012. Available: https://tools.ietf.org/html/rfc6481.

[RFC 6482]	M. Lepinski, S. Kent, and D. Kong, *A Profile for Route Origin Authorizations (ROAs)*, RFC 6482, February 2012. Available: https://tools.ietf.org/html/rfc6482.
[RFC 6484]	S. Kent, D. Kong, K. Seo, and R. Watro, *Certificate Policy (CP) for the Resource Public Key Infrastructure (RPKI)*, RFC 6484, February 2012. Available: http://tools.ietf.org/html/rfc6484.
[RFC 6486]	R. Austein, G. Huston, S. Kent, and M. Lepinski, *Manifests for the Resource Public Key Infrastructure (RPKI)*, RFC 6486, February 2012. Available: https://tools.ietf.org/html/rfc6486.
[RFC 6487]	G. Huston, G. Michaelson, and R. Loomans, *A Profile for X.509 PKIX Resource Certificates*, RFC 6487, February 2012. Available: https://tools.ietf.org/html/rfc6487.
[RFC 6488]	M. Lepinski, A. Chi, and S. Kent, *Signed Object Template for the Resource Public Key Infrastructure (RPKI)*, RFC 6488, February 2012. Available: https://tools.ietf.org/html/rfc6488.
[RFC 6490]	G. Huston, S. Weiler, G. Michaelson, and S. Kent, *Resource Public Key Infrastructure Trust Anchor Locator*, RFC 6490, February 2012. Available: https://tools.ietf.org/html/rfc6490.
[RFC 6492]	G. Huston, R. Loomans, B. Ellacott, and R. Austein, *A Protocol for Provisioning Resource Certificates*, RFC 6492, February 2012. Available: https://tools.ietf.org/html/rfc6492.
[RFC 6495]	R. Gagliano, S. Krishnan, and A. Kukec, *Subject Key Identifier (SKI) SEcure Neighbor Discovery (SEND) Name Type Fields*, RFC 6495, February 2012. Available: https://tools.ietf.org/html/rfc6495.
[RFC 6810]	R. Bush and R. Austein, *The Resource Public Key Infrastructure (RPKI) to Router Protocol*, RFC 6810, January 2003. Available: https://tools.ietf.org/html/rfc6810.
[RFC 6811]	P. Mohapatra, J. Scudder, D. Ward, R. Bush, and R. Austein, *BGP Prefix Origin Validation*, RFC 6811, January 2013. Available: https://tools.ietf.org/pdf/rfc6811.pdf.
[RFC 6907]	T. Manderson, K. Sriram, and R. White, *Use Cases and Interpretations of Resource Public Key Infrastructure (RPKI) Objects for Issuers and Relying Parties*, RFC 6907, March 2013. Available: https://tools.ietf.org/html/rfc6907.
[RFC 7115]	R. Bush, *Origin Validation Operation Based on the Resource Public Key Infrastructure (RPKI)*, RFC 7115, January 2014. Available: https://tools.ietf.org/html/rfc7115.

[RFC 7132]	S. Kent and A. Chi, *Threat Model for BGP Path Security*, RFC 7132, February 2014. Available: https://tools.ietf.org/html/rfc7132.
[RFC 7318]	A. Newton and G. Huston, *Policy Qualifiers in Resource Public Key Infrastructure (RPKI) Certificates*, RFC 7318, July 2014. Available: https://tools.ietf.org/html/rfc7318.
[RFC 7382]	S. Kent, D. Kong, and K. Seo, *Template for a Certification Practice Statement (CPS) for the Resource PKI (RPKI)*, RFC 7382, April 2015. Available: https://tools.ietf.org/html/rfc7382.
[RFC 7454]	J. Durand, I. Pepelnjak, and G. Doering, *BGP Operations and Security*, RFC 7454, February 2015. Available: https://tools.ietf.org/html/rfc7454.
[RFC 7674]	J. Haas, *Clarification of the Flowspec Redirect Extended Community*, RFC 7674, October 2015. Available: https://tools.ietf.org/html/rfc7674.
[RFC 7730]	G. Huston, S. Weiler, G. Michaelson, and S. Kent, *Resource Public Key Infrastructure (RPKI) Trust Anchor Locator*, RFC 7730, January 2016. Available: https://tools.ietf.org/html/rfc7730.
[RFC 7908]	K. Sriram, D. Montgomery, D. McPherson, E. Osterweil, and B. Dickson, *Problem Definition and Classification of BGP Route Leaks*, RFC 7908, June 2016. Available: https://tools.ietf.org/html/rfc7908.
[RFC 7909]	R. Kisteleki and B. Haberman, *Securing Routing Policy Specification Language (RPSL) Objects with Resource Public Key Infrastructure (RPKI) Signatures*, RFC 7909, June 2016. Available: https://tools.ietf.org/html/rfc7909.
[RFC 8097]	P. Mohapatra, K. Patel, J. Scudder, D. Ward, and R. Bush, *BGP Prefix Origin Validation State Extended Community*, RFC 8097, March 2017. Available: https://tools.ietf.org/html/rfc8097.
[RFC 8182]	T. Bruijnzeels, O. Muravskiy, B. Weber, and R. Austein, *The RPKI Repository Delta Protocol (RRDP)*, RFC 8182, July 2017. Available: https://tools.ietf.org/html/rfc8182.
[RFC 8205]	M. Lepinski and K. Sriram, *BGPsec Protocol Specification*, RFC 8205, September 2017. Available: https://tools.ietf.org/html/rfc8205.
[RFC 8208]	S. Turner and O. Borchert, BGPsec Algorithms, Key Formats, and Signature Formats. Available: https://tools.ietf.org/html/rfc8208
[RFC 8207]	R. Bush, *BGPsec Operational Considerations,* RFC 8207, September 2017. Available: https://tools.ietf.org/html/rfc8207.
[RFC 8210]	R. Bush and R. Austein, *The Resource Public Key Infrastructure (RPKI) to Router Protocol*, RFC 8210, September 2017. Available: https://tools.ietf.org/html/rfc8210.

[RFC 8481]	R. Bush, *Clarifications to BGP Origin Validation Based on Resource Public Key Infrastructure (RPKI)*, RFC 8481, September 2018. Available: https://tools.ietf.org/html/rfc8481
[RPKI ARIN]	*Resource Public Key Infrastructure (RPKI)*, American Registry for Internet Numbers, [website]. Available: https://www.arin.net/resources/rpki/index.html.
[Saarinen]	J. Saarinen, *itnews.com*, "Australia's Internet Hit Hard by Massive Malaysian Route Leak," June 15, 2015.
[Singel]	R. Singel, *Wired.com*, "Pakistan's Accidental YouTube Re-routing Exposes Trust Flaw in Net," February 25, 2008.
[V_Sriram]	V. Sriram and D. Montgomery, "Design and analysis of optimization algorithms to minimize cryptographic processing in BGP security protocols," *Computer Communications*, Vol. 106, pp. 75-85, DOI 10.1016/j.comcom.2017.03.007, July 2017. Available: https://www.sciencedirect.com/science/article/pii/S0140366417303365.

NIST SPECIAL PUBLICATION 1800-14C

Protecting the Integrity of Internet Routing:

Border Gateway Protocol (BGP)
Route Origin Validation

Volume C:
How-To Guides

William Haag
Applied Cybersecurity Division
Information Technology Laboratory

Doug Montgomery
Advanced Network Technologies Division
Information Technology Laboratory

Allen Tan
The MITRE Corporation
McLean, VA

William C. Barker
Dakota Consulting
Silver Spring, MD

June 2019

DISCLAIMER

Certain commercial entities, equipment, products, or materials may be identified by name or company logo or other insignia in order to acknowledge their participation in this collaboration or to describe an experimental procedure or concept adequately. Such identification is not intended to imply special status or relationship with NIST or recommendation or endorsement by NIST or NCCoE; neither is it intended to imply that the entities, equipment, products, or materials are necessarily the best available for the purpose.

National Institute of Standards and Technology Special Publication 1800-14C, Natl. Inst. Stand. Technol. Spec. Publ. 1800-14C, 61 pages, (June 2019), CODEN: NSPUE2

FEEDBACK

As a private-public partnership, we are always seeking feedback on our Practice Guides. We are particularly interested in seeing how businesses apply NCCoE reference designs in the real world. If you have implemented the reference design, or have questions about applying it in your environment, please email us at sidr-nccoe@nist.gov.

All comments are subject to release under the Freedom of Information Act (FOIA).

National Cybersecurity Center of Excellence
National Institute of Standards and Technology
100 Bureau Drive
Mailstop 2002
Gaithersburg, MD 20899
Email: nccoe@nist.gov

NATIONAL CYBERSECURITY CENTER OF EXCELLENCE

The National Cybersecurity Center of Excellence (NCCoE), a part of the National Institute of Standards and Technology (NIST), is a collaborative hub where industry organizations, government agencies, and academic institutions work together to address businesses' most pressing cybersecurity issues. This public-private partnership enables the creation of practical cybersecurity solutions for specific industries, as well as for broad, cross-sector technology challenges. Through consortia under Cooperative Research and Development Agreements (CRADAs), including technology partners—from Fortune 50 market leaders to smaller companies specializing in IT security—the NCCoE applies standards and best practices to develop modular, easily adaptable example cybersecurity solutions using commercially available technology. The NCCoE documents these example solutions in the NIST Special Publication 1800 series, which maps capabilities to the NIST Cybersecurity Framework and details the steps needed for another entity to recreate the example solution. The NCCoE was established in 2012 by NIST in partnership with the State of Maryland and Montgomery County, Md.

To learn more about the NCCoE, visit https://www.nccoe.nist.gov/. To learn more about NIST, visit https://www.nist.gov.

NIST CYBERSECURITY PRACTICE GUIDES

NIST Cybersecurity Practice Guides (Special Publication Series 1800) target specific cybersecurity challenges in the public and private sectors. They are practical, user-friendly guides that facilitate the adoption of standards-based approaches to cybersecurity. They show members of the information security community how to implement example solutions that help them align more easily with relevant standards and best practices, and provide users with the materials lists, configuration files, and other information they need to implement a similar approach.

The documents in this series describe example implementations of cybersecurity practices that businesses and other organizations may voluntarily adopt. These documents do not describe regulations or mandatory practices, nor do they carry statutory authority.

ABSTRACT

The Border Gateway Protocol (BGP) is the default routing protocol to route traffic among internet domains. While BGP performs adequately in identifying viable paths that reflect local routing policies and preferences to destinations, the lack of built-in security allows the protocol to be exploited by route hijacking. Route hijacking occurs when an entity accidentally or maliciously alters an intended route. Such attacks can (1) deny access to internet services, (2) detour internet traffic to permit eavesdropping and to facilitate on-path attacks on end points (sites), (3) misdeliver internet network traffic to malicious end points, (4) undermine internet protocol (IP) address-based reputation and filtering systems, and (5) cause routing instability in the internet. This document describes a security platform that demonstrates how to improve the security of inter-domain routing traffic exchange. The platform provides route origin validation (ROV) by using the Resource Public Key Infrastructure (RPKI) in a manner that mitigates some misconfigurations and malicious attacks associated with route hijacking. The example solutions and architectures presented here are based upon standards-based, open-source, and commercially available products.

KEYWORDS

AS, autonomous systems, BGP, Border Gateway Protocol, DDoS, denial-of-service (DoS) attacks, internet service provider, ISP, Regional Internet Registry, Resource Public Key Infrastructure, RIR, ROA, route hijack, route origin authorization, route origin validation, routing domain, ROV, RPKI

ACKNOWLEDGMENTS

We are grateful to the following individuals for their generous contributions of expertise and time.

Name	Organization
Tim Battles	AT&T
Jay Borkenhagen	AT&T
Chris Boyer	AT&T
Nimrod Levy	AT&T
Kathryn Condello	CenturyLink
Christopher Garner	CenturyLink
Peter Romness	Cisco Systems
Tony Tauber	Comcast
Jonathan Morgan	Juniper Networks
Carter Wyant	Juniper Networks
Oliver Borchert	NIST ITL Advanced Networks Technologies Division

Name	Organization
Kotikalapudi Sriram	NIST ITL Advanced Networks Technologies Division
Sean Morgan	Palo Alto Networks
Tom Van Meter	Palo Alto Networks
Andrew Gallo	The George Washington University
Sophia Applebaum	The MITRE Corporation
Yemi Fashina	The MITRE Corporation
Susan Prince	The MITRE Corporation
Susan Symington	The MITRE Corporation

The Technology Partners/Collaborators who participated in this build submitted their capabilities in response to a notice in the Federal Register. Respondents with relevant capabilities or product components were invited to sign a Cooperative Research and Development Agreement (CRADA) with NIST, allowing them to participate in a consortium to build this example solution. We worked with:

Technology Partner/Collaborator	Build Involvement
AT&T	Subject Matter Expertise
CenturyLink	1 gigabit per second (Gbps) Ethernet Link Subject Matter Expertise
Cisco	7206 VXR Router v15.2 ISR 4331 Router v16.3 2921 Router v15.2 IOS XRv 9000 Router v6.4.1 Subject Matter Expertise
Comcast	Subject Matter Expertise

Technology Partner/Collaborator	Build Involvement
Juniper Networks	MX80 3D Universal Edge Router v15.1R6.7 Subject Matter Expertise
Palo Alto Networks	Palo Alto Networks Next-Generation Firewall PA-5060 v7.1.10 Subject Matter Expertise
The George Washington University	Subject Matter Expertise

Contents

List of Figures

1 Introduction

The following guides show information technology (IT) professionals and security engineers how we implemented the example Secure Inter-Domain Routing (SIDR) Project solution for Resource Public Key Infrastructure (RPKI)-based route origin validation (ROV). We cover all of the products employed in this reference design. We do not recreate the product manufacturers' documentation, which is presumed to be widely available. Rather, these guides show how we incorporated the products together in our environment.

Note: These are not comprehensive tutorials. There are many possible service and security configurations for these products that are out of scope for this reference design.

1.1 Practice Guide Structure

This National Institute of Standards and Technology (NIST) Cybersecurity Practice Guide demonstrates a standards-based reference design and provides users with the information they need to replicate the SIDR RPKI-based ROV solution. This reference design is modular and can be deployed in whole or in parts.

NIST Special Publication (SP) 1800-14 contains three volumes:

- NIST SP 1800-14A: *Executive Summary*
- NIST SP 1800-14B: *Approach, Architecture, and Security Characteristics* – what we built and why
- NIST SP 1800-14C: *How-To Guides* – instructions for building the example solution **(you are here)**

Depending on your role in your organization, you might use this guide in different ways:

Business decision makers, including chief security and technology officers, will be interested in the *Executive Summary* (NIST SP 1800-14A), which describes:

- The challenges that enterprises face in implementing and maintaining route origin validation
- An example solution built at the National Cybersecurity Center of Excellence (NCCoE)
- Benefits of adopting the example solution

Technology or security program managers who are concerned with how to identify, understand, assess, and mitigate risk will be interested in NIST SP 1800-14B, which describes what we did and why. The following sections will be of particular interest:

- Section 4.4.3, Risks, provides a description of the risk analysis we performed
- Section 4.4.4, Cybersecurity Framework Functions, Categories, and Subcategories Addressed by the Secure Inter-Domain Routing Project, maps the security characteristics of this example solution to cybersecurity standards and best practices

If you are a technology or security program manager, you might share the *Executive Summary,* NIST SP 1800-14A, with your leadership team members to help them understand the importance of adopting the standards-based SIDR RPKI-based ROV solution.

IT professionals who want to implement an approach like this can use the How-To portion of the guide, NIST SP 1800-14C, to replicate all or parts of the build created in our lab. The How-To guide provides specific product installation, configuration, and integration instructions for implementing the example solution. We do not recreate the product manufacturers' documentation, which is generally widely available. Rather, we show how we incorporated the products together in our environment to create an example solution.

This guide assumes that IT professionals have experience implementing security products within the enterprise. While we have used a suite of commercial products to address this challenge, it is not NIST policy to endorse any particular products. Your organization can adopt this solution or one that adheres to these guidelines in whole, or you can use this guide as a starting point for tailoring and implementing parts of an RPKI-based ROV solution. Your organization's security experts should identify the products that will best integrate with your existing tools and IT system infrastructure. We hope that you will seek products that are congruent with applicable standards and best practices. Section 4.5, Technologies, of NIST SP 1800-14B lists the products that we used and maps them to the cybersecurity controls provided by this reference solution. A NIST Cybersecurity Practice Guide does not describe "the" solution, but a possible solution.

1.2 Build Overview

This NIST Cybersecurity Practice Guide addresses the challenge of using existing protocols to improve the security of inter-domain routing traffic exchange in a manner that mitigates accidental and malicious attacks associated with route hijacking. It implements and follows various Internet Engineering Task Force (IETF) Request for Comments (RFC) documents that define RPKI-based Border Gateway Protocol (BGP) ROV, such as RFC 6480, RFC 6482, RFC 6811, and RFC 7115, as well as recommendations of NIST SP 800-54, *Border Gateway Protocol Security*. To the extent practicable from a system composition point of view, the security platform design, build, and test processes have followed NIST SP 800-160, *Systems Security Engineering: Considerations for a Multidisciplinary Approach in the Engineering of Trustworthy Secure Systems*.

The ROV capabilities demonstrated by the proof-of-concept implementation described in this Practice Guide improve inter-domain routing security by using standards-conformant security protocols to enable an entity that receives a route advertisement to validate whether the autonomous system (AS) that has originated it is in fact authorized to do so.

In the NCCoE lab, the team built an environment that resembles portions of the internet. The SIDR lab architecture is depicted in Figure 1-1 and Figure 1-2. It consists of virtual and physical hardware, physical links to ISPs, and access to the Regional Internet Registries (RIRs). The physical hardware mainly consists of the routers performing ROV, workstations providing validator capabilities, and firewalls that protect the lab infrastructure. The virtual environment hosts the RPKI repositories, validators, and caches used for both the hosted and delegated RPKI scenarios. The architecture is organized into separate virtual local area networks (VLANs), each of which is designed to represent a different AS. For example, VLAN 1 represents an ISP with AS 64501, VLAN 2 represents the enterprise network of an organization with AS 64502, and VLAN 3 represents an ISP with AS 64503.

The configurations in this document provide a baseline for completing all the test cases that were performed for the project.

There are two environments that are used: test harness and live data.

- The test harness environment consists of physical/virtual routers, a lab RPKI repository, RPKI validators, and simulation tools (or test harness). The physical and virtual routers in this environment are from Cisco and Juniper. The lab RPKI repository is configured using the RPKI.net tool. The RPKI caches in this environment are the Réseaux IP Européens Network Coordination Centre (RIPE NCC) validator and the RPKI.net validator. The test harness simulates BGP routers sending and receiving advertisements and emulates RPKI data being sent from validators/caches. There are two components of the test harness: the BGPSEC-IO (BIO) traffic generator and collector, which produces BGP routing data, and the SRx-RPKI validator cache test harness, which simulates RPKI caches.

- The live data environment leverages many of the same components from the test harness environment. The difference is that this environment leverages live data from the internet, rather than uses emulated BGP advertisements and RPKI data. The physical and virtual routers in this environment are from Cisco and Juniper. The lab RPKI repository is configured using the RPKI.net tool. Repositories from the RIRs (American Registry for Internet Numbers [ARIN], RIPE NCC, African Network Information Center [AFRINIC], Latin America and Caribbean Network Information Center [LACNIC], and Asia-Pacific Network Information Center [APNIC]) are also used to receive real-world route origin authorization (ROA) data. The RPKI caches in this environment are the RIPE NCC validator and the RPKI.net validator. A physical wide area network (WAN) link is used to connect to CenturyLink to receive a full BGP table and to connect to the RIRs.

Figure 1-1 Test Harness Environment for SIDR RPKI-Based ROV Solution Testing

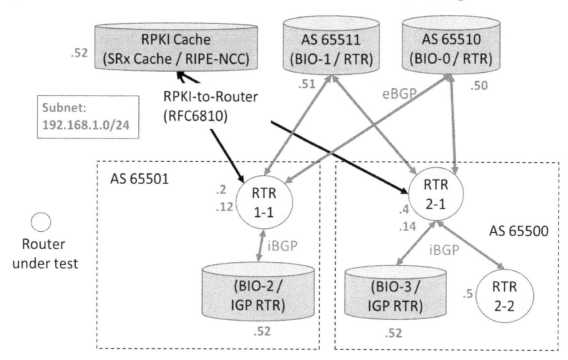

BGPSEC-IO (BIO) – BGP traffic generator & collector / RTR – CISCO or Juniper Router

Figure 1-2 Live Data Environment for SIDR RPKI-Based ROV Solution Testing

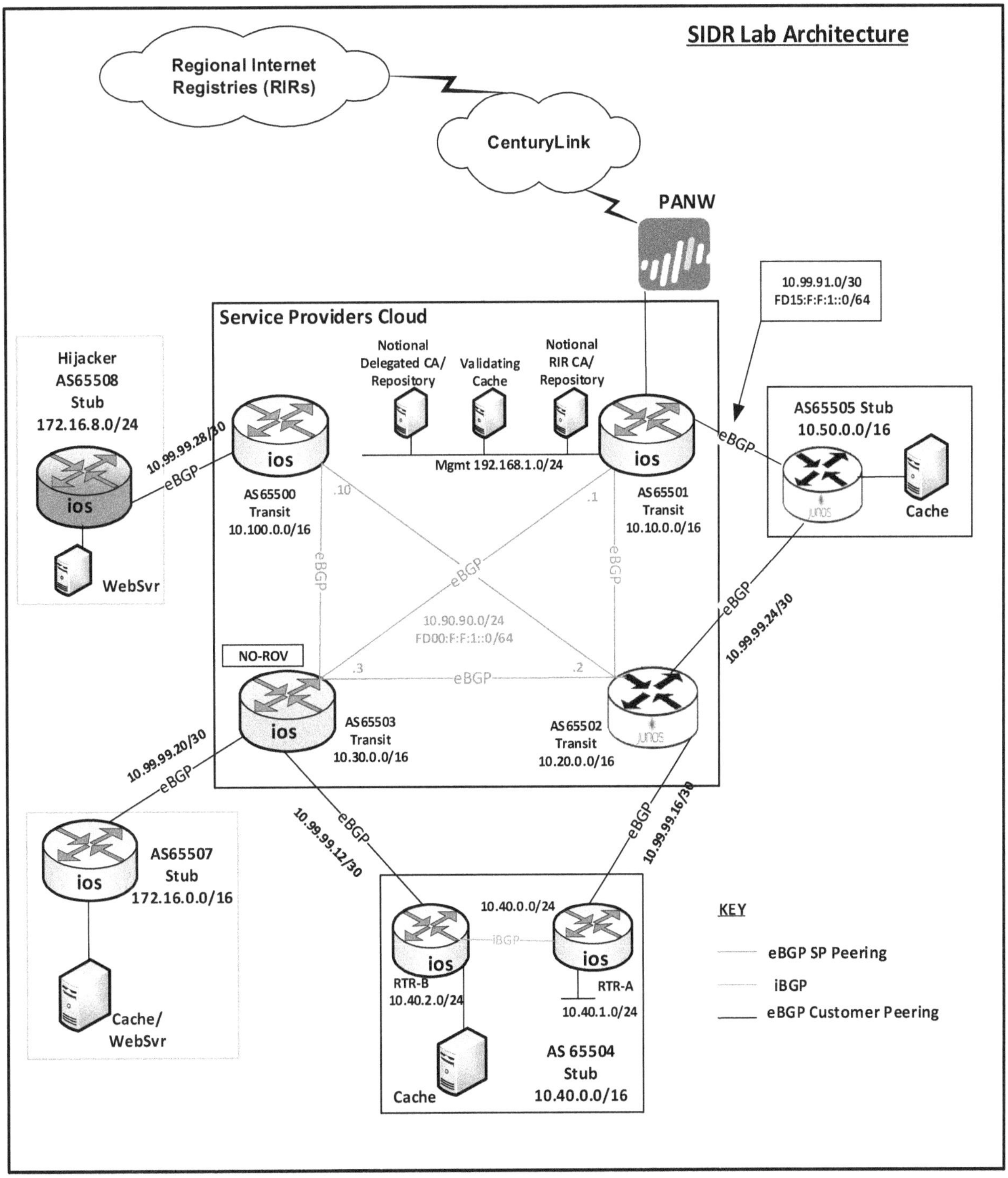

1.3 Typographic Conventions

The following table presents typographic conventions used in this volume.

Typeface/Symbol	Meaning	Example
Italics	filenames and pathnames references to documents that are not hyperlinks, new terms, and placeholders	For detailed definitions of terms, see the *CSRC.NIST.GOV Glossary*.
Bold	names of menus, options, command buttons, and fields	Choose **File > Edit.**
`Monospace`	command-line input, on-screen computer output, sample code examples, status codes	`Mkdir`
	command-line user input contrasted with computer output	`service sshd start`
	link to other parts of the document, a web URL, or an email address	All publications from NIST's National Cybersecurity Center of Excellence are available at http://www.nccoe.nist.gov

2 Product Installation Guides

This section of the Practice Guide contains detailed instructions for installing and configuring all of the products used to build an instance of the SIDR RPKI-based ROV example solution. The main components of the lab build consist of ROV-enabled routers, RPKI repositories, RPKI validators / validating caches (VCs), a live internet circuit, and firewalls.

2.1 RPKI Validators

The RPKI validator receives and validates ROAs from the RPKI repositories of the trust anchors and delegated repositories. Currently, there are five trust anchors, all of which are managed by the RIRs: AFRINIC, APNIC, ARIN, LACNIC, and the RIPE NCC. A subset of the data from ROAs, called validated ROA payload (VRP), is then retrieved from the local RPKI validator by an RPKI-capable router to perform ROV of BGP routes.

In this lab build, two RPKI validators (also referred to as VCs) are tested: the RIPE NCC RPKI validator and the Dragon Research RPKI.net validator.

2.1.1 RIPE NCC RPKI Validator Configuration/Installation

The RIPE NCC RPKI validator is developed and maintained by RIPE NCC [RIPE Tools]. This validator tool is free and open-source. The version used in the build is 2.24. It is available for download at https://www.ripe.net/manage-ips-and-asns/resource-management/certification/tools-and-resources.

System requirements: a UNIX-like operating system (OS), Java 7 or 8, rsync, and 2 gigabytes (GB) of free memory.

Lab setup: CentOS 7 minimal install, Java 8, rsync, one central processing unit (CPU), 6 GB memory, and running on a virtual machine (VM) on VMware ESXi.

For release notes, installation information, and source code, please view https://github.com/RIPE-NCC/rpki-validator/blob/master/rpki-validator-app/README.txt.

1. Use the CentOS template to create the VM with the system requirements provided above.

    a. Put the VM in the proper VLAN.

2. Install Java (must be Oracle 8) and open firewall to allow rsync.

3. In the VM, create a folder under home called "RPKI".

    a. `# mkdir RPKI`

    b. `# cd RPKI`

4. Download and install the RIPE NCC RPKI validator software in the VM.

    a. `# tar -xvf rpki-validator-app-2.24-dist.tar.gz`

5. Set *JAVA_HOME* (only if the application complains that it does not see the *JAVA_HOME* path).

    a. `# cd /etc/environment`

        i. `# nano environment`

      ii.   `# JAVA_HOME="/usr"`

   b.   Source it and check echo.

      i.   `# source /etc/environment`

      ii.   `# Echo $JAVA_HOME`

6. Reboot the server.

7. Start the RPKI cache.

   a.   `# ./rpki-validator.sh start`

8. Using a web browser, connect to the validator software that you just installed, by typing http://ip-address:8080 into the browser search window, replacing "ip-address" with the internet protocol (IP) address of the VM that you just created in step 1. (i.e., http://192.168.1.124:8080).

9. Once the validator is up, it receives data from the following RIR repositories: AFRINIC, APNIC, LACNIC, and RIPE NCC.

   a.   To retrieve ROAs from the ARIN repository, download the Trust Anchor Locator (TAL) file from https://www.arin.net/resources/rpki/tal.html.

   b.   Stop the validator.

      i.   `# ./rpki-validator.sh stop`

   c.   Put the file in the *TAL* sub-directory.

   d.   Restart the validator.

      i.   `# ./rpki-validator.sh start`

2.1.2 Dragon Research RPKI.net Validator Configuration/Installation

The Dragon Research Labs-developed RPKI.net toolkit contains both a VC and a certificate authority (CA). This section discusses the VC only.

System requirements: Ubuntu 16.04 Xenial server, 32 GB of hard disk, 1 GB of random access memory (RAM), and a minimum of one CPU.

Lab setup: Ubuntu 16.04 Xenial server, rsync, one CPU, 6 GB memory, and running on a VM on VMware ESXi.

For release notes, installation information, and additional information, please view https://github.com/dragonresearch/rpki.net/blob/master/doc/quickstart/xenial-rp.md.

```
# wget -q -O
/etc/apt/sources.list.d/rpki.list https://download.rpki.net/APTng/rpki.xenial.l
ist
```

You may get a message that says that there were errors (i.e., "the following signatures couldn't be verified because the public key is not available"). To fix this, use the following command, along with the key that showed up on the error:

```
# apt-key adv --keyserver keyserver.ubuntu.com --recv-keys 40976EAF437D05B5
```

Note: *40976EAF437D05B5* is an example. Use the exact key that showed up in the error.

Reference: https://chrisjean.com/fix-apt-get-update-the-following-signatures-couldnt-be-verified-because-the-public-key-is-not-available/.

```
# apt update
```

```
# apt install rpki-rp
```

This should install the VC. Next, access the VC by opening a browser and typing http://192.168.2.106/rcynic into the search window.

Note: It takes up to an hour to completely update. The proper Uniform Resource Locator (URL) will not show up until then. Just wait for it. You will see a parent folder directory in the URL during that time. Once it's ready, charts about the repositories from the different RIRs will show up.

Check to see if the VC is running by entering the following command:

```
# ps -aux | grep rpki
```

2.2 RPKI CA and Repository

The delegated model of RPKI for ROA creation and storage requires that two components be set up, operated, and maintained by the address holder: a CA and a repository. Currently, only the Dragon Research RPKI.net toolkit provides the components needed to set up a delegated model.

2.2.1 Dragon Research RPKI.net CA and Repository Configuration/Installation

The setup for the CA and repository is different from the setup for the relying-party VC.

System requirements: Ubuntu 16.04 Xenial server, 32 GB of hard disk, 1 GB of RAM, and a minimum of one CPU.

Lab setup: Ubuntu 16.04 Xenial server, rsync, one CPU, 6 GB memory, and running on a VM on VMware ESXi.

For release notes, installation information, and additional information, please view https://github.com/dragonresearch/rpki.net/blob/master/doc/quickstart/xenial-ca.md.

Steps for installing the rpki-ca (the CA software) toolkit for this lab build were different from the instructions provided by the GitHub documentation. Guidance for the lab build is provided below.

2.2.1.1 Assumptions

Prior to installing rpki-ca and rpki-rp (the repository software), ensure that you are working with two hosts running the Ubuntu Xenial server. In our setup, we will call one host *primary_root* (parent) and the other host *remote_child* (child); both are running the Ubuntu Xenial server.

2.2.1.2 Installation Instructions

Run the initial setup to install rpki-ca. Follow the steps in the Xenial guide up to "CA Data initialization".

Execute the steps under rcynic and rsyncd, specifically the "cat" commands that are listed.

2.2.1.3 Getting rcynic to Run

1. It's important to note that the rcynic software will NOT be installed correctly. You will need to add the following line to */var/spool/cron/crontabs/rcynic*:

   ```
   */10 * * * * exec /usr/bin/rcynic-cron
   ```

   a. This ensures that the rcynic software will be run periodically to update the certificates. This should be done on both hosts. Rcynic is designed to run periodically by default.

   b. Rcynic will error out when external TAL files are called. Delete all repository files in the trust-anchors folder. To do this, run the following command:

   ```
   # rm /etc/rpki/trust-anchors/*
   ```

   i. This should be done on both hosts.

2. The next step is to edit the */etc/rpki.conf* file.

   a. On the host that we will be calling *primary_root*, make the following changes:

   i. Change the handle to *primary_root*.

   ii. Change rpkic_server_host to *0.0.0.0*.

   iii. Change irdb_server_host to *0.0.0.0*.

   iv. Set run_pubd to *yes*.

   v. Change pubd_server_host to *0.0.0.0*.

   This should be sufficient for the changes on primary_root.

b. On the host that we will be calling *remote_child*, make the following changes to */etc/rpki.conf*:

    i. Change the handle to *remote_child*.

    ii. Change rpkic_server_host to *localhost*.

    iii. Change irdb_server_host to *localhost*.

    iv. Set run_pubd to *no*.

    v. Change pubd_server_host to *primary_root*.

This last change means that remote_child will look to primary_root as the publication server rather than running its own. To access primary_root, remote_child will need a Domain Name System entry for primary_root.

1) To create this, first find primary_root's IP address by running **ifconfig** on primary_root. In our setup, this IP address is 192.168.2.115.

2) Then, on remote_child, we add the following line to the */etc/hosts* file:

```
192.168.2.115: primary_root :(Replacing the IP address with
whatever IP address is currently assigned to primary_root.)
```

At this point, rcynic, rpkic, and rsyncd should all be set up.

3. On both hosts, run the following commands to reboot the services:

```
# systemctl restart xinetd
```

```
# systemctl restart rpki-ca
```

2.2.1.4 GUI Setup

1. Set up the graphical user interface (GUI) on both VMs by running the following command:

```
# rpki-manage createsuperuser
```

2. Fill in the details appropriately. Verify that each GUI is up by opening a browser and visiting https://127.0.0.1 on both hosts.

2.2.1.5 Root CA Repository Setup

1. For simplicity, create a folder named */root/CA-stuff* on both VMs. Change the directory into this folder for both VMs.

2. Now, we will set up primary_root as a root server for all resources.

a. On primary_root, run the following command:

```
# rpkic create_identity primary_root
```

This will produce a file named *primary_root.identity.xml*.

b. Next, run the following command:

```
# rpkic configure_root
```

This will produce a file named *primary_root.primary_root.repository-request.xml*. We will return to this file later.

c. Now, run the following command:

```
# rpkic -i primary_root extract_root_certificate
```

```
# rpkic -i primary_root extract_root_tal
```

These commands will respectively produce a *.cer* file and a *.tal* file.

d. Copy both of these files into the */usr/share/rpkic/rrdp-publication* folder. (Note: This step may not be necessary.)

e. Copy the *.tal* file to */etc/rpki/trust-anchors*. This step configures rcynic to look at this node as a repository.

f. Now, we will copy the *.tal* file from primary_root to remote_child. One way to do this is with rsync as follows:

  i. Copy the *.tal* file to */usr/share/rpki/publication* on primary_root.

  ii. On remote_child, run the following command to verify that rsync is working, replacing the IP address as appropriate in the command below:

```
# rsync rsync://192.168.2.115/rpki
```

  iii. If the above runs correctly, copy the *.tal* file, replacing <file> as appropriate in the command below:

```
# rsync rsync://192.168.2.115/rpki/<file>.tal /etc/rpki/trust-
anchors
```

Now, primary_root's *.tal* file should be on both VMs in the */etc/rpki/trust-anchors* directory.

g. We now want to update rcynic. To force it to synchronize, we run the following command on both VMs:

```
# sudo -u rpki python /usr/bin/rcynic-cron
```

    i. To verify that rcynic works, visit https://127.0.0.1/rcynic on both VMs.

h. We return to setting up primary_root.

    i. On primary_root, find the file named *primary_root.primary_root.repository-request.xml.* Once in the right directory, run the following command:

```
# rpkic configure_publication_client
primary_root.primary_root.repository-request.xml
```

    This should produce a file named *primary_root.repository-response.*

    ii. With this file, run the following command:

```
# rpkic configure_repository primary_root.repository-response
```

Now, primary_root should be set up.

i. On primary_root, visit https://127.0.0.1 and log in. You should see primary_root as a repository at the bottom of the page.

2.2.1.6 Child CA Repository Setup

1. Our next step is to set up remote_child as a child of primary_root. On remote_child, run the following command:

```
# rpkic create_identity remote_child
```

This will produce a file named *remote_child.identity.xml.*

2. We now want to copy this over to primary_root by using rsync.

    a. First, copy the file to */usr/share/rpki/publication* on remote_child.

    b. Next, on primary_root, run the following command:

```
# rsync rsync://192.168.2.116/rpki/remote_child.identity.xml ./
```

    (Replace *192.168.2.116* with remote_child's IP address in the command above.)

    This command will copy the child's identity file to the current working directory on primary_root.

c. Now, on primary_root, run the following command:

```
# rpkic configure_child remote_child.identity.xml
```

This will produce a file named *primary_root.remote_child.parent-response.xml*.

3. We will copy this file over to remote_child.

   a. To do this, first (on primary_root) copy the file to /usr/share/rpki/*publication*.

   b. Next, on remote_child, run the following command:

   ```
   # rsync rsync://192.168.2.115/rpki/primary_root.remote_child.parent-
   response.xml ./
   ```

   (Replace the IP address with the appropriate one for primary_root in the command above.)

   This command will copy the response to the current working directory on remote_child.

   c. With this file, we now run the following command on remote_child:

   ```
   # rpkic configure_parent primary_root.remote_child.parent-response.xml
   ```

   This will produce a file named *remote_child.primary_root.repository-request.xml*.

4. We will copy this file to primary_root with rsync.

   a. To do this, on remote_child, copy the file to */usr/share/rpki/publication*.

   b. Then, on primary_root, run the following command:

   ```
   # rsync rsync://192.168.2.116/rpki/remote_child.primary_root.repository-
   request.xml ./
   ```

   (Replace the IP address in the command above with remote_child's IP address).

   This will copy the file to the current working directory.

   c. Now, on primary_root, we run the following command:

   ```
   # rpkic configure_publication_client
   remote_child.primary_root.repository-request.xml
   ```

   This will produce a file named *remote_child.repository-response.xml*.

5. We will copy this file to the remote_child by using rsync.

   a. On primary_root, copy the file to */usr/share/rpki/publication*.

b. Then, on remote_child, run the following command:

```
# rsync rsync://192.168.2.115/rpki/remote_child.repository-response.xml
./
```

(Replace the IP address as necessary in the command above.)

This will copy the file to the current working directory.

c. Now, on remote_child, we run the following command:

```
# rpkic configure_repository remote_child.repository-response.xml
```

2.2.1.7 Run rcynic to Update Root and Child CA Repositories

This will complete the parent-child setup between primary_root and remote_child. Before verifying, we run the following commands on both VMs:

```
# rpkic force_publication
# rpkic force_run_now
# rpkic synchronize
# sudo -u rpki python /usr/bin/rcynic-cron
```

This should force both VMs to fully update everything, including running rcynic. At this point, you should verify that primary_root shows up as a parent on remote_child's GUI, and that remote_child shows up as a child on primary_root's GUI. Now, we can assign resources. On primary_root's GUI, assign some resources to remote_child. Given enough time, remote_child should update its GUI to reflect that it has been assigned resources under the resources header on the GUI.

2.2.1.8 Adding Resources

When adding resources using the GUI, run the following commands to ensure that rcynic runs to update the repository:

```
# rpkic force_run_now
# rpkic synchronize
# sudo -u rpki python /usr/bin/rcynic-cron
```

2.3 BGP-SRx Software Suite

BGP Secure Routing Extension (BGP-SRx) is an open-source reference implementation and research platform for investigating emerging BGP security extensions and supporting protocols, such as RPKI Origin Validation and Border Gateway Protocol Security (BGPsec) Path Validation [NIST BGP-SRx].

For the latest installation information, please use the Quick Install Guide:
https://bgpsrx.antd.nist.gov/bgpsrx/documents/SRxSoftwareSuite-5.0-QuickInstallGuide.pdf.

2.4 Firewalls

The firewall used for the lab build is the Palo Alto Next Generation Firewall. The firewall provides protection against known and unknown threats. In this deployment, only ports and connections necessary for the build are configured. All other ports and connections are denied.

System requirements: Palo Alto PA-5060 Next Generation Firewall running Version 7.1.10 software.

The configuration shown in Figure 2-1 addressed all ports that are allowed by the firewall. Ports that are allowed by the firewall are BGP, rsync, and RPKI Repository Delta Protocol (RRDP). All other ports are denied by the firewall. Figure 2-1 depicts the firewall rules.

Figure 2-1 Palo Alto Firewall Configuration

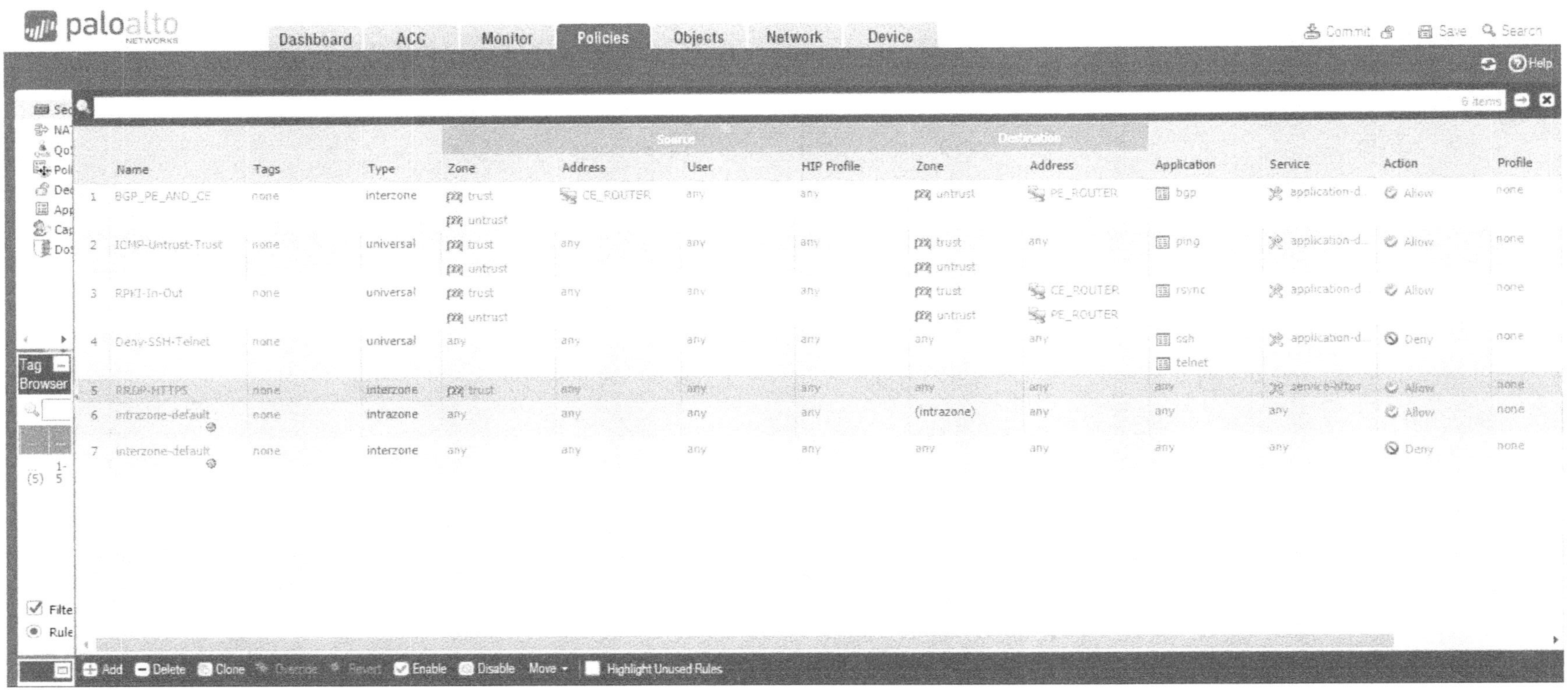

This publication is available free of charge from: http://doi.org/10.6028/NIST.SP.1800-14.

2.5 Test Harness Topology Configuration

The configurations provided in this section are the configurations that are used on each of the routers when operating in the test harness environment architecture provided in Figure 1-1 in Section 1.2. Initially, Cisco routers were used as routers RTR 1-1, RTR 2-1, and RTR 2-2 in that architecture to perform the functional tests. The same tests were then repeated, replacing the Cisco routers with Juniper routers as RTR 1-1, RTR 2-1, and RTR 2-2.

The systems and operating software used for the Cisco routers are as follows:

- Cisco 7206 running *c7200p-adventerprisrk9-mz.152-4.s7.bin*, with a minimum of 4-gigabit Ethernet (GbE) ports. Routers AS 65500 (RTR 2-1) and AS 65501 (RTR 1-1) use this system and OS.

- Cisco 4331 running *ISR4300-universalk9.16.03.04.SPA.bin*, with a minimum of 4 GbE ports. Router AS 65504A (RTR 2-2) uses this system and OS.

All Juniper routers have the following requirements: Juniper MX80 running on Juniper Operating System (JUNOS) 15.1R6.7, with a minimum of 4 GbE ports. Routers AS 65500 (RTR 2-2), AS 65503-J (RTR 2-1), and AS 65505 (RTR 1-1) use this system and OS.

The BGP-SRx Software Suite traffic generators can run on a CentOS Linux system with minimum requirements.

2.5.1 RTR 1-1 Configuration – Cisco

RTR 1-1 acts as an exterior border gateway protocol (eBGP) router receiving eBGP routes from BIO-1, as depicted in Figure 1-1. It updates its interior border gateway protocol (iBGP) peer, BIO-2, with iBGP updates. VRP data is provided to RTR 1-1 by the RPKI validator.

```
hostname AS65501

!

interface GigabitEthernet0/1

 ip address 10.90.90.1 255.255.255.0

 ipv6 address FD00:F:F:1::1/64

!

interface FastEthernet0/2

 description VLAN1

 ip address 192.168.1.2 255.255.255.0
```

```
!

interface GigabitEthernet0/2

 ip address x.x.x.x 255.255.255.252   #Actual IP address to CenturyLink removed.

 !

interface GigabitEthernet0/3

 ip address y.y.y.y 255.255.255.248   #Actual IP address to CenturyLink removed.

ipv6 address FD15:F:F:1::1/64


 !

router bgp 65501

 bgp log-neighbor-changes

 bgp rpki server tcp 192.168.1.52 port 8282 refresh 5

 neighbor 10.90.90.4 remote-as 65501

 neighbor 192.168.1.50 remote-as 65510

 neighbor 192.168.1.51 remote-as 65511

 neighbor 192.168.1.52 remote-as 65501

 neighbor 192.168.1.53 remote-as 65512

 neighbor FD00:F:F:1::3 remote-as 65503

 !

 address-family ipv4

  bgp bestpath prefix-validate allow-invalid

  no neighbor 10.90.90.4 activate

  neighbor 192.168.1.50 activate

  neighbor 192.168.1.51 activate

  neighbor 192.168.1.52 activate

  neighbor 192.168.1.52 send-community both
```

```
    neighbor 192.168.1.52 announce rpki state

    neighbor 192.168.1.53 activate

    no neighbor FD00:F:F:1::3 activate

   exit-address-family

    !

   address-family ipv6

     redistribute connected

     neighbor FD00:F:F:1::3 activate

   exit-address-family

  !

  ip prefix-list WAN-OUT seq 10 permit 65.118.221.8/29

  !

  route-map rpki permit 10

   match rpki invalid

   set local-preference 100

  !

  route-map RPKI-TEST permit 10

   match ip address prefix-list WAN-OUT

   set community 13698023

  !

  end
```

2.5.2 RTR 2-1 Configuration – Cisco

RTR 2-1 acts as an eBGP router receiving eBGP routes from BIO-0, and as an iBGP peer providing updates to RTR 2-2, as depicted in Figure 1-1. RTR 2-1 updates another iBGP peer, BIO-2, with iBGP updates. VRP data is provided to RTR 1-1 by the RPKI validator.

```
hostname AS65500

!

interface Loopback1

 ip address 10.100.0.1 255.255.0.0

 ipv6 address 2010:10:10:10::1/64

!

interface GigabitEthernet0/1

 ip address 10.90.90.10 255.255.255.0

  ipv6 address FD00:F:F:1::10/64

!

interface FastEthernet0/2

 ip address 192.168.1.4 255.255.255.0

!

interface GigabitEthernet0/2

 ip address 10.99.99.21 255.255.255.252

!

interface GigabitEthernet0/3

 description VLAN8

!

router bgp 65500

 bgp log-neighbor-changes

 bgp rpki server tcp 192.168.1.52 port 8282 refresh 5
```

```
bgp rpki server tcp 192.168.1.53 port 8282 refresh 5

neighbor 192.168.1.5 remote-as 65500

neighbor 192.168.1.50 remote-as 65510

neighbor 192.168.1.51 remote-as 65511

neighbor 192.168.1.52 remote-as 65500

neighbor 192.168.1.53 remote-as 65513
!
address-family ipv4
 bgp bestpath prefix-validate allow-invalid
 redistribute connected
 neighbor 192.168.1.5 activate
 neighbor 192.168.1.5 send-community both
 neighbor 192.168.1.5 announce rpki state
 neighbor 192.168.1.50 activate
 neighbor 192.168.1.51 activate
 neighbor 192.168.1.52 activate
 neighbor 192.168.1.52 send-community both
 neighbor 192.168.1.52 announce rpki state
 neighbor 192.168.1.53 activate
 exit-address-family
!
route-map 10 permit 10
!
end
```

2.5.3 RTR 2-2 Configuration – Cisco

RTR 2-2 acts as an iBGP router receiving iBGP routes from RTR 2-1, and as an eBGP peer providing updates to BIO-6, as depicted in Figure 1-1.

```
version 16.3

!

hostname AS65504A

!

interface GigabitEthernet0/0/0

 description VLNA5

 ip address 10.40.0.1 255.255.255.0

  ipv6 address FD34:F:F:1::4/64

!

interface GigabitEthernet0/0/1

 description VLN6

 ip address 10.99.99.18 255.255.255.252

ipv6 address FD24:F:F:1::4/64

!

interface GigabitEthernet0/0/2

 ip address 192.168.1.5 255.255.255.0

  ipv6 address 2004:4444:4444:4444::4/64

!

router bgp 65500

 bgp log-neighbor-changes

 bgp rpki server tcp 192.168.1.53 port 8282 refresh 5

 bgp rpki server tcp 192.168.1.52 port 8282 refresh 5

 neighbor 192.168.1.4 remote-as 65500
```

```
 neighbor 192.168.1.53 remote-as 65513

 !

 address-family ipv4

  neighbor 192.168.1.4 activate

  neighbor 192.168.1.4 send-community both

  neighbor 192.168.1.4 announce rpki state

  neighbor 192.168.1.53 activate

 exit-address-family

 !

 route-map NO-EXPORT permit 10

  set community no-export

 !

 end
```

2.5.4 RTR 1-1 Configuration – Juniper

RTR 1-1 acts as an eBGP router receiving eBGP routes from BIO-1, as depicted in Figure 1-1. RTR 1-1 updates its iBGP peer, BIO-2, with iBGP updates. VRP data is provided to it by the RPKI validator.

```
set system host-name AS65501

set system login user nccoe uid 2000

set system login user nccoe class read-only

set system login user nccoe authentication encrypted-password
"$5$8.Yu28ng$LbcoMQ9uqDO3.U4VaiG4bg5fWMeaMYAJjr09Aniu8c7"

set interfaces ge-1/3/0 unit 0 family inet address 192.168.1.12/24

set interfaces ge-1/3/1 unit 0 family inet

set interfaces ge-1/3/2 unit 0 family inet

set interfaces ge-1/3/3 unit 0 family inet

set interfaces lo0 unit 0 family inet address 127.0.0.1/32

set routing-options autonomous-system 65501
```

```
set routing-options validation group cache session 192.168.1.52 refresh-time 5

set routing-options validation group cache session 192.168.1.52 port 8282

set protocols bgp group external-as65511 type external

set protocols bgp group external-as65511 import validation

set protocols bgp group external-as65511 export allow-direct

set protocols bgp group external-as65511 peer-as 65511

set protocols bgp group external-as65511 neighbor 192.168.1.51

set protocols bgp group external-as65510 type external

set protocols bgp group external-as65510 import validation

set protocols bgp group external-as65510 export allow-direct

set protocols bgp group external-as65510 peer-as 65510

set protocols bgp group external-as65510 neighbor 192.168.1.50

set protocols bgp group internal-as65501 type internal

set protocols bgp group internal-as65501 neighbor 192.168.1.52

set protocols bgp group external-as65512 type external

set protocols bgp group external-as65512 import validation

set protocols bgp group external-as65512 export allow-direct

set protocols bgp group external-as65512 peer-as 65512

set protocols bgp group external-as65512 neighbor 192.168.1.53

set policy-options policy-statement allow-all from route-filter 0.0.0.0/0
orlonger

set policy-options policy-statement allow-all then accept

set policy-options policy-statement allow-direct term default from protocol
direct

set policy-options policy-statement allow-direct term default then accept

set policy-options policy-statement validation term valid from protocol bgp

set policy-options policy-statement validation term valid from validation-
database valid
```

```
set policy-options policy-statement validation term valid then local-preference
110

set policy-options policy-statement validation term valid then validation-state
valid

set policy-options policy-statement validation term valid then community add
origin-validation-state-valid

set policy-options policy-statement validation term valid then accept

set policy-options policy-statement validation term invalid from protocol bgp

set policy-options policy-statement validation term invalid from validation-
database invalid

set policy-options policy-statement validation term invalid then local-
preference 90

set policy-options policy-statement validation term invalid then validation-
state invalid

set policy-options policy-statement validation term invalid then community add
origin-validation-state-invalid

set policy-options policy-statement validation term invalid then accept

set policy-options policy-statement validation term unknown from protocol bgp

set policy-options policy-statement validation term unknown then validation-
state unknown

set policy-options policy-statement validation term unknown then community add
origin-validation-state-unknown

set policy-options policy-statement validation term unknown then accept

set policy-options community origin-validation-state-invalid members 0x4300:2

set policy-options community origin-validation-state-unknown members 0x4300:1

set policy-options community origin-validation-state-valid members 0x4300:0
```

2.5.5 RTR 2-1 Configuration – Juniper

RTR 2-1 acts as an eBGP router receiving eBGP routes from BIO-0, and as an iBGP peer providing updates to RTR 2-2, as depicted in Figure 1-1. It updates another iBGP peer, BIO-2, with iBGP updates. VRP data is provided to RTR 2-1 by the RPKI validator.

```
set system host-name AS65500-J

set interfaces ge-1/3/0 unit 0 family inet

set interfaces ge-1/3/1 unit 0 family inet address 192.168.1.14/24

set interfaces lo0 unit 0 family inet address 127.0.0.1/32

set routing-options autonomous-system 65500

set routing-options validation traceoptions file rpki-trace

set routing-options validation traceoptions flag all

deactivate routing-options validation traceoptions

set routing-options validation group cache session 192.168.1.52 refresh-time 5

set routing-options validation group cache session 192.168.1.52 port 8282

set protocols bgp group external-as65511 type external

set protocols bgp group external-as65511 import validation

set protocols bgp group external-as65511 export allow-direct

set protocols bgp group external-as65511 peer-as 65511

set protocols bgp group external-as65511 neighbor 192.168.1.51

set protocols bgp group external-as65510 type external

set protocols bgp group external-as65510 import validation

set protocols bgp group external-as65510 export allow-direct

set protocols bgp group external-as65510 peer-as 65510

set protocols bgp group external-as65510 neighbor 192.168.1.50

set protocols bgp group internal-as65500 type internal

set protocols bgp group internal-as65500 neighbor 192.168.1.52
```

```
set policy-options policy-statement allow-all from route-filter 0.0.0.0/0
orlonger

set policy-options policy-statement allow-all then accept

set policy-options policy-statement allow-direct term default from protocol
direct

set policy-options policy-statement allow-direct term default then accept

set policy-options policy-statement validation term valid from protocol bgp

set policy-options policy-statement validation term valid from validation-
database valid

set policy-options policy-statement validation term valid then local-preference
110

set policy-options policy-statement validation term valid then validation-state
valid

set policy-options policy-statement validation term valid then community add
origin-validation-state-valid

set policy-options policy-statement validation term valid then accept

set policy-options policy-statement validation term invalid from protocol bgp

set policy-options policy-statement validation term invalid from validation-
database invalid

set policy-options policy-statement validation term invalid then local-
preference 90

set policy-options policy-statement validation term invalid then validation-
state invalid

set policy-options policy-statement validation term invalid then community add
origin-validation-state-invalid

set policy-options policy-statement validation term invalid then accept

set policy-options policy-statement validation term unknown from protocol bgp

set policy-options policy-statement validation term unknown then validation-
state unknown

set policy-options policy-statement validation term unknown then community add
origin-validation-state-unknown

set policy-options policy-statement validation term unknown then accept
```

```
set policy-options community origin-validation-state-invalid members 0x4300:0:2

set policy-options community origin-validation-state-unknown members 0x4300:0:1

set policy-options community origin-validation-state-valid members 0x4300:0:0
```

2.5.6 RTR 2-2 Configuration – Juniper

RTR 2-2 acts as an iBGP router receiving iBGP routes from RTR 2-1, and as an eBGP peer providing updates to BIO-6, as depicted in Figure 1-1.

```
set system host-name AS65500

set interfaces ge-1/3/0 unit 0 family inet address 192.168.1.15/24

set interfaces ge-1/3/1 unit 0

set interfaces ge-1/3/2 unit 0

set interfaces ge-1/3/3 unit 0

set interfaces lo0 unit 0 family inet

set routing-options autonomous-system 65500

set routing-options validation group cache session 192.168.1.52 refresh-time 5

set routing-options validation group cache session 192.168.1.52 port 8282

set routing-options validation group cache session 192.168.1.53 refresh-time 5

set routing-options validation group cache session 192.168.1.53 port 8282

set protocols bgp group internal-as65500 type internal

set protocols bgp group internal-as65500 neighbor 192.168.1.14

set protocols bgp group external-as65513 type external

set protocols bgp group external-as65513 import validation

set protocols bgp group external-as65513 export allow-direct

set protocols bgp group external-as65513 peer-as 65513

set protocols bgp group external-as65513 neighbor 192.168.1.53

set policy-options policy-statement allow-all from route-filter 0.0.0.0/0
orlonger

set policy-options policy-statement allow-all then accept
```

```
set policy-options policy-statement allow-direct term default from protocol
direct

set policy-options policy-statement allow-direct term default then accept

set policy-options policy-statement validation term valid from protocol bgp

set policy-options policy-statement validation term valid from validation-
database valid

set policy-options policy-statement validation term valid then local-preference
110

set policy-options policy-statement validation term valid then validation-state
valid

set policy-options policy-statement validation term valid then community add
origin-validation-state-valid

set policy-options policy-statement validation term valid then accept

set policy-options policy-statement validation term invalid from protocol bgp

set policy-options policy-statement validation term invalid from validation-
database invalid

set policy-options policy-statement validation term invalid then local-
preference 90

set policy-options policy-statement validation term invalid then validation-
state invalid

set policy-options policy-statement validation term invalid then community add
origin-validation-state-invalid

set policy-options policy-statement validation term invalid then accept

set policy-options policy-statement validation term unknown from protocol bgp

set policy-options policy-statement validation term unknown then validation-
state unknown

set policy-options policy-statement validation term unknown then community add
origin-validation-state-unknown

set policy-options policy-statement validation term unknown then accept

set policy-options community origin-validation-state-invalid members 0x4300:2

set policy-options community origin-validation-state-invalid members 0x43:100:2

set policy-options community origin-validation-state-unknown members 0x4300:1
```

```
      set policy-options community origin-validation-state-valid members 0x4300:0
```

2.5.7 Traffic Generator BIO Configuration

```
      ski_file    = "/var/lib/key-volt/ski-list.txt";

      ski_key_loc = "/var/lib/key-volt/";

      preload_eckey = false;

      mode = "BGP";

      max = 0;

      only_extended_length = true;

      session = (

      {

          disconnect = 0;

          ext_msg_cap      = true;

          ext_msg_liberal = true;

          bgpsec_v4_snd = false;

          bgpsec_v4_rcv  = false;

          bgpsec_v6_snd = false;

   bgpsec_v6_rcv  = false;    update = (

                    );

          incl_global_updates = true;

          algo_id = 1;

          signature_generation = "BIO";

          null_signature_mode = "FAKE";

          fake_signature            = "1BADBEEFDEADFEED" "2BADBEEFDEADFEED"

                                        "3BADBEEFDEADFEED" "4BADBEEFDEADFEED"

                                        "5BADBEEFDEADFEED" "6BADBEEFDEADFEED"

                                        "7BADBEEFDEADFEED" "8BADBEEFDEADFEED"

                                        "ABADBEEFFACE";

          fake_ski              = "0102030405060708" "090A0B0C0D0E0F10"

                                        "11121314";

          printOnSend = {
```

```
        update      = true;
    };


    printOnReceive = {
      update.      = true;
      notification = true;
      unknown      = true;
    };
    printSimple     = true;
    printPollLoop  = false;
    printOnInvalid = false;
  }
);
update = (
        );
```

2.5.7.1 AS – Peer Configuration: BIO-0 (AS 65510) – RTR-1-1 (AS 65501)

```
asn           = 65510;
bgp_ident  = "192.168.1.50";
hold_timer = 180;


peer_asn   = 65501;
# For CISCO replace x with 2, For JUNIPER replace x with 12
peer_ip     = "192.168.1.x";
peer_port  = 179;
```

2.5.7.2 AS – Peer Configuration: BIO-0 (AS 65510) – RTR-2-1 (AS 65500)

```
asn           = 65510;
bgp_ident  = "192.168.1.50";
hold_timer = 180;


peer_asn   = 65500;
```

```
# For CISCO replace x with 4, For JUNIPER replace x with 14
peer_ip    = "192.168.1.x";
peer_port  = 179;
```

2.5.7.3 AS – Peer Configuration: BIO-1 (AS 65511) – RTR-1-1 (AS 65501)

```
asn          = 65511;
bgp_ident = "192.168.1.51";
hold_timer = 180;


peer_asn   = 65500;
# For CISCO replace x with 2, For JUNIPER replace x with 12
peer_ip    = "192.168.1.x";
peer_port  = 179;
```

2.5.7.4 AS – Peer Configuration: BIO-1 (AS 65511) – RTR-2-1 (AS 65500)

```
asn          = 65511;
bgp_ident = "192.168.1.51";
hold_timer = 180;


peer_asn   = 65500;
# For CISCO replace x with 4, For JUNIPER replace x with 14
peer_ip    = "192.168.1.x";
peer_port  = 179;
```

2.5.7.5 AS – Peer Configuration: BIO-2 (AS 65501) – RTR-1-1 (AS 65501)

```
asn          = 65501;
bgp_ident = "192.168.1.52";
hold_timer = 180;


peer_asn   = 65501;
# For CISCO replace x with 2, For JUNIPER replace x with 12
peer_ip    = "192.168.1.x";
peer_port  = 179;
```

2.5.7.6 AS – Peer Configuration: BIO-3 (AS 65500) – RTR-2-1 (AS 65500)

```
asn           = 65500;

bgp_ident  = "192.168.1.52";

hold_timer = 180;


peer_asn   = 65500;
# For CISCO replace x with 4, For JUNIPER replace x with 14
peer_ip      = "192.168.1.x";

peer_port  = 179;
```

2.5.7.7 AS – Peer Configuration: BIO-5 (AS 65512) – RTR-1-1 (AS 65500)

```
asn           = 65512;

bgp_ident  = "192.168.1.53";

hold_timer = 180;


peer_asn   = 65501;
# For CISCO replace x with 2, For JUNIPER replace x with 12
peer_ip      = "192.168.1.x";

peer_port  = 179;
```

2.5.7.8 AS – Peer Configuration: BIO-6 (AS 65513) – RTR-1-1 (AS 65513)

```
asn           = 65513;

bgp_ident  = "192.168.1.53";

hold_timer = 180;


peer_asn   = 65500;
# For CISCO replace x with 4, For JUNIPER replace x with 14
peer_ip      = "192.168.1.x";

peer_port  = 179;
```

2.6 Live Data Configuration

The configurations provided in this section are the configurations that are used on each of the routers when operating in the live data environment architecture shown in Figure 1-2. Live BGP data and RPKI data can be retrieved in this environment. The architecture is organized into eight separate networks, each of which is designed to represent a different AS.

The systems and operating software used for the Cisco routers are as follows:

- Cisco 7206 running *c7200p-adventerprisrk9-mz.152-4.s7.bin*, with a minimum of 4 GbE ports. Routers AS 65500, AS 65501, and AS 65503 use this system and OS.

- Cisco 4331 running *ISR4300-universalk9.16.03.04.SPA.bin*, with a minimum of 4 GbE ports. Routers AS 65504A and AS 65504B use this system and OS.

- Cisco 2921 running *c2900-universalk9-mz-SPA.152-4.M6.bin*, with a minimum of 4 GbE ports. Routers AS 65507 and AS 65508 use this system and OS.

- Cisco Internetwork Operating System (IOS) XRv 9000 router Version 6.4.1 running on VMware ESXi using the *xrv9k-fullk9-x.vrr-6.4.1.ova* file.

All Juniper routers have the following requirements: Juniper MX80 running on JUNOS 15.1R6.7, with a minimum of 4 GbE ports. Routers AS 65502 and AS 65505 use this system and OS.

RPKI validators and repositories are configured based on Section 2.1 and Section 2.2. Live ROV data is retrieved from the five trust anchors, and lab ROA data is retrieved from the lab delegated model of the local RPKI repository.

Note: Real IP addresses and AS numbers were removed from the configuration.

2.6.1 CenturyLink Configuration Router AS 65501 – Cisco

To receive a full BGP route table, CenturyLink provided a physical link connecting the NCCoE lab with an eBGP peering. The configuration below illustrates the eBGP peering. An additional configuration for this router, related to the lab build, is provided in Section 2.5.3.

```
version 15.2
!
hostname AS65501
!
ipv6 unicast-routing
ipv6 cef
```

```
!

interface GigabitEthernet0/1

  ip address 10.90.90.1 255.255.255.0

ipv6 address FD00:F:F:1::1/64

  !

interface FastEthernet0/2

  description VLAN1

  ip address 192.168.1.2 255.255.255.0

  !

interface GigabitEthernet0/2

  ip address a.a.a.a 255.255.255.252

  !

interface GigabitEthernet0/3

  ip address c.c.c.c 255.255.255.248


ipv6 address FD15:F:F:1::1/64

  !

router bgp aaa

 bgp log-neighbor-changes

 neighbor a.a.a.b remote-as bbb

  !

 address-family ipv4

  network c.c.c.d mask 255.255.255.248

  neighbor a.a.a.b activate

  neighbor a.a.a.b send-community

  neighbor a.a.a.b soft-reconfiguration inbound
```

```
    neighbor a.a.a.b route-map RPKI-TEST out

 exit-address-family

 !

ip prefix-list WAN-OUT seq 10 permit c.c.c.d/29

ipv6 router rip proc1

 !

route-map rpki permit 10

 match rpki invalid

 set local-preference 100

 !

route-map RPKI-TEST permit 10

 match ip address prefix-list WAN-OUT

 set community 13698023

 !

end
```

2.6.2 Router AS 65500 Configuration – Cisco

Router AS 65500 represents an ISP. For the lab build, this router originates BGP updates from its own AS and receives and sends routes to and from its eBGP peers.

```
hostname AS65500

 !

ip cef

ipv6 unicast-routing

ipv6 cef

 !

interface Loopback1

 ip address 10.10.0.1 255.255.0.0
```

```
 ipv6 address FD10:10:10:10::1/64

 ipv6 rip proc1 enable

!

interface GigabitEthernet0/1

 ipv6 address FD00:F:F:1::1/64

 ipv6 rip proc1 enable

!

interface FastEthernet0/2

 description VLAN1

 ip address 192.168.1.2 255.255.255.0

 ipv6 address FD01:F:F:1::2/64

 ipv6 rip proc1 enable

!

interface GigabitEthernet0/2

 ip address a.a.a.a 255.255.255.252

!

interface GigabitEthernet0/3

 ip address c.c.c.c 255.255.255.248

 ipv6 address FD15:F:F:1::1/64

!

router rip

 version 2

 network 10.0.0.0

 network 192.168.1.0

 no auto-summary

!
```

```
router bgp aaa
 bgp log-neighbor-changes
 neighbor a.a.a.b remote-as bbb
 !
 address-family ipv4
  network c.c.c.d mask 255.255.255.248
  neighbor a.a.a.b activate
  neighbor a.a.a.b send-community
  neighbor a.a.a.b soft-reconfiguration inbound
  neighbor a.a.a.b route-map RPKI-TEST out
 exit-address-family
!
ip route 10.20.0.0 255.255.0.0 192.168.1.3
ip route 10.30.0.0 255.255.0.0 192.168.1.3
ip route 10.40.0.0 255.255.0.0 192.168.1.3
ip route 10.50.0.0 255.255.0.0 192.168.1.3
ip route 10.70.0.0 255.255.0.0 192.168.1.3
ip route 10.80.0.0 255.255.0.0 192.168.1.3
ip route 10.90.90.0 255.255.255.0 192.168.1.3
ip route 10.97.74.0 255.255.255.0 192.178.1.1
ip route 10.99.99.0 255.255.255.0 192.168.1.3
!
ip prefix-list WAN-OUT seq 10 permit c.c.c.d /29
ipv6 router rip proc1
!
route-map rpki permit 10
```

```
 match rpki invalid

 set local-preference 100

 !

route-map RPKI-TEST permit 10

 match ip address prefix-list WAN-OUT

 set community 13698023

 !

end
```

2.6.3 Router 65501 Configuration – Cisco

Router AS 65501 represents an ISP. As indicated in Section 2.5.1, this router peers with the CenturyLink router to receive a full BGP routing table. For the lab build, this router originates BGP updates from its own AS and receives and sends routes to and from its eBGP peers. It is the gateway for all devices in the lab, allowing ROAs from RIRs to be retrieved by RPKI validators. It also peers with stub AS A65505.

```
hostname AS65501

!

ip cef

ipv6 unicast-routing

ipv6 cef

!

interface Loopback1

 ip address 10.10.0.1 255.255.0.0

 ipv6 address FD10:10:10:10::1/64

 ipv6 rip proc1 enable

!

interface GigabitEthernet0/1

 ipv6 address FD00:F:F:1::1/64

 ipv6 rip proc1 enable
```

```
!

interface FastEthernet0/2

 ip address 192.168.1.2 255.255.255.0

 ipv6 address FD01:F:F:1::2/64

 ipv6 rip proc1 enable

!

interface GigabitEthernet0/2

 ip address a.a.a.a 255.255.255.252

!

interface GigabitEthernet0/3

 ip address c.c.c.c 255.255.255.248

 ipv6 address FD15:F:F:1::1/64

!

router rip

 version 2

 network 10.0.0.0

 network 192.168.1.0

 no auto-summary

!

router bgp aaa

 bgp log-neighbor-changes

 neighbor a.a.a.b remote-as bbb

 !

 address-family ipv4

  network c.c.c.d mask 255.255.255.248

  neighbor a.a.a.b activate
```

```
   neighbor a.a.a.b send-community

   neighbor a.a.a.b soft-reconfiguration inbound

   neighbor a.a.a.b route-map RPKI-TEST out

 exit-address-family

!

ip route 10.20.0.0 255.255.0.0 192.168.1.3

ip route 10.30.0.0 255.255.0.0 192.168.1.3

ip route 10.40.0.0 255.255.0.0 192.168.1.3

ip route 10.50.0.0 255.255.0.0 192.168.1.3

ip route 10.70.0.0 255.255.0.0 192.168.1.3

ip route 10.80.0.0 255.255.0.0 192.168.1.3

ip route 10.90.90.0 255.255.255.0 192.168.1.3

ip route 10.97.74.0 255.255.255.0 192.178.1.1

ip route 10.99.99.0 255.255.255.0 192.168.1.3

!

ip prefix-list WAN-OUT seq 10 permit c.c.c.d /29

ipv6 router rip proc1

!

route-map rpki permit 10

 match rpki invalid

 set local-preference 100

!

route-map RPKI-TEST permit 10

 match ip address prefix-list WAN-OUT

 set community 13698023

!
```

```
end
```

2.6.4 Router AS 65502 Configuration — Juniper

Router AS 65502 represents an ISP using a Juniper router. For the lab build, this router originates BGP updates from its own AS and receives and sends routes to and from its eBGP peers. It also provides eBGP routes to stub AS 65504.

```
set system host-name AS65502

set interfaces ge-1/3/0 unit 0 family inet address 10.90.90.2/24

set interfaces ge-1/3/0 unit 0 family inet6 address fd00:f:f:1::2/64

set interfaces ge-1/3/1 unit 0 family inet address 10.99.99.17/30

set interfaces ge-1/3/1 unit 0 family inet6 address fd24:f:f:1::2/64

set interfaces ge-1/3/2 unit 0 family inet address 10.99.99.25/30

set interfaces ge-1/3/2 unit 0 family inet6 address fd25:f:f:1::2/64

set interfaces ge-1/3/3 unit 0 family inet address 10.20.0.1/16

set interfaces ge-1/3/3 unit 0 family inet6 address 2020:2020:2020:1::2/64

set interfaces lo0 unit 0 family inet address 127.0.0.1/32

set routing-options validation group cache session 192.168.1.146 port 8282

set policy-options policy-statement allow-all from route-filter 0.0.0.0/0
orlonger

set policy-options policy-statement allow-all then accept

set routing-instances rpki instance-type virtual-router

set routing-instances rpki interface ge-1/3/0.0

set routing-instances rpki interface ge-1/3/1.0

set routing-instances rpki interface ge-1/3/2.0

set routing-instances rpki interface ge-1/3/3.0

set routing-instances rpki interface lo0.1

set routing-instances rpki routing-options router-id 2.2.2.2

set routing-instances rpki routing-options autonomous-system 65502
```

```
set routing-instances rpki protocols bgp group external-as65500 type external

set routing-instances rpki protocols bgp group external-as65500 import allow-
all

set routing-instances rpki protocols bgp group external-as65500 export allow-
all

set routing-instances rpki protocols bgp group external-as65500 peer-as 65500

set routing-instances rpki protocols bgp group external-as65500 neighbor
10.90.90.10

set routing-instances rpki protocols bgp group external-as65500 neighbor
fd00:f:f:1::10

set routing-instances rpki protocols bgp group external-as65501 type external

set routing-instances rpki protocols bgp group external-as65501 import allow-
all

set routing-instances rpki protocols bgp group external-as65501 export allow-
all

set routing-instances rpki protocols bgp group external-as65501 peer-as 65501

set routing-instances rpki protocols bgp group external-as65501 neighbor
10.90.90.1

set routing-instances rpki protocols bgp group external-as65501 neighbor
fd00:f:f:1::1

set routing-instances rpki protocols bgp group external-as65503 type external

set routing-instances rpki protocols bgp group external-as65503 import allow-
all

set routing-instances rpki protocols bgp group external-as65503 export allow-
all

set routing-instances rpki protocols bgp group external-as65503 peer-as 65503

set routing-instances rpki protocols bgp group external-as65503 neighbor
10.90.90.3

set routing-instances rpki protocols bgp group external-as65503 neighbor
fd00:f:f:1::3

set routing-instances rpki protocols bgp group external-as65505 type external

set routing-instances rpki protocols bgp group external-as65505 import allow-
all
```

```
set routing-instances rpki protocols bgp group external-as65505 export allow-
all

set routing-instances rpki protocols bgp group external-as65505 peer-as 65505

set routing-instances rpki protocols bgp group external-as65505 neighbor
fd25:f:f:1::5

set routing-instances rpki protocols bgp group external-as65505 neighbor
10.99.99.26

set routing-instances rpki protocols bgp group external-as65504 type external

set routing-instances rpki protocols bgp group external-as65504 import allow-
all

set routing-instances rpki protocols bgp group external-as65504 export allow-
all

set routing-instances rpki protocols bgp group external-as65504 peer-as 65504

set routing-instances rpki protocols bgp group external-as65504 neighbor
10.99.99.18

set routing-instances rpki protocols bgp group external-as65504 neighbor
fd24:f:f:1::4
```

2.6.5 Router AS 65503 Configuration – Cisco

Router AS 65503 represents an ISP without ROV capabilities. For the lab build, this router originates BGP updates from its own AS and receives and sends routes to and from its eBGP peers without performing BGP origin validation. This router peers with two transit routers, AS 65500 and AS 65502, as well as two stub ASes, AS 65504 and AS 65507.

```
hostname AS65503
!
ip cef

ipv6 unicast-routing

ipv6 cef
!
interface Loopback1
  ip address 10.30.0.1 255.255.0.0

  ipv6 address 2003:3333:3333:3333::1/64
```

```
!

interface GigabitEthernet0/1

 ip address 10.90.90.3 255.255.255.0

 ipv6 address FD00:F:F:1::3/64

 !

interface FastEthernet0/2

 ip address 192.168.1.251 255.255.255.0

 !

interface GigabitEthernet0/2

 ip address 10.99.99.13 255.255.255.252

 !

interface GigabitEthernet0/3

 description VLAN7

 ip address 10.99.99.21 255.255.255.252

 ipv6 address FD37:F:F:1::1/64

 !

router bgp 65503

 bgp log-neighbor-changes

 bgp rpki server tcp 192.168.1.146 port 8282 refresh 10

 neighbor 10.90.90.1 remote-as 65501

 neighbor 10.90.90.2 remote-as 65502

 neighbor 10.90.90.10 remote-as 65500

 neighbor 10.99.99.14 remote-as 65504

 neighbor 10.99.99.22 remote-as 65507

 neighbor FD00:F:F:1::1 remote-as 65501

 neighbor FD00:F:F:1::2 remote-as 65502
```

```
neighbor FD00:F:F:1::10 remote-as 65500

neighbor FD34:F:F:1::4 remote-as 65504

neighbor FD34:F:F:1::7 remote-as 65507

!

address-family ipv4

 redistribute connected

 redistribute static

 neighbor 10.90.90.1 activate

 neighbor 10.90.90.2 activate

 neighbor 10.90.90.10 activate

 neighbor 10.99.99.14 activate

 neighbor 10.99.99.22 activate

 no neighbor FD00:F:F:1::1 activate

 no neighbor FD00:F:F:1::2 activate

 no neighbor FD00:F:F:1::10 activate

 no neighbor FD34:F:F:1::4 activate

 no neighbor FD34:F:F:1::7 activate

exit-address-family

 !

address-family ipv6

 redistribute connected

 neighbor FD00:F:F:1::1 activate

 neighbor FD00:F:F:1::2 activate

 neighbor FD00:F:F:1::10 activate

 neighbor FD34:F:F:1::4 activate

exit-address-family
```

```
!

ipv6 router rip proc1

!

end
```

2.6.6 Router AS 65504A Configuration – Cisco

Router AS 65504A represents an enterprise edge router for AS 65504. For the lab build, this router originates BGP updates from its own AS and receives and sends routes to and from its eBGP peer, AS 65502. It peers with Router AS 65504B to exchange iBGP routes.

```
hostname AS65504A

!

ipv6 unicast-routing

!

interface Loopback1

 ip address 10.40.1.1 255.255.255.0

!

interface GigabitEthernet0/0/0

 ip address 10.40.0.1 255.255.255.0

 ipv6 address FD00:F:F:1::40/64

 ipv6 address FD34:F:F:1::4/64

!

interface GigabitEthernet0/0/1

 ip address 10.99.99.18 255.255.255.252

 ipv6 address FD24:F:F:1::4/64

!

interface GigabitEthernet0/0/2

 ip address 10.40.4.1 255.255.255.0
```

```
 ipv6 address 2004:4444:4444:4444::4/64
!
router bgp 65504
 bgp log-neighbor-changes
 neighbor 10.40.0.2 remote-as 65504
 neighbor 10.99.99.17 remote-as 65502
 neighbor FD24:F:F:1::2 remote-as 65502
 !
 address-family ipv4
  redistribute connected
  redistribute static
  no neighbor 10.40.0.2 activate
  neighbor 10.99.99.17 activate
  no neighbor FD24:F:F:1::2 activate
 exit-address-family
 !
 address-family ipv6
  redistribute connected
  neighbor FD24:F:F:1::2 activate
 exit-address-family
!
ip route 10.40.2.0 255.255.255.0 10.40.0.2
!
route-map NO-EXPORT permit 10
 set community no-export
!
```

```
    end
```

2.6.7. Router AS 65504B Configuration – Cisco

Router AS 65504B represents an enterprise edge router for AS 65504. For the lab build, this router originates BGP updates from its own AS and receives and sends routes to and from its eBGP peer, AS 65503. It peers with Router AS 65504A to exchange iBGP routes.

```
hostname AS65504B

!

ipv6 unicast-routing

!

interface Loopback1

 ip address 10.40.2.1 255.255.255.0

 ipv6 address 4040:4040:4040:4242::1/64

!

interface GigabitEthernet0/0/0

 ip address 10.99.99.14 255.255.255.252

 ipv6 address FD34:F:F:1::4/64

!

interface GigabitEthernet0/0/1

 ip address 10.40.0.2 255.255.255.0

 ipv6 address FD40:F:F:1::2/64

!

router bgp 65504

 bgp log-neighbor-changes

 neighbor 10.40.0.1 remote-as 65504

 neighbor 10.99.99.13 remote-as 65503

 neighbor FD34:F:F:1::2 remote-as 65503
```

```
    neighbor FD40:F:F:1::1 remote-as 65504

    !

    address-family ipv4

     redistribute connected

     no neighbor 10.40.0.1 activate

     neighbor 10.99.99.13 activate

     no neighbor FD34:F:F:1::2 activate

     no neighbor FD40:F:F:1::1 activate

    exit-address-family

    !

    address-family ipv6

     redistribute connected

     neighbor FD34:F:F:1::2 activate

     neighbor FD40:F:F:1::1 activate

    exit-address-family

    !

    route-map NO-EXPORT permit 10

     set community no-export

    !

    end
```

2.6.8 Router AS 65505 Configuration – Juniper

Router AS 65505 represents an enterprise edge router. For the lab build, this router originates BGP updates from its own AS and receives and sends routes to and from its eBGP peers, AS 65501 and AS 65502.

```
    set system host-name AS65505

    set interfaces ge-1/3/0 unit 0 family inet
```

```
set interfaces ge-1/3/0 unit 0 family inet6

set interfaces ge-1/3/1 unit 0 family inet address 10.99.99.2/30

set interfaces ge-1/3/1 unit 0 family inet6 address fd15:f:f:1::5/64

set interfaces ge-1/3/2 unit 0 family inet address 10.99.99.26/30

set interfaces ge-1/3/2 unit 0 family inet6 address fd25:f:f:1::5/64

set interfaces ge-1/3/3 unit 0 family inet address 10.50.0.1/16

set interfaces ge-1/3/3 unit 0 family inet6 address 5050:5050:5050:1::5/64

set interfaces lo0 unit 0 family inet address 127.0.0.1/32

set routing-options autonomous-system 65505

set routing-options validation group cache session 192.168.1.146 port 8282

set protocols bgp group external-as65501 type external

set protocols bgp group external-as65501 import validation

set protocols bgp group external-as65501 export allow-direct

set protocols bgp group external-as65501 peer-as 65501

set protocols bgp group external-as65501 neighbor 10.99.99.1

set protocols bgp group external-as65501 neighbor fd15:f:f:1::1

set protocols bgp group external-as65502 type external

set protocols bgp group external-as65502 import validation

set protocols bgp group external-as65502 export allow-direct

set protocols bgp group external-as65502 peer-as 65502

set protocols bgp group external-as65502 neighbor 10.99.99.25

set protocols bgp group external-as65502 neighbor fd25:f:f:1::2

set policy-options policy-statement allow-all from route-filter 0.0.0.0/0
orlonger

set policy-options policy-statement allow-all then accept

set policy-options policy-statement allow-direct term default from protocol
direct
```

```
set policy-options policy-statement allow-direct term default then accept

set policy-options policy-statement validation term valid from protocol bgp

set policy-options policy-statement validation term valid from validation-
database valid

set policy-options policy-statement validation term valid then local-preference
110

set policy-options policy-statement validation term valid then validation-state
valid

set policy-options policy-statement validation term valid then accept

set policy-options policy-statement validation term invalid from protocol bgp

set policy-options policy-statement validation term invalid from validation-
database invalid

set policy-options policy-statement validation term invalid then local-
preference 90

set policy-options policy-statement validation term invalid then validation-
state invalid

set policy-options policy-statement validation term invalid then reject

set policy-options policy-statement validation term unknown from protocol bgp

set policy-options policy-statement validation term unknown then validation-
state unknown

set policy-options policy-statement validation term unknown then accept
```

2.6.9 Router AS 65507 Configuration – Cisco

Router AS 65507 represents an enterprise edge router for AS 65507. For the lab build, this router originates BGP updates from its own AS and receives and sends routes to and from its eBGP peer, AS 65503.

```
hostname AS65507

!

interface Loopback1

 ip address 10.70.0.1 255.255.0.0

 ipv6 address 7070:7070:7070:7070::1/64
```

```
!

interface GigabitEthernet0/0

 ip address 10.99.99.22 255.255.255.252

 ipv6 address FD37:F:F:1::7/64

!

interface GigabitEthernet0/1

 ip address 172.16.0.1 255.255.0.0

!

router bgp 65507

 bgp log-neighbor-changes

 neighbor 10.99.99.21 remote-as 65503

 neighbor FD37:F:F:1::3 remote-as 65503

 !

 address-family ipv4

  redistribute connected

  neighbor 10.99.99.21 activate

  no neighbor FD37:F:F:1::3 activate

 exit-address-family

 !

 address-family ipv6

  redistribute connected

  neighbor FD37:F:F:1::3 activate

 exit-address-family

!

access-list 23 permit 10.10.10.0 0.0.0.7

ipv6 router rip proc1
```

```
!

end
```

2.6.10 Router AS 65508 Configuration – Cisco

Router AS 65508 represents a hijacker masquerading as an enterprise edge router. For the lab build, this router originates BGP updates for routes that are held by other ASes (i.e., for routes for which it is not authorized to originate updates), in order to demonstrate route hijacks.

```
hostname AS65508

!

ipv6 unicast-routing

ipv6 cef

!

interface Loopback1

 ip address 10.80.0.1 255.255.0.0

 ipv6 address 8080:8080:8080:8080::1/64

!

interface GigabitEthernet0/0

 ip address 10.99.99.30 255.255.255.252

 ipv6 address FD00:F:F:1::61/64

 ipv6 address FD08:F:F:1::8/64

!

interface GigabitEthernet0/1

 ip address 172.16.8.1 255.255.255.0

!

router bgp 65508

 bgp log-neighbor-changes

 neighbor 10.99.99.29 remote-as 65500
```

```
neighbor FD08:F:F:1::10 remote-as 65500

!

address-family ipv4

 redistribute connected

 neighbor 10.99.99.29 activate

 no neighbor FD08:F:F:1::10 activate

exit-address-family

!

address-family ipv6

 redistribute connected

 neighbor FD08:F:F:1::10 activate

exit-address-family

!

ipv6 router rip proc1

!

end
```

2.6.11 Cisco IOS XRv Router Configuration

The Cisco IOS XRv software was also used to perform many of the functional tests, as many ISPs currently use it in their network environment. The baseline configuration is provided below. Depending on the test case, this router can replace any other router shown in <u>Figure 1-2</u>, in order to properly perform the test.

```
RP/0/RP0/CPU0:ios#sho run

!! IOS XR Configuration version = 6.4.1

!

interface MgmtEth0/RP0/CPU0/0

 ipv4 address 192.168.1.201 255.255.255.0

 ipv6 address fd00:f:f:1::201/64
```

```
!
route-policy pass-all
  pass
end-policy
!
router bgp 65501
 bgp router-id 1.1.1.1
 rpki server 192.168.1.146
  transport tcp port 8282
  refresh-time 15
  !
 address-family ipv4 unicast
  bgp bestpath origin-as allow invalid
  !
 address-family ipv6 unicast
  bgp bestpath origin-as allow invalid
  !
 neighbor 192.168.1.62
  remote-as 65501
  address-family ipv4 unicast
   route-policy pass-all in
   route-policy pass-all out
   !
  !
 neighbor fd00:f:f:1::62
  remote-as 65501
```

```
   address-family ipv6 unicast

    route-policy pass-all in

    route-policy pass-all out

  !

 !

!

end
```

Appendix A   List of Acronyms

Wide Area Network

Appendix B   References

BGP Secure Routing Extension (BGP SRx) Prototype, National Institute of Standards and Technology, [website]. https://www.nist.gov/services-resources/software/bgp-secure-routing-extension-bgp-srx-prototype

D. R. Kuhn, K. Sriram, and D. Montgomery, *Border Gateway Protocol Security*, NIST SP 800-54, July 2007. http://csrc.nist.gov/publications/nistpubs/800-54/SP800-54.pdf

Systems Security Engineering: An Integrated Approach to Building Trustworthy Resilient Systems, NIST SP 800-160 Second Public Draft, National Institute of Standards and Technology, November 2016. http://csrc.nist.gov/publications/drafts/800-160/sp800_160_second-draft.pdf

M. Lepinski and S. Kent, *An Infrastructure to Support Secure Internet Routing*, RFC 6480, February 2012. https://tools.ietf.org/html/rfc6480

M. Lepinski, S. Kent, and D. Kong, *A Profile for Route Origin Authorizations (ROAs)*, RFC 6482, February 2012. https://tools.ietf.org/html/rfc6482

P. Mohapatra, J. Scudder, D. Ward, R. Bush, and R. Austein, *BGP Prefix Origin Validation*, RFC 6811, January 2013. https://tools.ietf.org/pdf/rfc6811.pdf

R. Bush, *Origin Validation Operation Based on the Resource Public Key Infrastructure (RPKI)*, RFC 7115, January 2014. https://tools.ietf.org/html/rfc7115

Tools and Resources, RIPE Network Coordination Centre (NCC), [website]. https://www.ripe.net/manage-ips-and-asns/resource-management/certification/tools-and-resources

11.621 40689CB00019B/4089 [206127952]